A Concise History of Sweden

A comprehensive history of Sweden is much needed. Neil Kent's book sweeps through Sweden's history from the Stone Age to the present day. Early coverage includes Viking hegemony, the Scandinavian Union, the Reformation and Sweden's political zenith as Europe's greatest superpower in the seventeenth century, while later chapters explore the Swedish Enlightenment, royal absolutism, the commitment to military neutrality and Pan-Scandinavianism. The author brings his account up to date by focusing on recent developments: the rise of Social Democracy, the establishment of the welfare state, the country's acceptance of membership in the European Union and its progressive ecological programme. The book successfully combines the politics, economics and social and cultural mores of one of the world's most successfully functioning and humane societies. This is an informative and entertaining account for students and general readers.

NEIL KENT is Associate at the Scott Polar Research Institute in Cambridge and Professor at the St Petersburg State Academy of Art, Architecture and Culture. His latest publications include *Helsinki: A Cultural and Literary History* (2004) and *Trieste: Biography of a City* (2008).

CAMBRIDGE CONCISE HISTORIES

This is a series of illustrated 'concise histories' of selected individual countries, intended both as university and college textbooks and as general historical introductions for general readers, travellers, and members of the business community.

For a list of titles in the series, see end of book.

A Concise History
of Sweden

NEIL KENT

CAMBRIDGE UNIVERSITY PRESS
Cambridge, New York, Melbourne, Madrid, Cape Town, Singapore, São Paulo, Delhi

Cambridge University Press
The Edinburgh Building, Cambridge CB2 8RU, UK

Published in the United States of America by Cambridge University Press, New York

www.cambridge.org
Information on this title: www.cambridge.org/9780521012270

© Neil Kent 2008

First published 2008

Printed in the United Kingdom at the University Press, Cambridge

A catalogue record for this publication is available from the British Library

Library of Congress Cataloging in Publication data
Kent, Neil.
A concise history of Sweden / Neil Kent.
p.   cm. – (Cambridge concise histories)
ISBN 978-0-521-81284-9
1. Sweden – History. I. Title. II. Series.
DL649.K46   2008
948.5–dc22
2008005762

ISBN 978-0-521-81284-9 hardback
ISBN 978-0-521-01227-0 paperback

CONTENTS

ILLUSTRATIONS

MAPS

PREFACE

Sweden has long been a European country in a virtually unique position, both militarily and socially: it has avoided warfare for almost two hundred years and possesses a social welfare infrastructure that, decades ago, virtually eliminated extremes of poverty. To many, therefore, it may seem a land of milk and honey, a prosperous country in which people live in easy tolerance and harmony. The reality, though, is more earth-bound.

The Swedish social ethos which has informed its society and culture did not spring fully formed from the head of Zeus, but was moulded by the struggles, sacrifices, compromises and hard-bitten stamina of Swedes. The distillation is a society in which, at its best, the individual is expected to assume his or her civic responsibilities in the context of a highly ordered society. Individuality has its strict parameters and political strongmen rarely make headway. That said, the reigning dynasty of its constitutional monarchy was founded some two centuries ago by King Karl Johan, a powerful French field marshal and, before he changed sides, the protégé of Napoleon himself.

Of course, Swedish society has its own share of problems and these exert their own deleterious consequences. This is made clear, for example, by the so-called *Janteloven* (Law of Jante), as it is known in Swedish, first formulated by Axel Sandemose, the Danish author who settled in Norway, in his novel *A Refugee Crosses his Tracks*, published in 1933. He expresses the view that in Scandinavia, especially in the world of the provincial town, the individual impulse to stand out, to assert oneself, whatever the field, will meet with hostility, incomprehension and contempt. In this world, uniformity and the maintenance of collective security and stability will almost always win out over risk taking and genial creativity by the individual. This may, at least to some degree, be true, as many prominent Swedes from the world of the arts, business and academia have complained. Yet Sweden has by no means been bereft of people willing to struggle against the odds, in a plethora of ways, enabling the country to overcome enormous geographical, climatic and other handicaps over the centuries.

Vis-à-vis other European countries, Sweden's geographical position, at first sight, seems hardly likely to have been favourable for its development into a rich, peace-loving and socially cohesive nation state. Originally composed of four principal territories, Götaland, Svealand, Norrland and Österland – the last now independent Finland to the east – Sweden is located in the far north of Europe, on the eastern side of the Scandinavian peninsula, which it shares with Norway, but dominates in size. Covering an area of some 173,732 square miles (449,964 square kilometres), it extends approximately 1,000 miles (1,600 kilometres) north to south, a distance similar to that between the south of Sweden and Naples, in the south of Italy. From east to west, by contrast, it extends only about 310 miles (500 kilometres). Therefore, despite its length, it is by no means a large country, only slightly greater in size than the American state of California.

Its climate has hardly been inviting, even if warmer than in most other parts of the world situated at similar latitudes, like Alaska, Greenland and northern Siberia, for the effects of the Atlantic Gulf Stream exert a considerable warming effect in most parts of Sweden in winter. That said, 15 per cent of the country lies within the Arctic Circle, an inhospitable area where in winter temperatures frequently fall to minus 40 °C. Although in the summer temperatures can rise well above 30 °C (86 °F), frosts can occur there in all but the height of summer. Its soil, at least in the south in Scania, is often highly productive but that in Småland is stony, a poor till, glacial in origin, like that which covers so much of the rest of Sweden. The growing season is, in any case, usually short and the winters long and hard. In Haparanda, in the far north, temperatures in June average a meagre

15 °C (59 °F), and even in Malmö, in the extreme south, they are only 17 °C (63 °F). Crop failures have been frequent throughout Swedish history and famine was widespread well into the middle of the nineteenth century. Even now, arable land only makes up 7 per cent of the whole. Forests, on the other hand, predominate, covering almost 70 per cent of Sweden's land surface in the present day. In the far south, in Scania and along much of Sweden's western coast, they are deciduous, but in most of the rest of the southern and central parts of the country, they are mixed forests of typically northern European type. Only in Dalecarlia and Norrland do they become almost exclusively coniferous. While elk still abound in these forests in central and northern parts of Sweden, wolves have become a rarity and bears have long since disappeared.

Though crisscrossed by many rivers, of which the Göta, in the south, and the Torneå, in the north, are among the most notable, Sweden has no equivalent to the Rhine, in Germany, or the Mississippi, in the United States, in terms of significance for transport, since Swedish rivers can be frozen for almost half of the year. However, it does have three sizeable lakes, Vänern (2,156 square miles), Vättern (738 square miles) and Mälaren (440 square miles), all of which have considerable importance for the local communities round about them. Then there are the large Swedish islands of Gotland and, to a lesser degree, Öland, in the Baltic Sea, which in early days were by no means 'isolated', but were thriving centres of trade, only cut off when winter ice blocked the Baltic.

Its 2,000 miles (3,218 kilometres) of coastline, though useful for fishing, have made it vulnerable to attack by sea from neighbouring powers, in particular Denmark and Russia, with which it waged wars, off and on, for centuries, and in whose internal politics it often sought to interfere. It is, moreover, a fairly flat country, albeit with a mountain range along the extensive north-western frontier with Norway. There, in the far north, is Sweden's highest peak, Kebnekaise (Mount Kebne), which rises to a height of 6,926 feet (2,111 metres). Sweden, thus, has had no natural land defences, except in the north-west, with which to inhibit assault from beyond its borders.

Despite all these drawbacks, however, Sweden has managed to establish itself as one of the world's most economically developed nation states. Its market economy is thriving and the standard of its social welfare peerless, recent financial cuts notwithstanding. Its score on gender issues, especially the rights of gay and lesbian people, in particular, and women, in general, is also substantial. The decision of the current Swedish king, Carl XVI Gustaf, and his consort, Queen Silvia – the Brazilian-born daughter of a German businessman – in 1980, to make their eldest child, Princess Victoria (born 1977), heir to the throne proved to be a significant gesture in this regard, and served to increase popular support for the monarchy. Yet the most important fact remains Sweden's avoidance of active belligerent involvement in the violent conflagrations which have beset the world since the time of Napoleon, a status, in this respect, it shares in continental Europe only with Switzerland. It has also long served as a haven for hordes of refugees fleeing conflict in their own countries, not least Iraqis in our own day. These are no mean achievements and together they pose a fundamental question as to why and in which circumstances they came about.

I

From prehistory to Viking hegemony

In comparison with other parts of Europe, what is today Sweden, as a geographical entity with its modern coastal contours, is of relatively recent formation, its modern emergence the result of the end of the last Ice Age, which sheeted much of Europe until about ten thousand years ago. It began to emerge from its glacial covering of ice first in Scania, in the south. There the ice had disappeared by about 11,000 BC. Further north, the glaciers in and around what later became Stockholm vanished only around 8000 BC and it took a further four thousand years for the ice to disappear in most of the rest of the country. Indeed, in parts of Norrland, in the far north, some ice remained until just before the beginning of the Christian era. Therefore, it is only from this period that one can begin to speak of Sweden's prehistory, since there can remain no trace of any possible human presence from before the Ice Age.

The first human arrivals in Sweden in the aftermath of the Ice Age came predominantly from Denmark. They travelled across the Sound which today separates the two countries but, before the mid seventeenth century, was under Danish sovereignty on both sides for centuries. The earliest human settlement so far to be uncovered is that found in the far south of the country, at Segebro, near Malmö, which dates to about 10,000–9000 years BC. Another early settlement was that at Hensbacka, in Bohuslän, which can be dated to 7300–6600 BC. It was sustained by reindeer hunting, an important source of food for many of the Nordic region's inhabitants, even as far north as Pechenga (Petsamo, when it was Finnish between the two world wars), in what is today the far north-west of the Russian Federation. This common dependence on reindeer is an indication that a land route through the north of what is today Finland into Sweden may have been an important conduit, not only for reindeer but for migratory people as well. Other later settlements have been uncovered at Sandarna, where modern Gothenburg is now situated, and at Ageröd, in Scania. The former can be dated to between 6600 and 5000 BC, the latter more precisely to 6000 BC. Both communities lived largely by hunting and fishing, using implements of stone, clay, wood and bone.

The palaeolithic in Sweden persisted until the beginning of the third millennium BC, but the arrival of settled agriculture and animal husbandry in the neolithic led to dramatic changes in the life of the inhabitants. A massive influx of immigrants propelled by the westward migration of tribes from the east also further altered the social fabric of human life in the region. The most striking archaeological relics from this period are the massive stone burial tombs, some of which can be seen at Luttra, near Falköping, in Västergötaland, built, it is generally agreed, some two thousand years before the Christian era, even if the ethnic identity of their builders is still a matter of dispute.

BRONZE AGE SETTLEMENTS

Although situated on the northern periphery of Europe, the geographical area which is today Sweden was fully integrated into pan-European trading networks. The introduction of bronze around 1500 BC, made possible by the blossoming of maritime trade across the North and Baltic seas, had far-ranging consequences, especially with respect to trade. Imported bronze was exchanged for fur, slaves and gems. The metal itself was used not only for weapons, agricultural tools and other implements, but for decorative and symbolic purposes as well. Bronze jewellery was much sought after by powerful families and used to adorn woollen clothes, which had now come to supplant animal skins as the primary form of apparel.

Massive stone tombs, a feature of the beginning of this period, came to be supplanted by earth-covered ones, filled with a wide variety of artefacts, all of which were intended to accompany the dead into the afterlife beyond. The corpses themselves now generally came to be cremated, the ashes being placed in burial urns, which were, in turn, deposited within tombs. One so-called *hällristning*, that is, rock carving, an example of which can be seen at Vitlycke, in Bohuslän, is decorated with images, not only of sailing vessels and people, but of domestic animals and practical implements, in a variety of activities, presumed to be characteristic of the time.

THE IRON AGE

After the arrival of iron in Sweden, first introduced by the Celtic-speaking tribes who had migrated to Sweden across the Baltic Sea from the south, that metal rapidly superseded bronze because of its greater practical utility. Indeed, by 500 BC, its use had become so widespread that it effected profound changes on Swedish society and agriculture. Being much stronger than bronze, iron made not only more durable and efficient weapons but better household and agricultural implements as well.

Yet, if the Iron Age in Sweden had initiated improvements in agriculture, it was also a period in which the climate had become less hospitable. Indeed, the increasingly colder climate led not only to a diminution of the population, but, almost as significant for its survival, to a reduction in trade. Nonetheless, though now more limited in volume, mercantile links were by no means extinguished and archaeology demonstrates that a variety of valuable objects, including glassware and elaborately decorated pots now began to appear in Sweden from the Roman Empire during this period. Roman connections have also been demonstrated by the emergence of a Swedish runic language and script, which clearly shares many characteristics with the Latin alphabet. These similarities are evinced by more than fifty extant runic inscriptions from about the second century AD, which still intrigue archaeologists to this day. Initially, this old runic script was composed of twenty-four letters. However, by the seventh century, it had become more streamlined, reduced to only sixteen. It remained the written mode of expression for Swedes until after the country's Christianisation, when direct links with Rome came finally to be established. Thereafter, Latin rapidly superseded it, but by then the use of written language had become much wider in scope than its previous usage, largely limited to memorial inscriptions on wood, bone and stone.

As for domestic arrangements, the three-aisled longhouse was characteristic of this period. It typically contained several rooms for residential accommodation, along with a byre for livestock. The remains of such constructions have been found in various parts of Sweden, as far north as Ångermansland.

GROWTH OF CONTACT WITH THE ROMAN EMPIRE

By about AD 400, closer and more extended contacts had once again come to be formed with the Roman Empire, its political and economic decline during this period notwithstanding. Many imported commodities now passed through the hands of traders from the Germanic tribes which had begun to overrun Sweden and whose networks, largely economic, were spread southwards to the shores of the Mediterranean. Yet trade came from other directions as well, in particular from the east, and it is to this growing mercantile activity that the development of and consolidation of the nascent Swedish territorial state is largely indebted. Already, by the early sixth century, religious and other valuable objects from Asia were brought to Sweden along Russian river routes and then across the Baltic. Among the most interesting of these artefacts is a small Buddhist statue from India, now displayed in the Nordic Museum, Stockholm, a rare but fascinating example of trading links to the Asian subcontinent during this early period.

The Roman Empire throughout virtually all of its history was by no means unaware of the Nordic world and, during the early centuries of the Christian era, some Roman authors wrote about it. For example, according to the great Roman historian Tacitus, in the first century AD, the Sveas, who resided there, were a united people, with a king even in his day, but historians of our own time have come to the conclusion that a united kingdom of the Sveas can, in reality, be confirmed only from the ninth century. Perhaps Tacitus, then, in writing of northern peoples, was more interested in using contrived historical writing to influence events in Rome, rather than in remarking upon historical realities elsewhere.

Be that as it may, according to Procopius, a historian of the Eastern Roman Empire, writing in the early sixth century, the population of Sweden consisted of thirteen tribes, each with its own king. Later writers, however, saw the country as composed of primarily two peoples, the Sveas and the Goths, the former living to the north of the great forested belts of Kolmården and Tiveden, the latter to the south and on the island of Gotland. The matter is made more complicated by the fact that modern research concludes that the *Svitjod*, or lands of the *Sveas*, signified a more narrowly confined region, namely that which is today Uppland and parts of Västmanland, rather than a wider geographical area.

Swedish society at this time was highly hierarchical and its leaders commanded considerable political power. This they exerted in their political assembly or *Disartinget*, which helped to provide a focus for the formation of their common political identity. The primary purpose of the assembly had originally been religious, based on common sacrifices to the gods, but matters relating to government, law and trade were also discussed and decided there. The assembly also served to exert a unifying effect on the three local regions of which it was composed – Tiundaland, Attundaland and Fjärdhundraland – by increasingly forging a more unified political and economic identity than had previously been the case. Be that as it may, the existence of royal graves at Hågahögen seems to confirm that a united kingdom of the Sveas had, at least by the Scandinavian late Iron Age, certainly become a political reality. By then, it extended at least as far as Lake Mälaren to the south, the southern reaches of Norrland to the north, and the coastal regions of Finland to the east.

With trade expanding, especially eastwards, the Sveas were coming to enjoy considerable prosperity. This was characterised, in part, by the import of gold, possibly plundered from their neighbours to the south, the Goths, whose economic wellbeing was declining markedly during this period. Whether or not the ninth-century rune stone at Sparlösa, in Västergötland, can be taken to confirm decisively the hegemony of the Sveas in that province is a moot point. However, the report of the Scandinavian traveller Wulfstand to King Alfred of England, in 865, makes clear that by that year, Blekinge, Gotland

1 Carved and erected towards the end of the first millennium on the central Baltic island of Gotland, the centre of an important trading nexus, this runic stone at Hammars in Lärebo is richly adorned with depictions of horses, warriors and Viking vessels, but its precise meaning remains obscure. Photo: Else Roesdahl.

and Öland – along with much of the Baltic coastline – were all under the rule of the Sveas. That said, it was only under King Olof Eriksson Skötkonung, at the turn of the first millennium, that both the Sveas and the Goths living in today's modern provinces of Uppland, Västmanland, Östergötland, Småland and Västergötland were all united formally under one common acknowledged ruler, thereby creating the basis for a unified Swedish state. In the far north, however, Saami (Lapp) settlements were to be found, not only inland but at various sites along the western coast of the Gulf of Bothnia, of which Grundskatan and Hornslandet are the most notable. The recently discovered archaeological remains of these cobbled huts, four by five metres in size with central hearths, provide evidence of their presence from at least the beginning of the fifth century AD until the end of the thirteenth century.

THE VIKING AGE

From the beginning of the ninth century AD, the Vikings of Scandinavia – Sveas, Goths, Danes, Norwegians and others – were, through a combination of pillage and trade, making a dramatic impact economically and politically on much of Europe. It is for this reason that one can speak of a Viking hegemony in the north – the term 'Viking' signifying a person inhabiting the fjords which are so characteristic of Scandinavia's coastline. Yet, whereas many western Vikings pillaged and traded with the west, many Swedish Vikings did so in the east. There they were of great importance in what is today's Russia and Ukraine, assisting in the foundation of Novgorod (Holmgård, as it was known in old Swedish), in the mid ninth century, and Kiev, in the early tenth.

Even at home in Sweden, their activities profoundly changed local life and culture: villages came into being and new lands came under cultivation. Political and judicial administration tightened, as an increasingly centralised and invasive network of powerful military and political figures consolidated their authority over a territory which had become an increasingly unitary and centralised state, and one in which a king, elected by magnates of the most powerful families, had become the dominant power. This had, to a significant degree, been made possible by the increased wealth generated by a burgeoning trade with Russia and the east. This was by no means local or even merely trans-Baltic in scope, but was truly transcontinental in its dimensions. Indeed, by means of the rivers of Russia, Swedish Vikings were able to develop important mercantile links with Byzantium, successor to the Eastern Roman Empire, and the Arab world of the Middle East.

Towns, attracting merchants from throughout the region, became necessary for this trade and Birka, in the province of Uppland, not far from modern-day Stockholm, was Sweden's first, its *raison d'être* this very trade, which passed through the hands of its prosperous merchants. Extending over some twelve hectares, it thrived between 800 and 975, protected, as it was, by the fort that surmounted the hill to its south-west, the ramparts of which can still be seen. Its trade was from far afield, indeed, and items have been uncovered there from such far-removed places as England and the Middle East, an indication of its role as a major Baltic marketplace. It was from here, in all probability, too, that Swedish merchants went eastward to what is now Russia, through the trading centre of Roslagen, the name of which may have led them to be named the 'Rus', after they had established themselves across the Baltic Sea.

Frankish annals of the period, though, still called these Vikings Sveas and they fanned out both eastwards and southwards deep into Russia and beyond. They travelled down rivers, in particular the Volga and Dnepr, at least as far as the Black and Caspian seas, pulling their boats overland when geographical impediments, such as rapids, required it. Not a few reached Constantinople, capital of the Byzantine Empire, where some acquired considerable fortunes, not only through pillage but by employment in the imperial government. With Rome, in the west, on the other hand, to which transport links were poor, direct contacts remained minimal.

The relationship between the Byzantine imperial capital and the Swedes, while sometimes mutually beneficial, was also sporadically highly destructive: in 860, a surprise assault on Constantinople, the initiative for which emanated from Kiev, left the city plundered and weary of these Northmen. More generally, however, they were a source of profit for local people who greedily bought up their goods in the markets of the Byzantine Empire.

Another major centre of trade was Sweden's Baltic island of Gotland. Archaeological remains, both urban and rural, found scattered throughout its parishes, include objects of silver, among them many coins of Arab origins, with Kufic designs, as well as those of Byzantine mintage. These provide an indication of the wealth amassed through this trans-Baltic trade, which was largely carried out by the prosperous local landowners who frequently visited the overseas ports from which their trade emanated. Since many of their trading ships travelled in armed convoy, their defensive stance often transmogrified into open Viking marauding, when lucrative booty from poorly defended towns and countryside proved too tempting, beyond their shores. That said, such Swedish merchants often worked in peaceful tandem with the foreign peoples they encountered, especially those who facilitated the import and export of goods throughout Europe and beyond. This was, for example, the case with the Frisians of the North Sea coast to the west and the neighbouring Danes to the south, in particular those based at Hedeby, a major mercantile centre, where in the early tenth century a branch of the Swedish royal clan briefly succeeded in gaining political control.

Swedes traded a wide variety of goods, in all directions, but slaves, usually of Slavic ethnicity, furs and amber were the primary commodities. As for imports, these were various but silver featured prominently, highly fashionable for personal ornamentation.

Russia had by now become a land offering Swedish Vikings considerable potential political domination and, even more importantly, material gain. As the Nestor Chronicle relates, admittedly long after the events, the Swede Rörik, or Rurik, as he is known in Russia, established with his men Swedish hegemony, the so-called *Stora Svitjod*, in the lands settled by Slavs to the south and west. Archaeological remains confirm that Nordic colonists, travelling by way of Lake Ladoga and the rivers Ilmen, Volga, Don and Dnepr, were settled over a wide area, albeit concentrated therein in important seats of trade. These extended from Novgorod in the east, to Smolensk in the west and Kiev in the south. Archaeological relics, such as female jewellery, indicate that these immigrants were largely Svea from the Swedish heartland, by Birka and around Lake Mälaren, rather than from Gotland. The fact that the legal code which came to be established in Novgorod was that of the Sveas further strengthens this conclusion.

Suddenly, in 975, Birka disappeared from the chronicles as a noted trading centre. Probably it was destroyed by an enemy assault, though by whom or why precisely is not known. This did not mean, though, that its province of Uppland ceased to be an important centre for trade, since the newly established settlement of Sigtuna seems to have captured much of Birka's former trade in its stead. Moreover, Gotland's mercantile development also seems to have strengthened at this time. After the turn of the millennium, Lödöse, on Sweden's west coast, also became an important centre of trade, with an expanding network extending westwards across the North Sea to England and the Netherlands.

As economic integration with other parts of Europe increased, Sweden increasingly came under another profound pan-European influence: Christianity. In consequence, Sweden, too, would soon enter the ranks of Christendom and by so doing, its centuries-old religion would rapidly disappear. Nonetheless, its cultural influence would persist and, indeed, find a rich resonance surviving up to our own day.

RELIGIOUS BELIEFS

The Vikings of Sweden left many legacies to the world, both beneficial and destructive, yet some of the most lasting, at least in cultural terms, were elements of their system of religious beliefs. The religion of the ancient Swedes has long captivated not only historians, but poets and authors from around the world, in a multiplicity of cultures, fascinated by its complex mythology, rivalling and often influenced by that of the classical world. Nowhere was its influence greater than in the central European heartland of Germany almost a millennium after its heyday, in the course of the nineteenth century, as Wagnerian images of the ancient Norse gods, still popular today, demonstrate. Nonetheless, Nordic gods and goddesses, as evinced in Wagner's majestic and multifaceted operas, should not be taken as representative of genuine pre-Christian Nordic religious beliefs. True, the Æsa cult to which Swedes adhered towards the end of the first millennium AD was clearly related to ancient Germanic religious beliefs and customs. However, their own uniqueness and individuality, as distinguished from that of nineteenth-century concepts of them, cannot be overstressed.

By no means monolithic and dogmatic, it was a porous religious system which encompassed a plethora of gods and goddesses, who played roles related to all aspects of life. It also had no formalised priesthood in the Christian sense of the term. This was in part because, as in most of the world's religions, except for Christianity, the dividing line between the religious and the secular was non-existent. In consequence, major figures, political, military and economic, played roles in both religious and secular spheres. They evoked the help and protection of the gods and goddesses in a wide range of situations, social, cultural, agricultural and military. A broad spectrum of events – successful harvests or victorious military campaigns – all demanded their own appropriate religious invocations, many of which involved sacrifices of one form or another. In these, the Norse gods played key, if diverse, roles.

Among the most prominent Norse gods – and it should be remembered that their veneration was not restricted to Sweden but extended throughout Scandinavia and beyond – were Thor, Odin and Freyr.

Thor was invoked for a successful harvest and his protection was sought by farmers against the giants who were thought to reside in the mysterious realm of *Jotunheim*. While they battled with both gods and men, these giants also provided them with much wisdom and many skills. One of their number, Ymir, was considered to be the first living creature.

Thor was one of the most powerful of the gods and his domain was a world of order and stability in which chaos was kept at bay. The god Odin, in turn, was invoked when military campaigns were undertaken. He was deemed to be the protector, not only of the sword-bearing aristocracy, but also of the bards who sang of their exploits. However, like the gods of ancient Greece, he was a fickle divinity whose deviousness was feared, especially as he was also associated with death and the world of the dead.

Odin's handmaidens, the Valkyries, were the arbiters of the warriors who would die in battle, destined, therefore, to ride victoriously into Valhalla. This was a Nordic version of the Greek Mount Olympus, known as *Asgård* in Swedish. Archaeological excavations confirm that many warriors in the tenth century were buried with their weapons in seeming anticipation of a heroes' welcome in Valhalla. Once arrived in the afterworld, the deceased warriors were expected eventually to enter a new military affray, a confrontation in which, together with the gods, they would fight the chaos which threatened all order, both human and divine. This, it was believed, would occur at *Ragnarök*, in a Nordic version of the

German *Götterdämmerung*, that is, a spiritual apocalypse, which not only implied the doom of the gods themselves but also had overwhelming significance for the whole of human history. In this scenario, Thor and Odin also played major roles. This shattering event, however, was perceived not as the end of history, but rather as the occasion for its re-creation.

The gods themselves were divided up into two family groupings. Both Thor and Odin were of that known as the *æsir*. Freyr, by contrast, was from the family known as *vanir* and was the son of Njord, god of wind, sea and fire. He himself was the god of fertility – as well as lust – and much political clout was later made of the legend that maintained that the Swedish royal house of Yngve Frej was descended from him. Freyr's sister, in turn, was Freyja, associated with a cult of fertility, but, at the same time, linked to the world of the dead, where she welcomed newly arrived warriors fallen in battle.

Other goddesses included the Norns, a Nordic version of the Fates, who determined the length of every person's life span. There were also the *disir*, female beings to whom festive sacrifices, the so-called *blót*, were made, usually at the solstices, as reflected in extant examples of skaldic poetry of the time.

While the gods, goddesses and heroes resided in *Asgård*, humankind was confined to the middle realms of *Midgård*, that is, the earth. While all of creation was itself, in turn, encompassed by a giant sea serpent, its centre was by no means fixed, as in Christianity of the same period. That said, a central feature of this cosmology was the so-called *Yggdrasill* or World Tree, a mystical abstraction of considerable complexity. Ancient trees on individual farmsteads were frequently venerated in conjunction with it, thereby linking family life and wellbeing to the cosmic order itself. The natural world was, thus, inextricably intertwined in the religious world of pre-Christian Sweden, with a resonance which has inspired many, politically as well as culturally, in the centuries following and up to our own day.

THE CHRISTIANISATION OF SWEDEN

The conversion of Sweden to Christianity, largely completed in the twelfth century, exerted a profound influence not only on Swedish society and its spiritual life, but by assisting in the growth of the

Swedish state itself over the following centuries. Yet it was a long and arduous process and took several centuries to achieve. In 829, the French missionary Ansgar, later German Hamburg's first bishop, arrived in the Swedish trading centre of Birka, by way of the Danish settlement of Hedeby. His reception by the king of the Sveas was deceptively friendly. Granted land for the construction of Sweden's first church, he remained in Birka until the following year. However, after his departure, anti-Christian sentiment grew, ultimately leading to the massacre of a number of missionaries who had remained. In its immediate aftermath he undertook no further mission there, but eventually he returned to Birka in 850, remaining until the following year in an attempt to resuscitate Christianity. Although again its revival at this time proved short lived, Ansgar's role as an intrepid missionary was recognised and, not long after his death in 865, he was sanctified as a saint of the Catholic Church.

Fresh initiatives to convert Sweden were undertaken at various times thereafter but only in the eleventh century did Christianity begin to take firm root, as evinced by the appearance of contemporary runic stones embellished with Christian symbols. At first, it had seemed that the acceptance of Christianity by the Swedish warrior king Erik Segersäll (died *c.*994), during his sojourn in Denmark, would facilitate this process. However, he reverted to paganism after his return to his capital, Uppsala, the ancient centre of Swedish pagan religious practices. That said, his son, Olof Eriksson Skötkonung (*c.*980–1022), proved more steadfast in the new religion. He even introduced Christian symbols into Swedish coinage, taking English examples for stylistic inspiration. He also saw to it that English craftsmen and priests arrived in Sweden in considerable numbers to propagate Christianity, as well as to provide new skills for the construction of churches and religious artefacts. Unfortunately, this endeavour was undermined by his unhappy relationship with Norway, with which numerous wars ensued. Therefore, despite some short-term territorial gains, few lasting benefits to Sweden accrued in this regard through these endeavours. On the other hand, in the sphere of religion, success was ensured: Christianity, in its western Catholic form, became firmly established as the religion of the land.

2 Husaby Church, Västergötland. One of Sweden's oldest churches dating
from the eleventh century. Its massive tower, with round arched windows,
was originally attached to a wooden nave which was replaced in the
following century by a stone nave and choir. Its style is Romanesque, largely
derived from models in the German Rhineland typical of stone churches
built in Sweden at this time. Photo: Anna Nilsén.

Olof Eriksson's three sons, Anund Jakob, Emund and Stenkil, remained steadfast in their adherence to the new faith. Indeed, under Stenkil's initiative, after his succession to the throne, an episcopal seat was established at Sigtuna, not far to the south of Uppsala, to the great chagrin of many who still adhered to paganism. It would later be transferred to Uppsala itself, that former *hochburg* of paganism, in the middle of the twelfth century. Meanwhile, another episcopal seat, Sweden's first, had already been established at Skara, in 1015, but, for complex reasons, ecclesiastical and political, both remained vacant for many years.

It was the arrival of Adam of Bremen, during the 1070s, which proved crucial for the solid establishment of the Catholic Church in Sweden. Under his aegis, Christianity came to be adopted not only by powerful magnate families but by the general population, as well. That said, it still remained to deal the final deathblows to a fading paganism. New laws were now promulgated to achieve this effect, in particular *Upplandslagen* or the Law of Uppland, by which the worship of idols, groves of sacred trees and stones all came to be forbidden. Nonetheless, old habits and customs died hard in Sweden, as the English monk Aelnoth bore witness in the eleventh century. Moreover, the dangers of war, poor harvests, severe political and economic decline, along with the other calamities of the period, led to a revival of the old cults. To combat this, numerous churches were built, from which the teachings of Christianity were propagated and, over the following years, many ancient pagan practices came to be subsumed into Christian ones. Even so, many persisted in the guise of rustic superstitions well into the modern period.

2

The formation and growth
of the Swedish state

By the end of the first quarter of the twelfth century, the Catholic Church was firmly established in Sweden. In 1120, the permanent presence of a bishop on Swedish soil was finally secured and other seats were formally established throughout the country, at Linköping, Strängnäs, Västerås and Eskilstuna, even if the episcopal incumbents were not necessarily in residence. Few of them were, in any case, Swedish at this time, for most of the country's early missionary bishops were foreigners, predominantly English or, in other cases, German. Some suffered martyrdom, like Eskil, the 'apostle' of Södermanland, in whose honour the see of Eskilstuna was named. English and German Catholicism thus came to exert a significant influence on the Swedish Church in its early days, furthering cultural and economic links in the process. The foreign churchmen were, also, particularly useful in introducing coherent legal codes and administrative practices modelled on those in their native lands. Especially important, in this regard, was the evidential stress they gave to written documentation, in confirmation of land grants or other forms of voluntary donations. This paved the way for a judicial system, which further served to assist the growth of the Swedish state itself.

Swedish architecture at this time was almost exclusively dependent upon local building materials, in particular wood, even if many stylistic influences also came from abroad. Most of the early churches in Sweden, therefore, were, not surprisingly, built of wooden staves, but already by the beginning of the twelfth century, stone ones like that at Sigtuna were constructed, often based on Anglo-Norman models. This situation was in contrast to that of Scania, in the south, still under Danish hegemony, where churches tended to follow German models, in particular church design from the Rhineland.

If, in architectural terms, the Swedish Church was highly dependent on foreign prototypes, it, nonetheless, strove to achieve considerable autonomy in administrative terms, in particular from neighbouring Denmark. One of its first goals was therefore to establish an independent archiepiscopal see in Sweden. To achieve this goal, in the later twelfth century, King Karl Sverkersson sent an embassy to Pope Alexander III, asking for permission to establish an archiepiscopal seat at Uppsala, independent of the Danish one at Lund, itself set up at the beginning of the twelfth century. This was finally granted in 1164 but a proviso was appended, obliging the actual investiture of the Archbishop of Uppsala to take place in Lund, the incumbent of which remained primate of the Nordic region until the Reformation. Nonetheless, the establishment of a Swedish archiepiscopal see also served to strengthen the Swedish state itself.

A major issue, full of political and economic significance, which now confronted the Church in Sweden, as well as the king and his subjects, was its financial maintenance and support. Measures were therefore instituted so that the hierarchy of the Church supported itself not only from voluntary donations and the financial largesse of the king and the nobility, the formation of which was completed about 1300, but from tithes collected on all forms of property. These included not only land but animal husbandry as well. One third of these collected tithes went to the priests themselves, an obligation on the parishes which continued throughout the Reformation and into the nineteenth century. Land sufficient to provide for their everyday needs was also exempted from taxation by the secular authorities, but land in excess of this amount remained liable, unless relieved by royal authority. In 1281, King Magnus issued a letter of privilege, freeing the Church altogether of any obligation to pay secular taxes. However, after his death, the hostility of the nobility to this measure led to curtailments of this privilege. Thereafter, only old church lands, that is, those acquired before 1302, remained permanently free from taxation.

A variety of monastic orders now came to establish themselves in Sweden, much as they had done elsewhere in Catholic Europe. Along with the foundation of an ecclesiastical administrative structure in the country, these religious orders not only set up their own religious houses and infrastructure, but often laid claim to large tracts of forested land, with the intention of bringing it into cultivation. Among the first to arrive in the middle of the twelfth century were the Cistercians. They rapidly founded, with royal assistance, the monasteries of Byarum, Alvastra, Gudhem and Varnhem. The Benedictines also came during this period, establishing the nunneries of Börringe and Bosjökloster. The Cluniacs, in turn, founded a monastery at Lund and the Augustinian monks their own houses, at Lund and Dalby. That said, it was the later arrivals, in particular the Franciscans and Dominicans, who came increasingly to dominate the monastic scene in Sweden over the following centuries.

A complex system of ecclesiastical administration thus developed in Sweden during this period, modelled on that established throughout western European Christendom, which maintained a considerable degree of independence from the secular authorities. By the beginning of the thirteenth century, chapter houses for the administration of cathedrals, as well as ecclesiastical courts of justice, came to be founded, centralising church administration, while at the same time integrating it into the wider international fabric of the Church. The increasingly cosmopolitan education of students for the clergy encouraged this process, forging as it did closer links with a wide range of continental universities. Indeed, there were some thirty Swedish students in Paris alone in 1309. The number of Swedish students in major seats of European learning was considerable for more than two centuries, with at least eight hundred attending a variety of universities. Swedish students of theology and law, destined for the higher clergy, for example, were sent to the University of Bologna and later that of Paris during the course of the thirteenth century. At the same time, the lower clergy also benefited, as they now received two years of theological education at cathedral schools established for the purpose, often with teachers imported from abroad. New schools also began to serve the needs of the secular population, but these were limited in both scope and number. In any case, they were confined to such major cities and towns as Stockholm, Vadstena and Jönköping. In Finland, now fully integrated into the Swedish kingdom, Turku (Åbo in Swedish) became the centre of ecclesiastical and scholarly activities, a status, with respect to the former, it still maintains today.

The Christianisation of Sweden did not remain restricted to its heartlands but extended into the Arctic, as Norrland, Sweden's most northerly province, also embraced the religion during this period. Luleå, in coastal Västerbotten, became rapidly established as the most important ecclesiastical seat in the province. Its ancient church was founded in 1339 and was later enlarged in 1492, thereby becoming the largest church in Sweden north of Uppsala when it was inaugurated by the Archbishop of Uppsala. Constructed in the Gothic style, its vaulted interior was adorned with paintings by the renowned artist Albertus Pictor (*c.*1440–*c.*1507) and its inventory, as recorded in 1525, included a splendid altar imported from Antwerp. Such expensive embellishments were made possible financially by the town's prosperous local economy, based on a lucrative trade in dry fish, furs and tar. The parish it served was vast, covering an area encompassing a quarter of what is today Sweden. Much of its funding, however, came specifically from Uppsala, from the coffers of which the Swedish primate himself made donations. Yet the territorial expanse of the parish notwithstanding, the population it served was tiny and the regularity of church attendance limited. More than 700 of the 2,500 parishioners registered there in 1559 did not even attend services at Easter, the most important religious feast day in the church calendar. That said, the town's religious significance was considerable because Luleå served as a base for missionary activities for the rest of the north of the province. Indeed, it was the missionaries from Luleå who went forth to effect the conversion of the Saami people who, though they had formerly, in centuries gone by, lived on the coast, now resided in the deep interior of Lapland. This conversion process took many years to complete, for many of the Saami continued to practise their shamanistic religion, in which the drum and singing of *joiks* played a prominent ceremonial role for centuries to come, albeit with increasingly interwoven elements of Christian theology and customs.

The Christianisation of the region also served to integrate the far north more tightly into the Swedish state.

If the twelfth and thirteenth centuries formed a period of spiritual upheaval in Sweden, it was also one of major secular disturbances and changes. Dynastic upheavals were a constant problem, one in which competing claims for royal hegemony vied with one another. With the death of Inge the Younger, for example, the Stenkil dynasty had been extinguished, allowing his grandson through the female line, a Danish prince named Magnus Nielsen, to claim the Swedish throne. Yet although his authority over Götaland was undisputedly acknowledged, his sudden death at the Battle of Fotevik, in Scania, in 1134, paved the way for Sverker the Elder, a magnate from Östergötland now married to Inge the Younger's widow, success- fully to claim the throne. However, his scandalous murder by one of his gentlemen of the chamber, at Christmas 1156, on the way to attend church, opened the way for the eruption of a century-long violent contest to secure the royal throne between the two principal dynastic contenders: those descended from Sverker and those from Erik the Holy.

KING ERIK, SAINT AND MARTYR

With the accession, after a vote in Uppsala, of Erik the Holy (c.1120–60), the Swedish throne was occupied by a new and pious king who saw to it that the Catholic Church thrived in his dominions, in ways secular as well as spiritual. Stone churches, rather than wood, now came to be built throughout the southern and central provinces of the country, even if in Norrland wooden ones continued to be the rule. It was during his reign that the episcopal see of Uppsala was elevated to its archiepiscopal status. Of especial significance, too, were the missionary activities which he initiated, since these led to the conversion of Finland to Christianity. This was accomplished under the leadership there of his assistant, the English-born Bishop Henry, who was martyred about 1156. In consequence of their efforts, an episcopal see was

3 The official seal of Sweden's capital city, Stockholm, depicts one of the country's early monarchs and its patron saint, King Erik (*c.*1120–60). Also known as Erik the Holy, he helped to consolidate the Roman Catholic Church in the country, in both religious and political terms. He was martyred in Uppsala, the recently established see of the Catholic Church in Sweden, not by pagans, but by a disaffected Danish prince, Magnus Henriksen.

established at Turku, in the following century, which served as a radiating focus for further missionary activities throughout Finland.

In Sweden, King Erik himself was martyred, struck down during mass in Uppsala, not by pagans, but by a disaffected Danish prince, Magnus Henriksen. Rapidly declared a saint of the Church, Erik was soon adopted as the country's patron saint. A powerful magnate, Karl Sverkersson, then seized the Swedish throne, only to meet a violent end himself in 1167, cut down by Erik's son Knut, from whom he had usurped the throne. Only then did a lengthy period of relative stability follow, which lasted beyond Knut Eriksson's own natural death in 1196. A member of the rival dynasty, Sverker the

Younger, then once more took the throne. Upon the latter's death without issue, this was expected to revert to Erik's line. Nonetheless, after decisive battles in Västergötland, in 1208 and 1210, in which Norway and Denmark supported opposing sides, the former's champion won and Erik Knutsson ascended the throne. However, his death in 1216 and his failure to produce a male heir (his only son, Erik, was born after his death) enabled Johan Sverkersson to reclaim the throne for his line. Nonetheless, it was to prove a pyrrhic victory, for, when Johan Sverkersson in his turn died without an heir having never married, his dynasty was suddenly extinguished. Therefore, the young Erik Eriksson succeeded to the throne in 1222. Although he would reign until 1249, his kingship, too, was challenged and in the late 1220s a rebellion under the leadership of Knut Långe (the Long) briefly succeeded in forcing him to flee to Denmark. However, after Långe's death not long thereafter, Erik returned to claim the throne. He had no issue and political power soon came to be invested in a coterie of powerful Swedish earls, in particular Ulv Jarl (Earl in English). Upon Erik's death, therefore, it was his nephew, the son of Birger Jarl (*c*.1210–66), another earl who was amassing an ever stronger power base, who was elected king while still a child. The power behind the throne was, in reality, that of Birger Jarl. He continued to hold the reins of state, while strengthening them, until his death in 1266, accomplishing a number of major social and economic reforms, including the abolition of judicial ordeal by fire and the curtailment of serfdom.

THE SIGNIFICANCE OF THE HANSA IN SWEDEN

Foreign influences from across the Baltic Sea to the south were now also beginning to make themselves strongly felt in Sweden, in the economic as well as the architectural sphere. These emanated outwards from the north German Hansa cities, which were beginning to become enmeshed in Sweden's economic and political life at this time. The mid-Baltic island of Gotland was by now a thriving centre of mercantile activity, and its principal city, Visby, an important Hansa mercantile centre for cross-Baltic trade. Already by 1250, it was completely dominated by German merchants, some fifty-six of whom had immigrated there from the Rhineland and Westphalia.

Many of them rapidly assimilated with the resident Swedes, but others continued to maintain their German cultural and linguistic identity for centuries. This was especially the case in Kalmar, where German ethnic identity survived until the seventeenth century. German settlement was, of course, not confined only to Gotland and the coast of mainland Sweden. Germans also settled in Viborg (Vipuuri in Finnish but today known as Vyborg, after its incorporation into Russia towards the end of the Second World War), where one was appointed Bishop of Turku in the fourteenth century and where a German community continued to thrive until the early twentieth century. Hansa ships now regularly criss-crossed the Baltic and North seas, laden with goods, which more tightly integrated Sweden with major European trading centres than ever before. They also made the country increasingly dependent on the political and economic pressures of Hansa merchants, both those now settled in Sweden, as well as those residing in Lübeck, Hamburg and elsewhere.

It should also be added that these German settlements continued to leave an imprint, architectural, as well as mercantile, on the Swedish cities, towns and even villages where they were established: the magnificent Gothic churches of Gotland, more plentiful per square mile than in Tuscany, in Italy, clearly evince the architectural workmanship of Saxon craftsmen who were brought over to carry out the commissions. So, too, both the Maria Church at Sigtuna and Strängnäs Cathedral demonstrate that already in the fourteenth century German craftsmen were at work there, propagating the cutting edge of the continental architectural fashions which were now the hallmarks of their native lands.

Germans were also prominent as theologians and men of thought. When German lawyers and churchmen gained increasing prominence in Sweden in the course of the fifteenth century, the ground was laid for a receptive soil in which the later values of the German-led Reformation were able to thrive. This process was facilitated by the literary revolution which followed in the wake of the arrival of the first printing press from Lübeck, which took place possibly as early as 1480. When many Swedish students then spent extended sojourns in German centres of learning, this symbiosis was heightened further, lending itself to the ultimate triumph of the Lutheran Church in Sweden, and its submission to the Swedish king, which strengthened the growth of the state. However, that lay many years in the future.

THE BIRGER DYNASTY

With the establishment of the Birger dynasty, otherwise known as the *Folkunga* dynasty, many powerful noblemen felt themselves increasingly marginalised by the growth of royal power, which to a significant degree had been brought about by the king's increasing control of the legal and judicial system. This problem of a powerful nobility alienated from its king would become a recurrent theme in Swedish history, often with murderous consequences, right up to the assassination of King Gustaf III in the late eighteenth century. On this early occasion they resented not only the strengthened monarchy, but the growing influence of German settlers and the fact that Birger Jarl's sons had been granted semi-autonomous duchies. As a result, not long after Birger Jarl's death, open rebellion broke out which led to the enforced abdication of his son Valdemar Birgersson (*c.*1239– 1302). This occurred through Danish interference and achieved the election to the Swedish throne of Valdemar's brother, Magnus Ladulås (*c.*1240–90), more amenable to their wishes. Upon his death, Magnus's son Birger was, in turn, elected to succeed him. However, the reins of government actually came to be held by the magnate Torgils Knutsson (died 1306), for Birger was still a child and the powers of the ruling council established to govern during the regency were limited.

Yet when the young Birger finally achieved his majority, the principal threat to his rule came not from rival dynasties but from his own family. His brother Erik Magnusson led the revolt. Finally, though, in 1305, an accord was reached between the two. Although this led to the execution of Knutsson for treason, the familial rivalry remained and further strife ensued. This situation was further aggra- vated by Sweden's neighbours which, in the following year, fomented uprisings during which Erik was successful in grabbing the reins of power. Birger was seized and imprisoned at the estate of Håtuna, in Uppland, in an attempt to neutralise his power. Yet only in 1310 was a wider peace finally reached. It involved not only all of Scandinavia, but the north German coastal principalities as well, so deeply involved in Sweden's economic and political life. In conse- quence, a division of Sweden into separate political spheres was effected, each controlled by a different brother and with inheritance rights relegated to their male issue. This was a heavy price to pay, but formally, the unity of Sweden remained intact: Birger remained king in name and his brothers took an oath of loyalty towards him. It was a superficial solution to a deep-seated problem.

With such fractions below the surface, it is not surprising that this accord proved short lived. In 1317, Birger, having strengthened his political and economic position, turned the tables on his brothers, and sent them to prison, where, according to tradition, they starved to death the following year. Notwithstanding such draconian and brutal methods to bolster his power, his reign collapsed and he fled to Denmark where he died soon after.

ESTABLISHMENT OF THE ESTATES SYSTEM AND SWEDISH EXPANSIONISM

New political constellations were now in the offing, in reaction to changes which had occurred in the later decades of the previous century, which would lead, in the early years of the following century, to dramatic changes in Sweden's political life and ultimately, towards its end, to the Nordic Union.

Already, in 1280, the Decree of Alsnö helped to consolidate a feudal order in Sweden along continental European lines, while introducing the estate system, in which each of the estates, representing the nobility, the Church, the burghers and the peasants, had its individual role to play. It was unique, however, in a wider European context, in that the peasants were, to a considerable degree, free and in possession of rights which enabled them to play significant political roles. Thus, they were able to assist in the election of clergymen, as well as to take part in local and regional decision making, at first with respect to local *landskapslagar* (provincial laws) and later even state-wide legal codes.

On 8 July 1319, at Mora, in Uppland, Erik's young son, Magnus (1316–74), was elected to the Swedish throne in his place. Crowned king of Norway shortly before, a maternal inheritance from his grandfather Håkon Magnusson, Erik's accession meant that Sweden and Norway now became united in a personal union, the first of two in history which would unite the two countries under one crown. Herein lies the beginning of a Swedish expansionism within the

Nordic region, which persisted until the early sixteenth century. This election also had another significance, for it laid down many of the mutual obligations which king and country expected from one another. Not without reason, therefore, it has been called Sweden's own Magna Carta and, as such, provided the country with what was virtually a basic constitution until 1719.

To consolidate his position, the new king quickly proceeded along the so-called *Eriksgatan* (Erik's Road), a traditional route which went, roughly speaking, from the north-east to the south-west in Östergötland. Its significance lay in the tradition that newly elected Swedish kings passed along it, meeting with provincial assemblies of notables as they stopped in the towns of Enköping, Nyköping, Jönköping and the country's first episcopal seat, Skara, a series of events rich in ceremonial trappings which helped legitimise the assumption of political power.

Yet the king's power was by no means unlimited. Rather it depended on support from powerful nobles. From 1319 onwards, those of the Swedish nobility who were members of the governing Council of State were in a particularly strong position, able to advise the monarch on a wide range of matters, political and economic. This newly won power became more evident when, the following year, Magnus Birgersson, a contender for the throne, was captured and, by decision of the Council, executed. Additionally, when Duchess Ingeborg, the queen mother, now remarried to the Dane Knut Porse, attempted to strengthen her own position at the expense of her son's, sidestepping the Council in the process, the Council reacted swiftly. Meeting in Skara, in 1322, it introduced a range of measures to limit the duchess's power, appointing Knut Jonsson (died 1347) principal regent during the young king's minority, while placing the duchess's fortified castles, Varberg, Hunehals and Axvall, all under close Council supervision. The Council's attention then turned beyond the borders of Sweden, to focus increasingly on Danish territory to the south, which had already been drawn from the mid 1320s into civil strife and economic decline by the machinations of the princes of Holstein who stood to gain by its weaknesses. The prospects of Swedish territorial expansion in these circumstances proved too tempting to resist: shortly before the declaration of the king's majority, Scania and Blekinge were incorporated into the kingdom of Sweden, with support from the Danish Archbishop of Lund, then present in Kalmar, as well as from much of the local populace, alienated by German administrative intrusions. In exchange, Denmark received 34,000 silver marks, but its king remained determined to recoup his losses. Attempts by Valdemar Atterdag of Denmark, in the 1340s, to re-establish Danish territorial integrity led to years of hostility and unrelenting confrontation with Sweden.

In 1356, for example, a major rebellion broke out in the new Swedish provinces of Scania and Halland, so recently seized by Magnus Eriksson in his struggle against Denmark. It lasted until 1363, when the aristocracy, acting through the Council of State, finally deposed him. Yet Denmark and its king were not entirely to blame. In part, the revolt was a reaction to the failure of the king to satisfy the political ambitions of his sons, whose political inheritances he attempted to secure in his own lifetime, contrary to Swedish tradition and previous political settlements. The king's eldest son, with the assistance of Albrekt of Mecklenburg the Younger (1338–1412), ensured the success of his rebellion by increasing his support by professing to be acting in the name of his father. Consequently, Magnus Eriksson was obliged to divide his dominions between himself and this son. However, it was not Erik Magnusson, his sons and followers who proved to be the principal winners in this new political arrangement, but members of the Council and its ally Albrekt of Mecklenburg, who personally received as a fief for twelve years Scania, with neighbouring Falsterbo, provinces blessed with prosperous markets, much of the wealth from which now went into the latter's coffers. In consequence, the aristocracy of Sweden achieved a political pre-eminence of which few of their fellows in other European countries could boast.

However, Magnus Eriksson had left one other legacy that was to have immense consequences: his Land Law, the earliest draft of which dates back to 1343. It became, over time, the inviolable fundamental law of the Swedish realm, binding on both king and subject. It could be added to or modified, but only by general consent. As such, it provided a written constitution, however sketchy, in which the powers of the king are laid down, in conjunction with his obligations to heed the advice of the Council, members of which had to be native-born nobles. Subjects, thereby, obtained basic rights in regard to the role they had to play with respect to war and peace, conscription and supplementary taxation, among other guarantees. Thus, while encouraging a strong central government, it also served to foster local self-administration, which was, to a considerable degree, relegated to the *tings* (local courts), which met in regular session throughout the land. They were entitled to choose their own officers, and ultimate authority was invested in a jury of local peasant proprietors. The law, thus, profoundly contributed to the growth of the Swedish state at both national and grass-roots level. The strength of this law would increase further in 1608, after its codification that year in written form. Profoundly modified in 1734, it remains a part of Sweden's fundamental system of laws to this day, one which has, through the respect accorded it and its centuries-long continuity, helped to keep the country free from the traumas of revolution.

In the mid fourteenth century, however, its implications for the country's long-term future were not fully recognised and the king had other matters to preoccupy him. In 1359, Magnus Eriksson and his younger son, Håkon, ruling king of Norway since his majority in 1355, entered into an alliance with the Danish king, Valdemar Atterdag, according to which the latter would receive the town of Helsingborg, on the eastern coast of the Sound in Scania, in exchange for assisting Magnus and Håkon to regain the territories lost to his elder son. This endeavour proved unsuccessful, at first, but the sudden death of Erik the following summer enabled Magnus to regain all of his kingdom. However, his pragmatic tactic of changing sides to support Albrekt of Mecklenburg in his campaign against Valdemar Atterdag, while giving in to the constitutional demands of the Council, undermined his position. Valdemar had by now become a formidable military presence and rapidly proceeded not only to re-conquer all of Scania, Blekinge and the southern half of Halland for Denmark, but Gotland, as well. This last acquisition had been facilitated by the skilful manipulation of local politics: Visby, then in a state of confrontation with its agricultural hinterland, was offered protection by the Danish king, in return for loyalty to him, and so assisted in the transfer of the island's sovereignty to Denmark, along with a considerable contribution of money. The city was permitted to maintain its Hansa status, but its economic significance continued to decline.

THE GROWTH OF HANSA INFLUENCE

Despite these humiliating losses to Denmark, and more fearful of an increasingly hostile Council than the Danish king, Magnus Eriksson saw to it that Håkon entered into a marriage alliance with his erstwhile enemy's daughter. In 1363, his son married Margarete (1353–1412), Valdemar Atterdag's child. This single act successfully secured a long-term dynastic solution for the future union of all Scandinavia under one dynasty, while at the same time offering hopes of marginalising the alienated Council of State. In the short term, however, it only aggravated the situation. Since Margarete had no offspring at this time, the Council sent an embassy to Albrekt of Mecklenburg, offering the Swedish throne to his son, Albrekt the Younger. Albrekt accepted this offer and, in 1364, after Magnus Eriksson's enforced removal, he was duly elected king of Sweden at Mora. When the Hansa organised the Confederation of Cologne, supported by the Council of Sweden, in 1367, for the purpose of creating a united front against Denmark and Norway, Albrekt could rely on its military and economic might to strengthen his position further and so invaded the domains of Valdemar Atterdag. This success led, in 1370, to the Peace of Stralsund, according to which the Hansa secured Skanör, Falsterbo, Malmö and Helsingborg for another fifteen years. Nonetheless, after years of negotiations, in which anti-German voices within Sweden made themselves increasingly heard, the ousted king was finally, in 1371, grudgingly granted certain rights over Västergötland, Värmland and Dalecarlia. While at first this seemed a trifling sop to the former Swedish monarch, in reality it proved a great gift, since, administered from Norway by Håkon, the newly gained territory was for all intents and purposes incorporated into the kingdom of Norway after Håkon's father drowned in a shipwreck in 1374. When Valdemar Atterdag then died the following year, to be succeeded by Olof, son of Håkon and Margarete, Albrekt's attempts to secure the Danish throne for his own offspring clearly failed and further Hansa expansion was now effectively checked there.

In Sweden itself, on the other hand, Hansa influence continued to grow, as Germans, administrators, merchants and others, increasingly strengthened their control over the cities in which they resided.

Not only Albrekt the Younger, as king of Sweden, but his father, too, were now endowed with vast landholdings, which included not only the royal demesnes of Kalmar and Nyköping, among others, but the whole of Norrland, too. That said, the royal prerogative was by no means unlimited, since the wishes of the Council also had to be taken into consideration. Indeed, in 1371, Albrekt was obliged to transfer control of the royal castles and their demesnes directly to the Council. He was also obliged to promise to heed the Council's recommendations on important matters of state. The magnate Bo Jonsson Grip (died 1386) had by now become the most powerful personage within the Council and it was he who secured both the return of Albrekt of Mecklenburg's territorial loans, as well as a reduction of German political and economic influence.

When King Olof, still a minor, died in 1387, Margarete herself assumed the throne of Denmark. Her support in Norway and Sweden now grew, and, in 1389, at the Battle of Falköping, her troops were victorious over Albrekt, whom they succeeded in capturing. Margarete was then hailed as queen of the three Nordic kingdoms: the union of Sweden, Denmark and Norway. Yet strife continued, with Stockholm and Kalmar remaining in the hands of the Mecklenburgs. Indeed, violence in the Swedish capital erupted in the so-called Käpplinge Massacre, involving a militarised band of Germans, the Hätte Brothers, who murdered a number of Swedes. There were also piratical attacks by the Hansa on Swedish ships on the high seas, carried out by sailors formed into units of the Vitalie Brothers. These events proved that opposition to Margarete's claim to the throne of Sweden had by no means abated. Complex negotiations, lasting several years during the early 1390s, followed. As a result, an accord between the two dynastic factions was signed at Lindholm Castle, in Scania, according to which Albrekt was to be ransomed through the assistance of Lübeck and other Hansa cities, while Stockholm was to be turned over to Margarete's supporters. Signed in 1395, its implementation was completed the following year: Erik of Pomerania (1384–1459), a relation of Margarete who herself had no further issue, was then proclaimed, first, king of Denmark, and then, king of Sweden, after his adoption by her.

With such dynastic issues settled, a series of reforms could now be undertaken. That same year, therefore, the Nyköping Recess was promulgated, according to which taxation was authorised only by virtue of a royal warrant and the confiscation of private property to satisfy the tax demands was prohibited, with the assurance made that goods previously so confiscated would be returned. Lands improperly incorporated into the estates of the Church and the nobility since 1363 were also to be returned to their rightful owners.

THE KALMAR UNION

On 17 June 1397, the Kalmar Union was officially proclaimed, with monarchical rule now established over all three kingdoms. While the laws of each of the three countries remained distinct, a person convicted of a crime in one was deemed to have been convicted in the other two as well. Stockholm was finally relinquished by the Mecklenburgers through the assistance of the Hansa, in 1398, but only after a wide range of privileges was accorded them. Opposition in Norrland and Finland ceased shortly thereafter. Only Gotland continued to resist, finally submitting in 1408, after a considerable sum of money had been paid to Visby, but irretrievably shorn of its economic power and its membership of the Hansa a thing of the past.

Margarete continued to rule the Union for the rest of her life, indeed, even after Erik of Pomerania assumed his majority in 1401. Therefore, it was only after her death that he undertook a journey throughout his kingdom, in 1412, in the traditional attempt to strengthen his monarchical position. He also widened his political influence by two important marriage alliances, himself taking the hand of Princess Philippa, daughter of England's King Henry IV, in marriage, and giving the hand of his sister Katerina to Johann of Bavaria, son of the Holy Roman Emperor. These actions served to cement his position more firmly within the ranks of Europe's most powerful rulers.

MEDIEVAL SOCIETY

As in the rest of Europe by the twelfth century, Swedish society had been highly hierarchical. With power concentrated in the hands of monarch and the magnates of powerful clans, the majority of the population had lived in thraldom, a form of serfdom, through the country, subject to the will of their masters living in the manors, on the estates of which they worked. While serfs were frequently granted manumission, an action encouraged by the Church, this, on its own, did not grant complete personal freedom. Since, by ancient tradition, land was owned by clans rather than by individuals, the acceptance of a thrall into a clan was required in order to complete the process of emancipation. That said, as the Middle Ages progressed serfdom rapidly gave way to a free peasantry and, in 1335, a royal decree finally abolished it completely. In its final days, with the Church ever more vociferously condemning the enslavement of Christians, unconverted Saami came to be among the last in Sweden to be held in subjugation. Therefore, already by the High Middle Ages, the whole agrarian population of Sweden, like that in the rest of Scandinavia, had come to be free. The land which they held in tenure now came to be based on legally binding agreements, both lease- and freehold. This meant that the foundations of the tenancy system were stable, giving both farm labourer and landowner relative economic security and the freedom to engage in other useful economic activities.

While freedom offered many obvious benefits, there were also disadvantages, one of the greatest of which was taxation by the king. Farmers labouring on land for the Church and nobility, the so-called *frälsebönder*, were, however, exempted from royal taxation, in theoretical exchange for military services, whether or not, in fact, these were actually rendered. From the end of the fourteenth century until the early 1520s, the proportion of land so freed from taxation remained stable, as the nobility were forbidden to purchase taxable property during this period. This served to strengthen not only the monarch vis-à-vis the nobility, but the growth of the state itself by continuing the flow of taxes into the government's coffers.

Sweden remained an overwhelmingly rural society in this period, with the majority of people living in the countryside, in small hamlets of three to five farms. Agriculture was their mainstay and crops were various. Barley and oats were among the most important agricultural staples in most places, but wheat was also cultivated, albeit only in the south of the country. Rye remained rare and cereals were, in general, imported from Tallinn (Reval, in German). Flax and hemp were grown for domestic purposes.

Every other year, a portion of the land, usually half, was allowed to remain fallow, serving the needs of animal husbandry, before being returned for sowing of the usual crop. In the south, two crops were often sown, before being turned to fallow. Agricultural tools remained primitive. Indeed, it was only in Västergötland that the turning plough was introduced during this period and its implementation in more northern parts of Sweden took a further couple of centuries.

Fishing was, of course, of considerable significance in Sweden, with its vast coastlines and lakes. Already, by the 1100s, salmon fishing played a significant role and provided for centuries a commodity enjoyed in plenitude by wide sections of the coastal population. Hunting and gathering were other activities and, in those areas less suited to agriculture, mining and quarrying were also important sources of employment.

Trade was also thriving, as we have seen, frequently depending on networks developed by the Hanseatic merchants and shippers of northern Europe. Kalmar, in particular, by the 1100s had become one of Sweden's most important ports, but in the following century, other mercantile centres were also developing, in particular Söderköping, Norrköping and Nyköping, to its north. Jönköping and Örebro were also of considerable significance, but especially prominent was Visby, reaping the benefits of trade from all corners of the Baltic and beyond. In all of these centres of trade, German merchants came to play a major role, embedded as they were within the Hansa, in the thirteenth and fourteenth centuries. Their access to relatively large sums of capital and the use of large trading vessels made them especially competitive vis-à-vis Swedish merchants, not only on Gotland but elsewhere in mainland Sweden. That said, this very success in coastal mainland Sweden undermined Gotland's own role, as the island became increasingly marginalised, with trade between Sweden's major Baltic trading partners, such as Lübeck, no longer in need of the interim staging post which Visby had long provided.

As trade thrived and population increased, so Swedish cities not only grew in number and size to include about 5 per cent of the country's population, but underwent a development which led to their greater political autonomy. This trend was not unlike that which also occurred in Denmark, but offers a contrast to the situation in Norway, far more sparsely populated. Since urban social life was to a considerable degree characterised not only by trade but also by crafts, the guilds, into which many city dwellers were divided, according to their métier, were able to acquire not only considerable wealth but local political power. They also had important religious and social functions, which spilt over into the political sphere. The introduction of the guilds into Sweden was largely effected by Germans. The first record of one was that of the tailors, in Stockholm, in 1356. The guilds maintained high standards of workmanship, while, at the same time, restricting competition perceived as undesirable by its members and maintaining prices which ensured them on-going prosperity.

THE BLACK DEATH

Yet if cities and towns were centres of thriving trade, they also suffered under profound disadvantages vis-à-vis life in the countryside, for health and hygiene was poor in Sweden throughout the Middle Ages, but nowhere more so than in urban areas. Throughout the period, both endemic diseases and the onslaught of plagues, at varying intervals, ravaged the country in general and towns in particular. Leprosy was a constant presence, while diseases such as smallpox tended to break out in periodic epidemics. None, however, was as devastating as the arrival of the mortal illness known as the Black Death, or bubonic plague, in the late 1340s. A scourge throughout almost all of Europe, it wiped out at least one third of Sweden's population – albeit leaving Finland relatively unscathed – along with huge swathes of the other various peoples who lived on all sides of the Baltic and North seas. By eliminating a major section of the working population, it also came to exert a dramatic effect on all aspects of society, especially agriculture. For the decimation of the labour force meant that large tracts of land fell out of cultivation and remained so until the end of the Middle Ages. This diminished the taxable resources available to the crown, while also reducing the income of the landed nobility. That said, there were benefits for the labouring people who survived it, for it meant that demand for labour increased, raising the incomes of those who remained to till the soil and serving to increase their political influence. This was a trend which occurred not only in Sweden, of course, but in much of the rest of north-western Europe which had also suffered from plague. Surviving landowners, by contrast, found there wealth diminished, as less of their land was now able to be cultivated and their outgoings were greater for that which was. Many of them, therefore, looked eastwards, for new opportunities, in terms of both land acquisitions and trade.

BALTIC EXPANSION

As the growth of the Swedish state continued during the course of the fourteenth century, the country found itself in increasing confrontation with Russia, politically and militarily. The Peace of Nöteborg, in 1323, was the first territorial agreement between Sweden and Russia, establishing a border between the two countries, which would soon prove as contentious as those with Denmark and Norway. The growth of trade with Russia also created its own sources of friction. The River Neva, at the bottom of the Gulf of Finland, was a tempting channel through which to trade northwards through Lake Ladoga and southwards into the heartland of Russia. However, Sweden was as yet in no position to secure the mouth of the Neva. It was, however, able to capitalise on trade with the great Russian mercantile city of Novgorod, about a hundred miles to the south of this estuary. Unfortunately, this growth in trade led to growing friction with the Hansa League as well, an increasingly Baltic-wide economic confrontation, which eventually stretched from Denmark to Russia. It was also no complete panacea for the Swedish king's perennial need for money, since it failed to mitigate in any major way the financial difficulties in which the crown found itself during these years through its overextension. During his reign, Magnus Eriksson, for example, was obliged to seek loans from his father-in-law, Albrekt of Mecklenburg, in return for the income from a variety of Scanian customs duties granted to him in compensation.

However, the eastern littoral of the Baltic was now providing compensations. By the later fourteenth century, eastern Baltic trade was increasing to such a degree that the king was obliged to turn his attention eastwards. Ports, such as Tallinn and Riga, as well as

Danzig (Gdańsk in Polish) to the south, were proving increasingly competitive to Lübeck as major trading partners. This circumstance benefited Stockholm as a growing centre of trade to these ports, without intruding significantly upon the activities of the older Swedish coastal ports, such as Kalmar. For this reason then, the king could only see advantages in extending Swedish influence in an easterly direction, for the more ports there were able to absorb Swedish export commodities, the more full the royal coffers could be expected to be.

Swedish exports were by no means limited to a few staple products. On the contrary, they were highly various during this period, though several stood out as among the most important: iron had been mined and exported from at least the thirteenth century, albeit in a quantity which never exceeded a thousand tons per year. Copper, from Dalecarlia, one of Europe's few sources of this metal, was also of major significance. The ancient trade in furs from the north and dairy produce from the south also continued. In reverse, salt, a necessity for the preservation of meat and fish, and cloth were imported in considerable quantities. The upper clergy and nobility also eagerly purchased such luxury items as wine and spices.

When the defeat of the Teutonic Order at Tannenberg (in what was long East Prussia but today lies within Poland) in 1410 created a vacuum, Sweden was keen to intrude, politically and economically. Since Erik of Pomerania had, of course, his inherited north German Baltic dominions, it was only logical that he should wish to extend his territories further eastward, in the hope of securing the whole of the Baltic coastline. To facilitate this, he built the new fortress of Elsinore, in Denmark, while strengthening fortifications at Kärnan, by Helsingborg, on the other side of the Sound. These measures gave him complete hegemony over the entrance to the Baltic. They also provided a rich source of income, for they enabled him, henceforth, to impose tolls on passing ships. Needless to say, more friction was thereby created with the Hansa League. The latter's growing hostility became an ever more serious problem for Sweden, as Erik of Pomerania's confrontations increased. They only began to decrease when internal difficulties at home sapped his strength. The fact that Erik, by 1430, had illegally bestowed almost all of his castles (except for those in Finland), with their demesnes, to foreigners, usually

Danes and Germans, but on one occasion even an Italian, aroused considerable resentment: the old Swedish nobility saw their political and economic power severely eroded thereby.

Another action of the king also aroused much resentment, namely the debasement of the currency which was implemented to compensate for the crown's growing need of money. Copper coins were by now all too frequently given the nominal value of silver ones, with merchants coerced to accept them. As a result, Sweden's higher quality coinage, already of lesser value than that used by the Hansa and foreign merchants in general, became increasingly depleted. This damaged trade.

DISCONTENT, THE ENGELBREKT REVOLT AND THE QUEST FOR BALTIC HEGEMONY

As in secular politics, so in the politics of the Church, Erik of Pomerania was keen to consolidate his power. Like his adoptive mother, Margarete, before him, he used his cordial relations with the Pope to secure his own people in important ecclesiastical positions, often in direct opposition to the wishes of the Swedish cathedral chapter houses. Yet royal authority with respect to the Church was limited. Although Margarete had succeeded in having her preferred candidate, Jöns Gerekesson, elevated to the archiepiscopal see of Uppsala in her time, it was a short-lived benefit, for the prelate was eventually removed from his see on the grounds of gross misconduct. However, after the brief incumbency of another churchman, Erik chose Thomas Simonsson, Bishop of Strängäns, for the vacant seat. This the chapter house rejected, selecting its own dean, Olof Laurensson, instead. Further elections followed, with resignations and open conflict ensuing. Ultimately, the dispute was sent to an assembly of ecclesiastics in Basle for arbitration. Rather than settling the matter, however, the issue spilt over into the political arena and open revolt resulted. It was in Dalecarlia that hostility to Erik was greatest.

Dalecarlia was a very rich and important province, in economic terms, as well as being the area in which, by tradition, the king of Sweden was elected, took his oath and set forth on his progress around the land. So the fact that it was precisely there that animosity towards the king was at its height was most alarming. Under the leadership of Engelbrekt Engelbrektsson (*c.*1390s–1436), a minor noble involved in mining, an activity which had suffered severely under Erik, vociferous opposition towards him grew. This was, in part, exacerbated because of the desire of the Dalecarlians to have Jösse Eriksson, sheriff of Västerås, removed from office. Two of the ecclesiastical city's most important secular officials, Nils Gustavsson Rossvik and his son Erik Puke, took Engelbrekt's side. Even Norrland came under their sway through the efforts of the latter, and, by July, Engelbrekt arrived safely at the gates of Stockholm. With a truce negotiated there, he was then free to move southwards, neutralising various fortresses on his way to Vadstena, where many members of the Council, both lay and ecclesiastical, were gathered together. To what degree they merely submitted under threats to his superior strength is not clear, but in the end, they were obliged to support Engelbrektsson in his missive to the king. They thus, in effect, legitimised the revolt and helped to enable the rebels to undermine Erik's position. Rebels soon occupied most of the south of Sweden, from where attempts were then made to expel Erik's sheriffs, most of whom were foreign, from the country.

In response, Erik mobilised his troops in Denmark and, in late autumn 1434, took his fleet to Stockholm. In desperation, he sought support from the only place he could hope to find it: his erstwhile enemies, the Hansa League. Engelbrekt, by this time, had secured his camp and forces at Långholm, in central Sweden. He now endeavoured to bolster a wider support. Although a truce was secured, representatives, not only of the nobility and Church, but of the merchant classes as well, assembled at Arboga, in January 1335, to deal with the matter. They chose Engelbrekt as their leader, with the special remit of protecting Stockholm and Uppland. From this position of strength, an accord was finally reached with Erik of Pomerania in Halmstad, on 3 May 1435, by which he accommodated some of the demands made on him by the rebels. When, in July of that year, the king also reached an accord with the Hansa League, he felt empowered once again to send his fleet to Stockholm.

Yet the compromise left neither side happy. Nonetheless, Erik did promise to respect Swedish law and to reserve most of his castles and their demesnes for Swedes. However, those of Stockholm, Nyköping and Kalmar, three of the most important in the country, were exempted from this restriction. Discontent, therefore, grew and, as taxes continued to prove ever more burdensome, confrontation increased. In consequence, yet another convocation was invoked at Arboga and military forces assembled. Leadership of the forces was granted jointly to both Engelbrekt and Karl Knutsson Bonde, but unity among the rebels proved impossible. In fact, local friction between the two leaders became so severe, that when the former was murdered on the way to an assembly called in Stockholm in 1436, the killer, Magnus Bengtsson, was given protection by Karl Knutsson.

Once again an accord was reached with King Erik and Karl Knutsson's position was strengthened. After a renewed open rebellion, Erik Puke was seized and beheaded in 1437. The family of Engelbrekt's killer, Bengtsson, meanwhile, had secured for themselves various fortresses along Sweden's Baltic coast, but, since during the following year Karl Knutsson had become the undisputed leader of the Council, he took action against them, obliging them to relinquish their new acquisitions, appeals to King Erik notwithstanding.

Resentment remained and, in 1439, the conflict intensified. Arson attacks wrought havoc and in Västerås and Uppsala the rebels gained the upper hand, assisted once again by Nils Gustavsson Rossvik.

King Erik, meanwhile, now found himself undermined by his own Danish Council, which, in the summer of 1439, abjured its allegiance to him, in favour of his nephew, Christopher of Bavaria (1416–48), as the compromise choice. When the latter then assumed the powers of government, the Swedish Council, also, shifted its allegiance to him, feeling that it could more easily dominate him than his predecessor. In 1440, therefore, Christopher was formally proclaimed king of Denmark and, in 1441, he was elected king of Sweden. By this time, though, both Sweden and Norway were in a process of disintegration, with Denmark increasingly the dominant power. That said, the Council of State became increasingly powerful and even Christopher was obliged to approve the revision of the law pertaining to the creation of a regency in his absence, castellans' letters of obligations when he should die, as well as its own renewal, all initiated by the Council itself.

The restraints put by the Council on Christopher were far more rigorous than those which it had attempted to impose on Erik. No longer was a king permitted to export income from wealth of the kingdom which had accrued to him, but it was to be deposited in a newly created State Treasury until needed for purposes within Sweden's borders. As for Karl Knutsson, he was compensated with demesnes in Finland, but obliged to reside there in the Castle of Turku, in what was a veritable enforced exile, even if Borgholm and the rest of the island of Öland were also granted to him as a form of security.

Yet the hopes of the Council notwithstanding, Christopher's reign in Sweden provided few benefits over that of Erik for the country's magnates and the wider population. Crop failures led to a general impoverishment, while Christopher himself was accused of plundering Swedish estates for his own exclusive benefit. Even more gravely, he was charged with attempting to sidestep the Council in his governmental decisions, relying instead on his Bavarian advisers. He had, moreover, shown himself to be militarily weak, unable to recapture Gotland from Erik. That said, Christopher did promulgate a new legal code in 1442, as the Council had desired, and accepted the principle that the demesnes of Sweden's castles should be granted to the Council and its favourites, rather than to his own German people. In consequence, some support for him remained, undermining the opposition. By 1448 the revolt seemed to have subsided. However, Christopher's death that same year not only ended aristocratic hegemony in the Nordic Union but opened the door to a renewed attempt by Karl Knutsson to secure the three thrones for himself. When, though, the Danish Council supported Christian of Oldenburg (1426–81) as king of Denmark and Norway in his stead, he was obliged to accept as definitive the decision of a congress at Halmstad in 1450, drawn from representatives from all three countries. While the Union was to be revived in the future, the de facto arrangement was, nonetheless, to remain in place. Karl Knutsson was thus obliged to content himself with the Swedish throne alone, acknowledging Christian of Oldenburg as king of Denmark and Norway.

This was, of course, a precarious situation and, under Karl Knutsson, Sweden was soon under attack from rebels within and enemies without. Christian proceeded to attack Sweden's southern borders, in an attempt to regain lost Danish territories, while hostile factions which had formed around Jöns Bengtsson, Archbishop of Uppsala, a member of the powerful Oxenstierna family which felt itself marginalised by Karl Knutsson, rose up within the country. They united with other disgruntled magnates in an open revolt against the Swedish king, supported by a wide swathe of the country's population, including not only the many powerful merchants of Stockholm – the city now had a population of some five thousand – but small farmers in Dalecarlia and Uppland, antagonised by military levies, a reduction in the tax-free land of Church and nobility, as well as general economic decline. In consequence, Karl Knutsson was deposed and, in 1457, Christian of Oldenburg was elected king of Sweden. This strengthened the position of the Church, in general, and the Oxenstierna family and their Vasa cousins, in particular, sometimes in symbiosis, the one with the other. However, Christian, too, was obliged to impose burdensome taxes on the nobility, to pay for his wars in Holstein. When Archbishop Bengtsson, then, switched sides and endeavoured to secure the recall of Karl Knutsson, Christian seized the prelate and, after attacking rebels under Kettil Karlsson in Västmanland, won a decisive victory. This, however, did not prevent the Council from now re-electing Karl Knutsson as king. A series of complex and prolonged negotiations then ensued, as a result of which, in 1464, Archbishop Bengtsson was released, Karl Knutsson once again cast out, and Christian reconfirmed as king of Sweden. Real power in Sweden, though, now lay in the hands of Archbishop Bengtsson, head of the Council and representative of the interests of the Oxenstierna and Vasa families, rather than with the monarch.

Their position, though, was soon to be threatened by the intrusion upon the scene of another powerful family, the Thotts, with Danish roots admittedly, but with aspirations for greater political and economic power in Sweden, in whose border regions they had come to reside. One of their members, Ivar Axelsson, had married Magdalena, Karl Knutsson's daughter, an alliance of great political significance for the Thotts. This became apparent when, shortly thereafter, Archbishop Bengtsson lost his position as head of the Council and Erik Axelsson, Ivar's brother, was elected in his stead.

While relations with Christian improved, those with the mining population of Dalecarlia and the merchants of Stockholm deteriorated. Their leader, Nils Bosson Sture, now joined forces with Erik Axelsson, encouraging Karl Knutsson to return to Sweden. This he did and, in 1467, he was elected Swedish king for the third time. Now, it was the Thotts who were the power behind the throne. Yet on the death of Karl Knutsson, in 1470, it was Nils Bosson Sture, now married to a Thott daughter, who seized control of the Council, along with the principal castles of the kingdom. The magnates of Uppland were outraged to such a degree that they now took sides with the Oxenstiernas and Vasas. Hostilities erupted.

The arrival of King Christian with his fleet at Stockholm seemed to bode ill for Sture and the Dalecarlians, but, at the Battle of Brunkeberg, on 10 October 1471, they proved victorious. The Oxenstiernas were defeated and Christian fled back to Denmark.

Christian's death in 1481, though, led to a renewed attempt by the Council to asset its authority and in 1483, the Kalmar Recess was promulgated, in which the supremacy of the Council was asserted. In 1487, Sten Sture the Elder concentrated his efforts on removing the Thotts as rivals and laid siege to their castles, Stegeborg, Borgholm and Raseborg. Defeated, they fled to Denmark and Sten Sture's authority in the Council was now uncontested.

From a position of strength, Sten Sture now turned his attentions eastward. In 1493, he concluded an accord with the Livonian Order, in the north of present-day Latvia, with a view both to blocking Russia's westward expansion, and to undermining King Hans, who had now succeeded his father, Christian I, and formed an alliance with Russia. This pitted Sweden against both Denmark and Russia, a political and military fault line which would henceforth persist for centuries. In 1495, Russia attacked the eastern settlements of Viborg and Nyslott, recently founded in the 1470s. Two years later, peace was made between the two powers.

With the pressure relieved on his eastern flank, Sten Sture refused to be cowed by King Hans. Therefore, when the Archbishop of Uppsala, in support of Hans, endeavoured to break Sten Sture's authority, the latter fomented an assault against his properties. The ecclesiastic, in response, excommunicated him. Hans intervened with troops and Sten Sture was forced to negotiate. Yet from these negotiations Sten Sture reaped considerable benefits: he was given numerous demesnes, including the plum castles of both Turku and Nyköping.

Sten Sture died in 1503, and, the following year, Svante Nilsson assumed the leadership of the Council. Confrontation with Denmark, though, failed to resolve itself, for two castles still remained in Danish hands, those of Kalmar and Borgholm. In the autumn of 1510, Swedish forces attempted their capture. Internal disputes took their toll and, when Nilsson died unexpectedly in the winter of 1512, deep fissures remained and the leading figure of opposition to his policies, Erik Trolle, was elected leader. Sten Sture's son, Sten Sture the Younger, was determined not to accept his election and, from a power base of fortified demesnes scattered throughout the kingdom, including Stockholm, Turku and Borgholm, saw to it that a new vote was organised and that he himself was elected. Soon, though, the new archbishop, Gustaf Trolle, son of the opposing candidate for the leadership of the Council, who was invested in Rome in 1514, began to form a formidable focus for dissension against the machinations of Sten Sture the Younger. As a result, confrontation between the two heightened, enabling Christian II of Denmark (1481–1559) to use the situation to justify the arrival of his naval forces at Välda, near Stockholm, in 1517 and intervention in support of the Swedish prelate. However, the Danes were defeated and obliged to flee. The Council therefore felt itself strong enough to convoke an assembly in November 1517, in which treasonous accusations were made against the archbishop. In consequence of this, the archbishop was assailed at his archiepiscopal fortress and obliged to retire. Once again, in the summer of 1518, the Danish fleet, in response, appeared off Stockholm, this time at Brännkyrka, with the Danish King Christian II himself at its head. Although they were once again defeated and their assault on Kalmar resisted, their forays into Västergötland and Öland proved successful. Excommunications and a general interdict on Sweden, promulgated from the Danish sees of both Lund and Roskilde, further bolstered their support. Further military action followed, as the Danes undertook a major campaign in Östergötland in 1520. In a battle on the ice near today's Ulrikehamn, Sten Sture the Younger was mortally wounded and he died on the journey back to Stockholm. Serious military opposition now collapsed and the former Archbishop Trolle himself led the negotiating team to restore harmony with Christian II.

The victorious Christian II now saw fit to re-enter Stockholm and in early November was crowned king of Sweden. Festivities followed, concluded by 'a feast of another sort', as the reformer Olaus Petri later put it, which left its indelible mark on Swedish history, mythologised as the greatest outrage ever perpetrated against the country: the Bloodbath of Stockholm. On 8 and 9 November 1520, about a hundred people who had opposed Christian II were massacred, including two bishops, scores of noblemen and many Stockholm merchants. To what degree Archbishop Trolle played a major role in its execution remains a subject of controversy. Certainly his role was used by many of his opponents to discredit the Catholic Church in Sweden. So, although the State Council thereafter hailed Christian II (1520–1) as king of Sweden, it proved an illusory victory for the Danes. Rather than crushing the growing power of the magnate Gustaf Vasa, who was a relation of the Stures by marriage, it removed his principal Swedish rivals. The stage was now set, not only for the establishment of the new long-lasting hereditary dynasty of the House of Vasa, but for the Protestant Reformation which severed Sweden from Catholic Europe, within which the country had now for several centuries been fully integrated. The event also paved the way for the consolidation of Sweden itself as a territorial state, one among others in a wider European framework.

MEDIEVAL LITERATURE

The integration of Sweden into Europe had long been established in terms of culture, and, in particular, the realms of literature. Early writings in Sweden were in Latin, just as they were throughout western Christendom, and, in similar fashion, were generally of an ecclesiastical nature. The first significant secular literary expression in Sweden was the Erik Chronicle, written by an anonymous author or authors in or around 1330. Based on a literary tradition of the previous century with roots in Germany, it is an epic in rhyme based on the life of Duke Erik Magnusson, focusing upon his fraternal strife with Dukes Erik and Valdemar. As such, it draws upon real events from the second half of the twelfth century and first two decades of the thirteenth. Considerably influenced by continental European courtly epics, it was written on parchment and, though paper was first used in Sweden in the fourteenth century, parchment continued to be used long afterwards for manuscripts.

It was followed, in the middle of the following century, by the Karl Chronicle, in which twelve authors collaborated to produce an epic tale in rhyme, the theme of which was Queen Margarete's ascent to the throne of the Scandinavian Union, and it carries on until 1454. Many powerful magnates resented it, in particular, King Karl Knutsson, after he first ascended the throne in 1464. Its purpose had clearly been political and it may have drawn much of its content from an earlier Engelbrekt Chronicle which deals with similar issues. This, in turn, was followed by the Sture Chronicle, also written by numerous authors, possibly clergymen, which appeared in 1500 and focuses upon less controversial political and military events of the previous decades until 1496.

More modern in tone is the Chronicle of the Gothic Kingdom (*Chronica regni gothorum*), written by Ericus Olai, a professor at the newly founded University of Uppsala, from 1477. He had studied at Rostock, in northern Germany, and later Siena, and was substantially inspired by continental historical writings of the period.

A considerable quantity of religious literature was now also making its appearance, emanating, in particular, from St Birgitta's Convent, at Vadstena, and the monastery of the Grey Brothers, in Stockholm. Writings from St Birgitta's Convent often took a mystical tone. The convent had been the seat of Birgitta (*c*.1303–73), daughter of magnate Birger Persson and widow of Ulf Gudmarsson, who for much of her later life was highly critical of King Magnus Eriksson and his court, a stance she felt was justified by her religious visions. Over the years her spiritual reputation grew to such an extent that she became the leading model of Swedish feminine sanctity. Indeed, her reputation for saintliness spread far beyond Sweden's borders. She founded a new religious order and already, in 1370, Pope Urban V had confirmed its rule. By this stage, she had long resided in Rome with her daughter Katerina, but made a pilgrimage shortly before her death to Jerusalem. Pope Boniface IX canonised her in 1391.

In the following century, many considered the rebel Engelbrekt himself to be a martyred saint and Bishop Thomas of Strängnäs, in 1439, composed his lyric poem 'Freedom is the Best of Things' in his honour, while glorifying the miracles said to have taken place by his graveside. Yet tastes were changing and by the late fifteenth century, the courtly tales so popular earlier had fallen out of fashion, replaced by a more robust, down-to-earth form of storytelling. These corresponded more to the tastes of those literary men of humble background who were now asserting themselves in the wider world, politically, economically and ecclesiastically.

The foundation of Uppsala University, in 1477, helped to create yet another source of literary output, albeit one which would go into temporary abeyance in the early years of the Reformation, when the university was shut down. Yet it was the spiritual and theological literature emanating from Germany that was to have the greatest input in Sweden in the early sixteenth century and which would pave the way for the Reformation which followed.

ART AND ARCHITECTURE

The arts, too, in Sweden during this period were fully integrated into a wider European tradition. During the second half of the fifteenth century and into the sixteenth Albertus Pictor (*c*.1440–*c*.1510) was arguably Sweden's most prominent artist, famed for his frescoes, especially those at Härkeberga Church, in Uppland, with their alluring devils and wheel of fate. The altar of Stockholm's Great Church, in one of the panels of which the Virgin Mary is depicted with St Elizabeth, was painted in Lübeck in 1468 and further evinces the fact that this great Hansa city exerted on Sweden an enormous cultural influence, which went hand in hand with its economic influence. This characteristic is also demonstrated in a plethora of important woodcarvings done at the time, such as that of *St George and the Dragon*, also in Stockholm's Great Church, from 1489, again by an artist from Lübeck. These carvings have an idealising quality about them, which harks back to Renaissance classical idealism. However, the 1470 carving of *Karl Knutsson Bonde as a Benefactor*, in Gripsholm Castle, is Sweden's first realistic portrait. Here such idealism has been eschewed in favour of

4 The statue of St Olof, early king of Norway and its patron saint, adorns
the thirteenth-century Gothic façade of Uppsala Cathedral, the country's
most important place of worship and historic see of its primate and
archbishop. Although this building was not consecrated until 1435, Uppsala
had an ancient religious association: the village of Old Uppsala, nearby, had
once been the site of Sweden's most important pagan temple. Photo: Uppsala
Domkyrka.

Germanic-inspired realistic depiction of the sitter, who was so generous in his donations to the Franciscan monastery church on
Riddarholmen, in the heart of Stockholm, where he himself was
buried that year.

Architecture during the Middle Ages in Sweden also evinces its
German roots. The construction of Uppsala Cathedral had commenced in the late thirteenth century, but was only completed a
century and a half later. Finally consecrated in 1435, it was carried
out in the Gothic style, the largest of its type in Sweden. Lund
Cathedral, under Danish suzerainty throughout this period, had
been built in the twelfth century in the earlier Romanesque style
emanating from Lombardy, in the north of Italy, but reinterpreted
by way of the German Rhineland. Although its high altar was consecrated as early as 1145, the richly carved choir stalls erected in
front of it are in the Gothic style from the 1370s. If high ecclesiastical
architecture, therefore, was deeply influenced by stylistic trends
filtered through Germany, the same was true of major secular buildings, including Turku Castle from the 1280s and the Palace of
Alsnöhus, in Uppland, from about the same time. Indeed right up
until the Reformation and in the decades beyond, German stylistic
trends were decisive in helping to pave the way for other forms of
German influence – theological, economic and administrative – all
of which helped to forge, in sometimes unexpected ways, the emerging and expanding Swedish state which blossomed in its wake.

3

The territorial consolidation of Sweden

The final collapse of the Nordic Union led, in the decades which followed, to the consolidation of the country as a territorial state. It joined the ranks of the other emerging European states under the leadership of Gustaf Vasa (1496–1560), against the backdrop of the Protestant Reformation which he successfully utilised for his own political purposes. In January 1521, this powerful magnate, a close relation to Kristina Gyllenstierna (1494–1559), the widow of the late regent Sten Sture the Younger, who had escaped from Danish captivity two years before, had been elected leader of the disgruntled Dalecarlians, many of whom had supported the Stures. Attacked by Didrik Slagheck, the new pro-Danish governor in Stockholm, at the ferry crossing nearby at Brunnbäck, Vasa was victorious in his resistance and proceeded to crush Gustaf Trolle, Archbishop of Uppsala (1488–1535), on his own territory in Uppland. Winning, therefore, the support of most of the Council of State, Gustaf Vasa was elected its leader in August 1521. By the following year, much of Sweden had been secured, albeit not the key cities of Stockholm and Kalmar, nor the Finnish fortresses. In this the Hansa League came to his aid, but only on condition that its ships would be granted freedom from duties in Sweden and a promise that Swedish ships would remain in Baltic waters rather than compete for trade now carried by the Hansa. Bolstered by their support and the

49

SIC·REX·GVSTAVS
ROSOVE
FOELIX IMPERIO

VVLTV·QVE·HVME
FEREBAT:
SVECIA MAGNATVO
1542

5 King Gustaf Vasa (1496–1560) was one of Sweden's most influential monarchs. He introduced not only a hereditary monarchy, which continues to this day, but the Protestant Reformation. He dispossessed the Roman Catholic Church, enriching both the crown and nobility thereby, and furthered the consolidation of Sweden as a territorial state while developing its administrative bureaucracy. Portrait by Jacob Binck (1542), oil on canvas. Uppsala University Art Collections.

growing general opposition to Christian II of Denmark in wide segments of the population, Gustaf was able to bring almost all of Sweden under his control by the late spring of 1523. In consequence of these circumstances, he was elected king of Sweden, at Strängnäs, on 6 June of that year. If his alignment with the Hansa had paid dividends, a rebellion in Denmark, fomented by the Hansa, had also aided him, since it further undermined the already weakened and contested kingship of Christian II in that country. As a result, the latter's uncle, Duke Frederik of Schleswig-Holstein, had been able to secure the throne, which he ascended as Frederik I, and Christian himself had been forced to flee the country.

When five years later, in 1528, Gustaf Vasa was crowned king of Sweden in Uppsala Cathedral, as Sweden's first hereditary monarch, the political scenario was radically different from what it had been only seven years before and he could feel himself relatively secure. For, as would become apparent over the following two and a half centuries in Poland, a country with an elected monarchy would remain terminally weak and subject to the machinations of greedy neighbours. Thus, the establishment of the hereditary principle served to consolidate not only the position of the monarch, but that of the territorial state itself. Indeed, by the 1530s, Gustaf Vasa could even dispense with the assistance of the Hansa League. In particular, he could jettison the support he received from them in Lübeck, having strengthened his own fleet and having obtained considerable assistance from Danzig, Lübeck's rival.

Dynastic alliances also helped to strengthen the foundations of the new dynasty, as well as the territorial integrity of Sweden itself. In particular, the king's second marriage to Margareta Leijonhufvud enabled him to bolster his support from another native magnate family, rather than from a foreign princely house with no actual power base in Sweden.

Equally important for the consolidation of the Swedish state was the import, during the 1530s, of skilled bureaucrats from the continent, in particular, from the German states of the Holy Roman Empire, to administer various facets of the government. When Conrad von Pyhy (died 1553), a former courtier at the court of the Holy Roman Emperor Charles V, became director of the royal chancellery in 1538, Gustaf Vasa acquired a highly skilled administrator who not only successfully helped to centralise and make more efficient the king's administration, but reaped many benefits in his negotiations with foreign states, not least his erstwhile enemy, Denmark.

In 1536, an accord beneficial to Sweden was finally reached with Denmark, now ruled by its new king, the Lutheran Christian III. He had emerged victorious after the conclusion of *Grevens Fejde*, a civil war which had raged in Denmark from 1534 to 1536 and in which he had allied himself with Gustaf Vasa. This support, in conjunction with Prussian assistance, had enabled an attack instigated by Lübeck against Sweden to be successfully resisted. From this position of strength, Gustaf Vasa was then able to revoke what remained of the privileges previously granted to Lübeck for its earlier support, secure in the perception that this German city would now be powerless to object.

Meanwhile, the import of other German administrators from the court of the Holy Roman Empire continued apace, fostering the centralisation of Gustaf Vasa's governmental bureaucracy. This meant that he could assert his authority more effectively than previously, while achieving greater economic liquidity. Using German legal codes as models, he also introduced a wide range of new civil laws, including the transfer of jurisdiction of a number of crimes from ecclesiastical to secular courts. By this stage, though, the Catholic Church in Sweden had already been dispossessed, an act which greatly benefited Gustaf Vasa and the consolidation of his political power.

DISPOSSESSION OF THE CHURCH AND STRENGTHENING OF THE CROWN

Discontent with the Catholic Church had, in the third decade of the sixteenth century, become a powerful force in Sweden among those who sympathised with such German Protestant reformers as Martin Luther and Philipp Melanchthon. Some Swedes had become radicalised to such a degree that, during the 1520s, iconoclastic disturbances broke out in both Stockholm and Malmö, the latter still under Danish sovereignty. With popular support for the

Reformation growing, the king, though personally uninterested in matters of theology, used this groundswell for his own pragmatic purposes. He saw that the vast material resources of the Catholic Church in Sweden could be used to the benefit of the crown, by their confiscation and redistribution, in particular, to himself and the nobility, whose loyalty, through material self-interest, could thus be secured. He also saw that with the power of the Church undermined, both the independence of the Swedish state and his own authority in ruling over it would be strengthened. Moreover, he could draw upon a groundswell of Protestant support from below, especially from those who stood to gain by the new opportunities for office, both clerical and state, which now became available.

It is against this background that the convocation of the Council in Västerås in 1527 should be seen, for it exerted a dramatic effect politically, as well as on the Church's temporal position in Sweden. For one thing, the estates which gathered there proclaimed the establishment of the Swedish *Riksdag* (Parliament). For another, the Council severed the Church in Sweden from that of Rome, while embedding it within the state itself, enabling the king to seize most of its economic assets. Key, at least in symbolic terms, was the legendary debate which took place there between the reformer Olaus Petri (1493–1552), who had studied at the University of Wittenberg, and the Catholic Peder Galle (died 1537 or 1538), an event said to have occurred in the presence of Gustaf Vasa himself. Petri was deemed to have triumphed, and therefore was able to carry out his Lutheran reforms, among them the crushing of the mendicant orders he so despised, with relatively little opposition.

The ecclesiastical congregation held in Örebro, in 1529, under the initiative of Olaus Petri, introduced further reforming measures. These served to advance the interests of Swedish churchmen from humble backgrounds at the expense of those of noble origins, since it was among that segment of the clergy that the greatest Reformist zeal was to be found. Such measures, in combination with growing economic and political discontent among some segments of the old nobility, however, incited the revolt of powerful magnates in Västergötland. This uprising also drew upon existing discontent in the north of Småland and in Västergötland, where the seats of its leaders, Magnus Haraldsson, the Bishop of Skara, and Ture Jönsson, the king's Lord Steward, were to be found. Nonetheless, the uprising failed to find widespread support among the general population and Haraldsson and Jönsson fled to the Danish ex-king Christian's court in exile. More serious as a threat to the new order was the deleterious reaction in Dalecarlia the following year, when King Gustaf Vasa attempted a general confiscation of church bells, as a form of local tax. Yet, this, too, was crushed, and its ringleaders were summarily executed, the king's promises of amnesty notwithstanding.

In the meantime, in 1531, the Lutheran Laurentius Petri (1499–1573), Olaus Petri's brother, was appointed Archbishop of Uppsala, shortly before the king's first marriage, to the German Katarina of Sachsen-Lauenburg, also of a family converted to the teachings of Martin Luther, and the rupture with Rome became irreparable. Yet relations between the reformer brothers and the king were hardly smooth. Indeed, in 1539–40, both Olaus and Laurentius Petri found themselves on trial, accused of treason by Pyhy. Though condemned to death, their punishment was ultimately commuted to a hefty fine and both were ultimately rehabilitated. But henceforth, a non-ecclesiastical governmental superintendent was placed in charge of church affairs, making it clear that the king would brook no competition, even from committed Lutheran reformers. Another German Lutheran, Georg Norman (died 1553), whose family seat was on Rügen, was made first Superintendent over the Swedish Church, with broad judicial rights over its hierarchy. He was appointed to the Council of State in 1541 and also increasingly undertook delicate diplomatic missions, most famously that which led to Sweden's alliance with France, the first of a number which over the following centuries became bulwarks of Swedish foreign policy.

At grass-roots level, the provincial church administration now came to be run by specially appointed priests, in conjunction with lay officials, rather than by the bishops themselves. The crown also proceeded to confiscate more of the Church's remaining worldly treasures, such as silver reliquaries and monstrances, under the watchful eyes of Norman.

The political importance of the Reformation's consolidation in Sweden became clear for all, when, in 1540, Gustaf Vasa was able, at an assembly of the leading secular and ecclesiastical figures in Örebro, to have himself declared king by Divine Right, with loyalty to himself and his descendants sworn by all. By now, the king had succeeded in fully consolidating his power over the Church. Indeed, while the philo-Catholic factions had not been entirely eliminated, the civil strife which they instigated in 1542 provided a further excuse for the king to suppress adherents of the old religion and to strive to block their attempts to revive it.

Economic stresses were now making themselves apparent in the Swedish body politic, as much as religious ones. Indeed, they were proving as disruptive of the old order as the religious ones had been. Thus, when the strife of 1542 became a fully fledged rebellion in Småland, it focused around the disaffected Nils Dacke, who bemoaned not only the increasing burden of taxation and the rise in price of necessary commodities, but the restrictions which had come to be placed on the export of goods abroad. This had occurred because of the king's fear of alienating further his erstwhile former ally Lübeck, a city by now one of northern Europe's most important ports, with a population of some 25,000, huge by the standards of the time and dwarfing Stockholm's meagre tally of 6,000. Of course, the despoliation of the Church and the introduction of Protestant forms of worship also played a role. That said, the matter was soon resolved. A temporary truce was declared and Gustaf Vasa succeeded through skilful manipulation of conflicting political, religious and economic factions in undermining Dacke. He was killed in 1543 and the rebellion collapsed.

Gustaf's skilful but deeply unpopular German administrator, Pyhy, could now be dispensed with, in turn. Despite having helped successfully to negotiate an alliance between Sweden and France, in opposition to the Holy Roman Emperor, in 1543, he was suddenly arrested for administrative and economic misdeeds. Swiftly convicted, he was sentenced to life imprisonment in Västerås Castle, where he died not long after. With his departure, the 'Germanisation' of the Vasa government came to an abrupt end. The Council was re-established and, although Norman remained as Superintendent, bishops were reinvested with considerable ecclesiastical administrative powers. Shorn of their vast estates, in financial terms, however, they remained highly dependent upon royal good will. For this reason, the confiscation of church land remained an important priority of Gustaf Vasa throughout his life. Whereas in 1521, at least 21 per cent of landed estates and up to one third of all arable land had belonged to the Church, by 1560, these had been virtually completely reallocated, to a large extent to aristocratic supporters of the king. That said, major financial benefits also accrued to the crown, which increased its share of landed estates from 5.5 per cent to 28.2 per cent. This furthered not only the consolidation of the monarchy itself, but that of the Swedish state.

Meanwhile, in 1544, a convocation of representatives of the Swedish nobility and clergy had been called at Västerås, each representing the interests of their own estates. It confirmed the new hereditary royal tenure of the House of Vasa, in the process granting ducal titles and landed patrimonies to the king's younger sons, while leaving these territories fully integrated within the unitary kingdom of Sweden. Thus, Johan was given the province of Turku, in south-western Finland, Karl Södermanland, Närke and Värmland, and Magnus, Dalsland, along with large swathes of Öster- and Västergötland. In consequence, the fate of the House of Vasa increasingly became identified with that of the Swedish state.

THE QUEST FOR IDENTITY WITHIN THE SWEDISH CHURCH

Across the Gulf of Bothnia in Finland, a fully integrated part of the Swedish kingdom, the Reformation was also introduced from above and with it a closer integration was achieved with the rest of Sweden. There the Reformist movement was led by Mikael Agricola (c.1510–57), also a follower of both Luther and Melanchthon under whom he had studied at Wittenberg. As a result of his reformist policies, the vernacular was introduced into religious services in 1537, the same year Lutheranism was formally established as the state religion in Denmark. Agricola also completed, in 1548, the groundbreaking literary accomplishment of translating the New Testament into Finnish, which furthered the cause of Protestantism among the general population. Six years later, he was elevated to the see of Turku and, when a new see was later created in its eastern stretches at Viborg, he saw to it that the Reformist priest Paavali Juusten (1516–76), a student at Wittenberg from 1543 to 1546, became its bishop. Both kept a watchful eye against a resurgence of Catholicism. At the same time, they were also wary of an Orthodox threat from the east, from lands under Russian hegemony lost to the western Church in 1054. The bitter war that broke out against Russia in 1555 increased their fears and exacerbated matters political and economic. Neither country benefited: while Russia wrought havoc on Sweden's Baltic coast, this had brought it no lasting gains when the peace was finally signed in 1557. As for Agricola, he himself died on his return home from a diplomatic embassy to Moscow, in which a strengthening of the cause of the Lutherans both at home and abroad was an important element. However, Tsar Ivan the Terrible's abhorrence of Protestantism, which he equated with Judaism in terms of its perceived godlessness, prevented any rapprochement. Indeed, diplomatic attempts to improve the lot of Protestants in Russia may have aggravated the problem, for, in 1564, the tsar massacred followers of both religions at Polotsk, in what is today Belarus, but was then under Russian sovereignty. Ivan also stepped up his attempts to proselytise Orthodoxy in Finland. Only with the elevation of Ericus Erici Sorolainen (1546–1625) to the episcopal seat of Turku in 1583 did the situation ameliorate. Thereafter, new modest attempts at dialogue were initiated between the two branches of Christendom, supported by the Swedish king Johan III, who was hoping to extend both his political tentacles and Protestantism itself within Russia.

On the western side of the Gulf of Bothnia, the Swedish Church also strengthened its power and promulgated a stricter religious formulation than had previously been the case since the advent of the Reformation. The saying of requiem masses, adoration of the saints and use of incense were all prohibited. The new ecclesiastical order, with its Swedish liturgy, was also confirmed. That said, the growing conflict between Lutheran and Calvinist elements, the latter strengthening from the 1560s onwards, remained unresolved until the end of the century. Only then can it be said that Lutheranism definitively triumphed. When it did, Sweden joined the ranks of the other by now Lutheran countries of the Nordic region, ensuring them a common religion, which would foster, despite frequent political and military conflict, a remarkable religious, cultural and social unity which has persisted until today.

THE ECONOMY

The successful consolidation of Sweden, of course, depended not only on the confiscation of disposed church property, but on a productive Swedish economy, in which trade grew and flourished. As such, it rested on two principal pillars: agriculture and animal husbandry, which continued to be central to the Swedish economy throughout the sixteenth century, much as they had been since time immemorial. The latter, indeed, was especially strong, three times greater in this period than it would become even in the eighteenth century. Mining, too, was of major importance, especially in Dalecarlia: copper from Stora Kopparberg and Garpenberg was sought after throughout Europe. Silver, too, albeit to a much lesser degree, was also mined in Dalecarlia, at the ancient mines of Västersilverberg and Östersliverberg. However, a new one, at Sala, where mining had begun in 1510, increasingly supplemented them. Also of significance, especially for the future, was the mining of iron, which now came to be carried out not only in Dalecarlia, but in the upland areas of Västmanland, Uppland, Södermanland and Östergötland. Production of iron increased dramatically towards the end of the Middle Ages, after massive ovens were introduced in place of the smaller and less efficient *blaster* ones. This facilitated the production of technologically advanced cannons, famed for their quality, during the 1500s.

By the middle of the sixteenth century, and in contrast to the situation in almost all of continental Europe, the majority of land, some 51.7 per cent, was in the hands of ordinary farmers, merchants and others, rather than those of the Church, crown or nobility. That said, the massive reallocations of ecclesiastical property which followed in the wake of the Reformation had exerted little effect on the position of ordinary farmers. Indeed, over the following four decades, their share of the whole was to remain remarkably constant, only declining slightly to 49.9 per cent by 1560. When at that time a major influx of new settlers did occur, brought in to satisfy the growing needs of a standing Swedish military, new provisions had to be made. These led to the introduction of the so-called *avelsgård*, or large royal demesne, in every third parish in the land, for the purposes of providing the standing army, now needed to defend the territorial state, with necessary provisions. Moreover, while the export of comestibles continued to be prohibited, the import of goods for the maintenance of the military now came to be encouraged. This, in turn, had a major effect upon the industrial economy, for it increased the need for the production and export of bar iron, facilitated by Gustaf Vasa's encouragement of the immigration of ironsmiths to Sweden. These iron bars increasingly came to be sold through the more easterly Hanseatic port of Danzig, rather than through Lübeck, as had previously been the case.

Taxation was onerous for the peasantry and mercantile elite, but, with reference to the still small cities and towns of Sweden, it was limited in scope. In fact, in 1523, only three hundred residents of Stockholm were obliged to pay tax. On the other hand, members of guilds with strong ecclesiastical links were disadvantaged. Guild confraternities were the most severely affected and those with a spiritual focus were abolished altogether and their property confiscated. That said, the *skrå*, or secular guilds, continued to function, maintaining a role of considerable prominence in Stockholm, albeit less so in the provincial towns, for centuries to come.

LITERATURE

As the Protestant Reformation in Sweden proved an important catalyst for the development of the Swedish territorial state, so it encouraged a wider literary use of the Swedish language and the development of its literature which also fostered its needs. Ericus Skinnerus's poem in hexameter *Epithalamion*, composed in honour of Johan III's marriage to Gunilla Bielke, was one of a number of literary high points of the time. However, other consequences were deleterious. For example, Uppsala University, which had been a hotbed of Catholicism, ceased to function during Gustaf Vasa's reign, a tragic victim of the Reformation as much as the Catholic bishops of Sweden who had been condemned to death. That said, some of Sweden's most prominent reformers were also among its most noted alumni. This was certainly the case with Olaus Petri, whose *Swedish Chronicle* (*c*.1540) focused upon the period 1450 to 1520, seen, on the one hand, through the eyes of a Swedish ecclesiastical reformer, but on the other, with an eye to the vices of King

Gustaf Vasa, his introduction of the Reformation to Sweden notwithstanding. Of even greater significance was the publication of the
first complete edition of the Bible in Swedish, in 1541, under the
direction of the Archbishop of Uppsala. From this time, the Bible
became ever more central to literate Swedish households as a spiritual and literary resource from which all could derive inspiration,
though it would take more than a further century and a half for its
presence to finally become ubiquitous in them.

Olaus Magnus (1490–1557), brother of Bishop Johannes Magnus
(1488–1544), was perhaps the most highly cultured literary figure of
the period. A Renaissance scholar and diplomat, he devoted himself
to the study of geography and history, having journeyed with his
brother to Rome in 1523. His maps of Scandinavia, published in
Venice, were of considerable importance, providing as they did the
first reasonably accurate depiction of the region's geographical contours. Yet he is most famous for his historical works, in particular
Historia de gentibus septentrionalibus (History of the Nordic
People), published in 1555. Richly illustrated with more than five
hundred woodcuts, this work idealised Sweden as a sovereign
princely state on a par with those of the other major powers of
Europe. It also stressed the unique role of Sweden within a divine
plan, at the same time focusing attention on little known peoples,
like the Saami of Lapland. As such, it would exert considerable
influence on European culture and philosophical values, not only in
Sweden, but elsewhere in the Christian world, at a time when northern European countries, newly converted to various forms of
Protestantism, were attempting to consolidate themselves as autonomous territorial states.

4

Towards a centralist and military state

After the death of Gustaf Vasa, Sweden underwent a lengthy period of turbulence which eventually gave way in the following century to a period of consolidation, on a wide variety of levels. In 1560, Erik XIV (1533–77) succeeded his father as king of Sweden, the second in the dynastic line of Vasa. However, the transition was less than smooth since relations with his brother Johan, later Johan III (1537–92), were troubled by the latter's marriage to the Catholic princess Katarina Jagellonica (1526–83) of Poland and the education of their son Sigismund (1566–1632) as a Catholic. This circumstance would open the door to Sweden's growing political and military involvement in continental European affairs, in particular those which involved Poland. Unwilling to bend to the will of Erik, Johan was imprisoned for four years. Yet his temporary removal left a wide range of problems unresolved for Erik. His morganatic marriage to his mistress Karin Månsdotter (1550–1612) in 1568 was especially unpopular. The key role played by the jurist Jöran Persson (c.1530–68) in his political decisions also won him many enemies, a situation which the latter's torture and murder failed to abate. For the murders, in 1567, of members and associates of the powerful, noble Sture family, including Nils, Svante and Erik Sture, as well as Abraham Stenbok, by Erik and his henchmen had been blamed on Persson's political machinations. In consequence, Erik was removed from

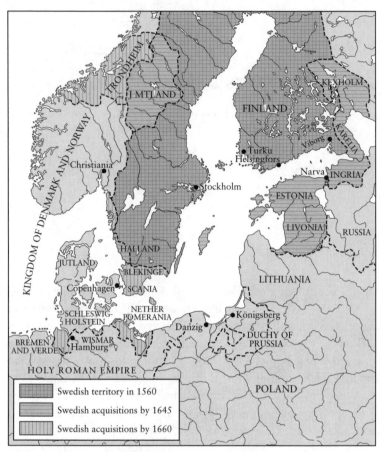

Map 1 Sweden, extending across the Baltic Sea, 1560–1660. As Sweden
consolidated and extended its territory during this period, particularly by
military conquest, it rapidly became one of Europe's most powerful states,
making the Baltic a veritable Swedish lake, in economic and military terms.

power in 1568, imprisoned, and Johan placed upon the throne in
his stead. The following year, King Johan III, as a means of appeas-
ing the nobility, promulgated a decree releasing them from military
obligations. However, relations with the nobility were also troubled,
not least because of Johan's attempts to re-establish Catholicism in
Sweden by stealth. In particular, his introduction of the so-called
Red Book, a new but more Catholic liturgy, in 1576 met with

considerable opposition. Although in 1571 a new series of pro-Reformation ecclesiastical laws eliminated many of the old Catholic holy days from the calendar, the Protestant Reformers themselves were riven by theological disagreement, as Lutherans and Calvinists vied with one another to dominate the Swedish Church. The former proved ultimately victorious, but the latter left a lasting imprint, since Erik XIV had himself been deeply influenced by them, his two tutors as a child, Dinysius Beurreus and Jan van Hervoville, both having been committed Calvinists.

The strength of the Protestants notwithstanding, Johan, encouraged by his Catholic wife, strengthened his effort to implement an ecclesiastic realignment in the direction of the old religion. These initiatives were limited in scope. A Catholic chapel was opened at court for the queen's spiritual needs and the Jesuits were invited to Stockholm to establish a new academy, under the directorship of their priest Nicolai Laurentius Nicolai. Nonetheless, both Lutherans and Calvinists looked on this turn of events with horror, especially when it became apparent that the crown prince, Sigismund, was being raised as a Catholic. His assumption of the kingship of Catholic Poland in 1587 further augmented fears among much of the Swedish clergy, now overwhelmingly Protestant, that Sweden was being reintegrated into the Catholic fold by stealth. The wider Swedish population also shared their anxiety, since they, too, had now come to accept the Lutheran confession, their views having been moulded by the yearly visitations of the reformed clergy, in which its catechism was expounded.

ECONOMIC DIFFICULTIES

If matters of religion remained a source of growing conflict between the Church and crown, the Swedish economy was also in difficult straits already under Erik XIV. The availability of sufficient funds to pay the military was an ever growing problem, especially as the employment of foreign, usually German, mercenaries was increasingly important in the defence of the realm. Indeed, by the 1550s, between a half and two thirds of all royal cash expenditures were used for this purpose. Since a permanent naval fleet had also now been assembled, this became a major issue for the king. While at first the silver confiscated from the churches helped to pay for Erik XIV's military activities, income from the silver mines at Sala was eventually utilised as well, though the mines became increasingly depleted as the century wore on. As a result, increased taxes and other forms of income derived from trade of various sorts became a necessity.

The growth of Swedish trade abroad also necessitated improved mercantile relations, in particular with such western maritime powers as England and the Netherlands, seeking to free itself from Habsburg hegemony. As a result, Sweden's small but only North Sea port Älvsborg took on an increasingly important role in the country's economy. Therefore its seizure by Denmark during the middle of the century proved a major setback. On the other hand, the acceptance by Estland (now Estonia) of Swedish sovereignty in 1561 ameliorated the situation, facilitating, as it did, trade with Russia and the east.

The situation in the west also improved after the Treaty of Stettin, in 1570, re-established peace with Denmark, and a more stable order, based on the de facto arrangement originally established by Gustaf Vasa, came to be accepted. Älvsborg was returned to Sweden in exchange for a payment of 150,000 silver *dalers* over the following three years. Most importantly, King Frederik II of Denmark relinquished his claim on Sweden. In return, Johan relinquished his on Norway.

THE CONGREGATION OF UPPSALA AND ITS DYNASTIC IMPLICATIONS

The attempts of Johan to foster Catholicism in Sweden increasingly polarised most of the now Lutheran clergy and alienated his popular support. His death in 1592 and the succession to the throne of the committed Catholic Sigismund was leading, as well, to not only theological but political confrontation. In response, in 1593, the clergy of the now Lutheran Church assembled at Uppsala, and issued a series of declarations which defined the tenets of the Church in Sweden, while going on to prohibit the practice of Catholicism. Another consequence was the revival of Uppsala University in 1595. Not only did this restore opportunities for higher learning in the traditional sense, but it provided a means by which future diplomats and other governmental figures could be educated and trained for their future roles, many of which took them abroad to the royal and princely courts of Europe, from which political and intellectual power emanated.

Yet in the immediate aftermath, it was the confrontation with Sigismund, who arrived in Sweden in September 1593, which was of greatest import, since the king gave clear indication that the decisions of the Council on religious matters would not find royal assent. Indeed, he ordered Catholic masses to be said in Stockholm and attempted in other ways to assert his will against both them and the implementation of their reforming measures. However, the opposition of both his uncle Duke Karl (1550–1611) and the estates, gathered together for the funeral of Johan III, proved so strong that Sigismund was obliged to confirm the decisions. He then returned to Poland, leaving Karl, in concert with the Council, as regent, nationally, but with the independent provincial governors appointed by himself. Some of these proved highly unpopular, not only with Karl but the local wider population. In particular, Klas Fleming, the governor in Ostrobothnia, in Finland, who enjoyed the king's full support, was so hated that a revolt broke out among the peasants in 1596.

Yet Karl was by this stage embroiled in hostilities not only with Sigismund but with his own nobility, many of whom objected to his attempts to consolidate his power at their expense. However, the matter was resolved in September 1598 after Sigismund and his men, who had arrived in Kalmar in July, were defeated by Karl's own military forces at Stångebro. Sigismund and his men then fled back to Poland. Therefore, from a position of strength, in July of the following year, the *Riksdag* in Stockholm officially declared Sigismund's dethronement in Sweden. This body, the composition of which changed from time to time, now consisted of four estates – the nobility, Church, burghers and peasants – but the first two dominated. It now remained for enemies at home to be dealt with. Drawing upon widespread commoner support, Karl prepared to attack those magnates keen to make the Council of State once again the main focus of governmental authority. This resulted in 1600 in the so-called Linköping Bloodbath, in which Karl's aristocratic opponents, Ture Bielke, Erik Sparre, and Gustaf and Sten Banér were put to death, all by order of the *Riksdag*.

Only in 1603, at a meeting of the estates at Norrköping, was Karl finally confirmed as king of Sweden, with hereditary rights to the throne granted to his descendants. He assumed the name Karl IX the following year, but was obliged to waited a further three years for his coronation in Uppsala Cathedral. Once this had been accomplished, he was then able to turn his attention to foreign affairs, as well as to strengthen his position politically and economically. This he did not only by increasing populist support for his absolutism, but by focusing upon opportunities of aggrandisement against Russia, now in a state of political turmoil.

The Treaty of Teusina in 1595 had delineated the northern border between Sweden and Russia in Lapland, so the old dispute over the frontier was no longer an issue. Rather, it was Karl IX's desire to diminish Polish political influence to the benefit of Sweden which lay at the heart of his interference in Russian affairs, especially those relating to the establishment of a new dynasty there to replace that so recently and brutally extinguished. His attempts to strengthen Swedish–Russian trade led him into open conflict with Denmark, not only in the Baltic Sea but to the north in the Arctic Ocean as well, and in Lapland, where the border with Danish-controlled Norway was also in dispute. As a result, during the early years of the seventeenth century, Sweden had become involved in three wars with its neighbours, as it attempted to dominate the Baltic littoral to an ever greater degree. Its defeat at Kirkholm, in Livonia, near the southern border of Swedish-held Estland, was demoralising enough, but the Kalmar War which broke out against Denmark in 1611 was, in reality, more threatening, especially since the port city was soon lost to the Danes. True, Sweden occupied Norwegian-held Jämtland and Härjedalen, but that was of little consolation for the loss of such a valuable window on the Baltic. With the appointment that year of Axel Oxenstierna (1583–1654) as chancellor, however, the king secured one of Sweden's most able administrators. Yet the challenges were many and he had numerous difficulties with which to contend: in 1612, the Danes once again seized Älvsborg, cutting off Sweden from the North Sea trade, and the fortress of Gullberg was captured as well.

ECONOMIC EXPANSION AND ITS MILITARY IMPLICATIONS

This conflict dragged on for a further two years, but in 1613, the Treaty of Knäred was finally signed, negotiations for which were facilitated by England, with its own maritime agenda. However, its demands were onerous: Älvsborg was to be returned to Sweden, but only upon payment of a million *riksdalers*, a huge sum equivalent to two thirds of the value of the country's yearly agricultural produce, with parts of Västergötland to remain in Danish hands until this was effected. The accomplishment of this onerous task took more than six years, largely achieved through earnings brought in by the export of Dalecarlian copper, but loans were also taken from Holland, whose ship-owning merchants were keen to see Danish maritime power reduced. Swedish–Dutch relations were further strengthened by a military alliance signed in The Hague in 1614. That said, Denmark's military might was by no means routed, for the far northern province of Finnmark, seized from Norway, had to be relinquished again by Sweden in line with the Treaty of Knäred just signed with Denmark.

Still Dutch support was highly beneficial to Sweden and not just in terms of military support, for its merchants and manufacturers helped to provide the necessary expertise required by a burgeoning Swedish industry, so important for the expansion of its military might and, at this stage, inferior to that of rival Denmark. Much of this depended on income from mining. Yet, while the export of copper grew markedly in the 1580s, it was the iron industry and its mining sector that proved over the longer term to be the more significant. In this the Dutch played a key role. For example, during that decade, the Dutch entrepreneur Willem van Wijck assisted Johan III to such an extant that iron production increased from an export value of 27,501 naval pounds in 1549, to 48,355 by 1604. Holland was a major importer of the iron, but England rapidly superseded it in sales, in terms of the quantity purchased. Indeed, so important did this burgeoning industry become that new administrative measures were introduced to facilitate its functioning. These led to the foundation of the *Bergskollegium* (College of Mining) in 1637, by crown initiative. It proved so successful in its supervision and administration of the industry that it continued to function until 1828.

With iron mining in such demand, other mining ventures were also undertaken. In 1636, during the early years of the reign of Queen Kristina, a silver mine was brought into production at Nasa, in Swedish Lapland, not far from the Norwegian border. There Saami herdsmen were pressed into service, hauling the ore with their reindeer. However, it proved unviable economically and was eventually closed down. On the other hand, copper mining continued to be extremely important. Indeed, the mines of Stora Kopparberg, near Falun in Dalecarlia, enabled Sweden to supply almost all of Europe's and later America's copper throughout the seventeenth century. It also encouraged the government to introduce copper as a standard for coinage. Some of the Swedish copper coins which now came to be minted were so extraordinarily large – a foot in length and more than forty pounds in weight – that their transport became difficult and new methods of payment were devised. Taxation, moreover, was still largely paid in produce. If proof were needed, these circumstances demonstrated that Sweden was still not a fully 'monetarised' society, even if, as far back as 1601, the country had become the first European country to issue paper money. That said, in 1644 Sweden began formally to print banknotes, fifty years before the first Bank of England note was issued.

Already towards the end of the sixteenth century, Johan III had provided the initiative for a variety of other mercantile endeavours, not least of which involved the foundation of several new cities in Sweden: Karlstad, Mariestad and Mariefred. Increasing resources in the royal coffers had military importance for they enabled Sweden's standing army to be increased in size, up to 24,500 Swedish men in peacetime, an extraordinarily large number compared with the tiny force that had previously served the country in such circumstances. These numbers were swelled yet further in wartime by mercenaries, usually of English, Scottish or German ethnicity. Many of these frequently stayed on in Sweden after the completion of their service, usually fulfilled in the eastern Baltic campaigns. Elevations to the hereditary nobility increased concomitantly, as did the allocation of land freed from the burden of taxation during such times. Thus, under Johan III, no less than 19 per cent of all cultivated land was so privileged, an increase of

4 per cent over the amount in the reign of Erik XIV, useful in the short term for military needs, but boding ill in the long term for the financial stability of the state and its growing centralisation.

THE FOUNDATION OF NEW CITIES

During the later sixteenth century, Sweden remained an overwhelmingly agricultural country with a sparsely settled population. According to a tax register of 1571, the country's population, excluding Finland, amounted to approximately 750,000. Of these, only about 5 per cent lived in urban areas, but they played an important role in mercantile activities. Stockholm was the largest city and most important trading emporium, but its population still hardly exceeded six thousand. Situated as it was on its Baltic archipelago, it was inclined over the centuries, like Sweden itself, to look more to the east and south, rather than in other directions, for its principal markets. However, by the seventeenth century, with its increasing maritime links to western Europe, the need for an eastern Swedish port facing the North Sea became a pressing priority. In consequence, a new city, Gothenburg, was founded in 1607 to fill this gap. Not surprisingly, it was Dutch merchants who came to dominate the new city, with ten on the city's new governing council. Seven Swedes and a Scot made up the rest. This Dutch connection is hardly surprising, since it was money from the Netherlands that assisted in facilitating the return of nearby Älvsborg to Sweden. That said, in its earliest years, Gothenburg remained under the domination of Stockholm, the country's capital and through which all international trade was obliged to pass. However, in 1621, Gothenburg was granted permission to carry out international trade directly, thereby opening a new chapter in Sweden's maritime history, giving it privileged links not only with the rest of Europe but with the wider world beyond. For the following decades, this city of predominantly Dutch and Scottish merchants served as a filter allowing foreign investors and entrepreneurs to enter the country, bringing with them the human and material resources Sweden's underdeveloped economy so desperately needed.

On the northern and eastern frontiers of Finland new settlements were also founded, albeit of a more modest nature and of more limited scope for trade. For Finland remained sparsely populated, with only about half a million inhabitants in 1690. Of these, one third were landless peasants, most of whom eked out their livelihood as farm labourers on the landholdings of others. Many, though, in quest of improving their lot, increasingly sought their fortunes on the frontier periphery with Russia, where virgin lands were available to be brought into cultivation, but at a price: for Russia viewed their growing presence as a threat and the invasions of Russian troops in the many wars with Sweden made these settlements precarious. In fact, in consequence of the ravishing forays by the Russians, a growing emigration took place, which saw many Finns seeking refuge in the northern and central provinces of Sweden across the Gulf of Bothnia. Many came to reside, in particular, in Värmland, where they were invited to open up forested land for cultivation. They arrived in considerable numbers, and even today the names of many villages there still attest to their former presence. That said, the dangers of Russian incursions notwithstanding, new towns also sprang up in Finland's frontier 'colonial territories', in Karelia, Savo, Kajani and Finnish Lapland.

THE THIRTY YEARS WAR

Sweden's success in consolidating itself as a highly centralised, militarised territorial state was soon to be brought to the test. The outbreak of a general war in central Europe in 1618 at first only affected Sweden peripherally. But, in 1630, when Sweden entered the affray, it assumed an important military and political status which it had never achieved before and has not done since. It had become what in modern parlance would be termed a superpower, or at least, it assumed the appearance of one, for, in reality, it had neither the manpower nor the wealth to sustain that position for long.

In part, the country owed its new position to the acumen of its new king, Gustaf II Adolph (1594–1632), who had acceded to the throne in 1611. Rapid military gains in the east had helped, in the short term, to consolidate his military and economic strength. In 1617, the year of his coronation, Sweden had acquired, by virtue of the Peace Treaty of Stolbova, the provinces of both Kexholm, in northern Karelia, and Ingria, in what is today Russia's Leningradskaya

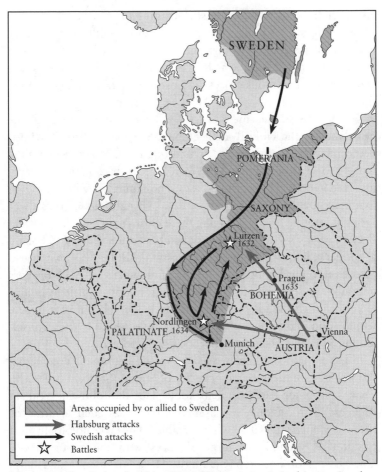

Map 2 Sweden during the Thirty Years War, 1618–48. At this time Sweden, ruled by the warrior-king Gustaf II Adolph, possessed one of Europe's most powerful military machines which, under its skilful generals, enabled it to dominate much of the German heartlands of central Europe, making the state a highly formidable player in European politics.

Oblast, where St Petersburg is situated. A devoted Lutheran and interested in creating a more unitary state, Gustaf II Adolph encouraged a growing centralisation of the state bureaucracy and more efficient management of its resources, which was assisted by the Swedish Church itself. Conformity and homogeneity, both religious and social, became characteristic features of society. Now both Catholicism and Orthodoxy were criminalised, with exile and confiscation of property the consequence for those who continued to adhere to the old faith which, the King felt, independent of his genuinely held religious objections, also threatened the unity of the state.

When in 1618, the Thirty Years War broke out, tearing apart the heartlands of the Holy Roman Empire, Sweden, at first, remained neutral, biding its time before committing itself. However, with the renewal of war with Poland in 1621, Sweden became more deeply involved in central European politics. The campaign, which began in Livonia, soon led to the capture of Riga. Then, in 1626, Prussia was brought into the fray, war raging there until 1629.

In 1629, a six-year truce was signed between Sweden and Poland at Altmark. Relieved on this front, Gustaf II Adolph was able to lead Sweden into the Thirty Years War the following year, with the goal not only of assisting his fellow Protestants, but of acquiring valuable territory on the southern shores of the Baltic. This, it was hoped, would soon allow the sea to become a Swedish lake, truly consolidating Sweden's position as Europe's great power.

In 1630, Swedish forces arrived in Pomerania, rapidly conquering the wealthy southern Baltic port city of Stettin (Szczecin in Polish). Their first major battle, though, took place the following year, at Breitenfeld, in Saxony, a major victory for Sweden against the Habsburg General Tilly, which enabled Gustaf Adolph, from a position of strength, to forge alliances with the major Protestant powers of northern Germany. These included Magdeburg, Brandenburg and Saxony. Although a devoted Lutheran, his tolerance of divergent forms of Protestantism had practical political benefits, for many of his Protestant allies were Calvinist. The scope of his military operations soon widened and the Swedish campaigns in central Europe came, over the better part of the next two decades, to extend south from Stralsund, in the north, to Leipzig, Frankfurt-am-Main and Munich, in the south. Even Vienna was threatened.

Catholic France was delighted and Cardinal Richelieu, its prime minister, relished the fact that his Protestant ally was threatening France's arch-enemy in war, the Habsburg Empire. Therefore, in January 1631, France promised Sweden 400,000 *riksdaler*, per annun, were it to wage war against the Habsburgs with an army of 36,000 men. This it did and by April, Sweden had conquered Erfurt and Frankfurt-an-der-Oder from imperial forces.

Both sides suffered losses. In 1632, on 5 April, the Habsburg General Tilly was mortally wounded at Lech. Then, on 6 November 1632, Gustaf Adolph himself fell at the Battle of Lützen. He was succeeded by his daughter Kristina (1626–89), but, as she was a mere child, arrangements had to be made for a regency. The Council of State then assumed the reins of power in Sweden, establishing the regency under Axel Oxenstierna until such time as Kristina should come of age.

Meanwhile, the wars in Germany continued apace. In 1634, the Habsburg General Albrekt von Wallenstein was assassinated in Bohemia. Then, in 1635, Saxony and Brandenburg made an independent peace with the Habsburgs, while a twenty-six-year truce was agreed between Sweden and Poland. Only now did France abandon its proxy war and finally, in 1636, it declared war on the Habsburg Empire. This assisted Sweden which, in September, was victorious at the Battle of Wittstock, in the north of Brandenburg, under General Johan Banér.

Banér died suddenly in 1641, but new talented military men now came to the fore. By the middle of 1642, the Swedish armies were being led by Field Marshal Lennart Torstensson (1603–51), who was in effect now *generalissimo* of the Swedish military forces in the empire. At the Second Battle of Breitenfeld that same year, he virtually annihilated the Habsburg imperial troops with whom he had engaged in battle. He then went on in the field from strength to strength. When once again, in 1643, war broke out between Sweden and Denmark, he rushed to Jutland where he served to check the Danes, before returning to the empire, where a series of battles enabled him to clear the way to the Danube and beyond. However, there he himself was checked by imperial forces. At this stage, therefore, crippled by gout, he returned to Sweden.

In 1644 Queen Kristina reached the age of majority and rapidly took the reins of power into her own hands. She was assisted by Axel Oxenstierna, who remained the most powerful man in Sweden. This was especially true with respect to the handling of foreign affairs and the conduct of the war in Germany, which, on the whole, proved highly successful for Sweden and its allies. Peace was again made at

Brömsebro, in 1645, by virtue of which Denmark lost the provinces of Jämtland, Härjedalen and Halland, as well as the islands of Gotland and Ösel, all of which were annexed to Sweden for a period of thirty years. Freedom from tolls in the Sound and the Belt was also granted, a privilege which would continue in effect until 1720. Most importantly, in 1645, Swedish forces defeated those of the imperial troops to the south-east of Prague. A year later, one of the war's greatest generals, Carl Gustaf Wrangel (1613–76), assumed control of Swedish military forces. He prepared himself for the final onslaught and in 1648, Prague itself, the *hochburg* of the Habsburg Empire, and the capital of Bohemia where the war itself had begun thirty years before, was captured by Swedish forces, just as the Treaty of Westphalia was being signed in Munster concluding thirty years of vicious hostilities in the ravaged heartlands of central Europe. As a result, through this brilliant *fait accompli* at the eleventh hour, Sweden received not only parts of Pomerania, Rügen, Usedom, Bremen and Verden for its territorial expansion, but the fabulous booty of the Rudolphine court in Prague, Europe's most important collection of art treasures.

SWEDISH POMERANIA

With the incorporation of Swedish Pomerania into the realm, the Swedish monarch in his capacity as Duke of Pomerania became subject to the Holy Roman Emperor. That said, this subservient position was purely nominal, for the Swedish king could levy taxes, grant land and appoint administrators, including the governor general and other ministers. German remained the language of the general population and government, with the former measurements and coinage still in place, but the affairs of the Treasury were, henceforth, conducted in Swedish. The old legal system was maintained, but the High Court of Sweden now superseded the old German one, a new courthouse being built in the capital, Stralsund, as if symbolically to emphasise this fact. Sweden's Baltic hegemony seemed to be becoming a reality.

To safeguard this and the other German territorial acquisitions by Sweden, the Swedish architect Erik Dahlberg was commissioned to construct an iron necklace of fortresses along the new continental frontier, to both the south and east. The most important of these bastions was at Wismar, but others included Stade, near Bremen, in the west, and Nöteborg, on Lake Ladoga, in the east.

Sweden's expectations that its new German possessions would be contested militarily proved justified. Already, in 1675, Denmark, supported by its ally Brandenburg, captured Wismar, but Sweden's ally France demanded its restitution to Sweden. As for the enforced cession by Sweden of much of Nether Pomerania to Brandenburg, it could not be reversed. Moreover, Stralsund was conquered in 1715, and the capital was transferred to Stettin. Five years later, only a narrow sliver of territory belonging to Hinter Pomerania, situated north of the River Peene, remained in Swedish hands. Once again, though, Stralsund was given to Sweden, and the administrative seat of government was once again transferred there in this now truncated province. The Swedish government then proposed a beautification of the city in line with its restored status. In response, a new palace for the governor general, Count Meijerfedt, was constructed in the Baroque style, designed by the Netherlandish architect Cornelius Loos, who accompanied Karl XII during his exile at Bender, in what is now Mordova, after his forces were defeated by the Russians under Peter the Great. A mansion for the city's military commander was also built, along with a new post office, embellished with a mélange of architectural features, which seemed to marry, like the political settlement, Swedish and German elements of design.

THE ARTS AS A POLITICAL STATEMENT

After the conclusion of the Thirty Years War, it was General Wrangel, rather than the Swedish monarchy, who entertained the most lavish architectural undertakings, not only in the southern Baltic province but in mainland Sweden itself. Having assumed the governorship of Swedish Pomerania, Wrangel, in 1654, commenced the building of the palace of Skokloster, on the shores of Lake Mälaren, not far from Stockholm. Some of northern Europe's most important architects, including Nicodemus Tessin the Elder (1615–84), a native of Stralsund, Jean de la Vallée (1620–96) and Caspar Vogel, assisted in its construction. The edifice as completed evinces the influence of such German prototypes as Friedenstein Castle, in

Gotha, and the Johannisburg Palace, in Aschaffenburg, rather than specifically Swedish ones. Yet, although much of the booty he had seized in the course of the Thirty Years War had found its way, by the 1660s, to Skokloster, now his family seat, the vast edifice was never completed. In any case, it was by no means Wrangel's only place of residence: the Wrangel Palace he built in Stockholm was one of the city's most splendid mansions. He also had other residences constructed in Swedish Pomerania. The Wrangel Palace in Stralsund was built by the Swedish architect Nils Eosander (1635–1705) in a Swedish style, the hallmark of which was a sloping roof on its principal façade, as opposed to the old German gabled tradition of roof building. Eosander also undertook major restoration of the Spycker Castle, on Rügen, around 1670. Surrounded by a moat when it was first built in the sixteenth century, it was provided with flanking corner towers and painted Falun red, a by-product of the copper mines of Falun, in Dalecarlia, in characteristic Swedish fashion. It became his favoured residence and Wrangel died there in 1676.

If art and architecture played an important political role in seventeenth-century Sweden, so, too, did music, seen as vital for the country's improved status. A key figure in this new found flourishing was Gustaf Düben (1628–90), who had succeeded his father, the German Andreas Düben (1590–1663), as both director of the Royal Swedish Court Orchestra and organist of the German St Gertrud Church in Stockholm. Based at the newly built Palace of Drottninghom, such pieces as his *Three Dances* and *Sarabande* were widely acclaimed and demonstrated that Sweden could hold its own with other major European courts in terms of its music.

RENEWAL OF WAR WITH RUSSIA

If Sweden's superpower status in the western Baltic was insecure, it was even more so in the eastern part. Already, in 1656, Russia again attacked Sweden's eastern Baltic territories. Making matters worse, Denmark declared war on Sweden the following year, desirous of annulling the gains which had accrued to its enemy by virtue of the Treaty of Brömsebro. In response, Karl X Gustaf (1622–60), who had succeeded his cousin Kristina, led his forces which were stationed in Poland through northern Germany and into Denmark.

His troops, after making their way into Jutland, crossed the ice of the Little Belt channel to Funen, from where they made their way across the Great Belt to Zealand. Encamped outside Copenhagen, the threatening Swedish military presence obliged Denmark to capitulate. As a result, Sweden gained not only Scania, Halland, Blekinge and Bohuslän, but the Baltic islands of Bornholm and the Norwegian province of Trøndelag. Nonetheless, greedy for more territory, Karl X shortly thereafter once again threatened Copenhagen. This time he was less successful. The following year, after a lengthy siege and unsuccessful assault, the Swedes were successfully repulsed. Peace was finally made in 1660, in consequence of which Bornholm and Trøndelag were returned to Denmark-Norway. Peace was also made with Poland and, most importantly, Russia.

FURTHER ECONOMIC DEVELOPMENTS

The demobilisation of the Swedish forces in Germany, even if a large proportion were foreign mercenaries, created both logistical and financial problems. For one thing, the donations of crown land to officers returning from the Thirty Years War had deeply impoverished the country's coffers. This situation was further exacerbated by the fact that, by the end of Queen Kristina's reign, some 63 per cent of agricultural land had come to belong to the nobility and was therefore free of taxation. Therefore, when Karl X assumed the throne in 1654, after the queen's abdication the year before, a new law obliging the reduction of the land of the nobility was enacted. As a result one quarter of all land loaned out to them since 1632, along with that land deemed necessary for the maintenance of the crown, was reclaimed, that is some three thousand homesteads in total. This action served to strengthen both the growing centralisation of government and the absolutism of the monarchy itself.

While rural life thereby underwent significant changes administratively, the mining industry continued to function smoothly and remain lucrative. Copper and iron remained in constant demand abroad, totalling some 80 per cent of all goods exported by the country during this period. Until the mid-1620s, copper predominated. While it had traditionally been exported as raw copper, more recently it had been processed into *garkoppar*, an especially refined form of the metal cleansed of small impurities. Its increased production, as we have seen, encouraged, from 1625, the use of copper in coinage, which lessened the amount of silver required, on the one hand, but debased the currency further, on the other. As the century wore on, however, iron took on an increasingly important role as an export commodity. Indeed, by the end of the seventeenth century, its international market had grown dramatically, with England alone purchasing approximately 65 per cent of all the iron exported by Sweden.

Brass also became an important Swedish export commodity. The German immigrant Momma brothers assisted in its industrial production, becoming so successful that they were able to amass considerable riches, while being elevated to the nobility, under the new name of Reenstierna.

Louis De Geer (1587–1652), from Wallonia in what is now Belgium, also followed a similar path to riches and high status after his arrival in Sweden in 1627. He built up his own weapons factory and brass production at Holmens bruk, by Norrköping, becoming one of the leading industrialists of his age. He also provided much of the necessary accoutrements for the Swedish military during the country's involvement in the Thirty Years War, going on to found an entrepreneurial dynasty which would long play a major role in his adopted country's economy.

The value for the Swedish economy of shipping through Stockholm was also increasing dramatically. From a value of 17,100 shipping pounds (one such pound equalled about 170 kg), in 1615, it grew to 58,500 in 1640, and 102,800 by 1650. Stockholm remained the principal port of export with its burgeoning international trade. Trade at Gothenburg, by contrast, remained modest: from 15,200 shipping pounds in 1640, it grew to only 17,000 by 1650.

Yet if the Baltic had by now become a veritable Swedish lake, it was not the Swedes who benefited predominantly, but the Dutch. They reaped the greatest rewards and their ships carried most of the Swedish realm's export commodities. Indeed, in the early 1650s, some 65 per cent of shipping passing through the Sound sailed under the Dutch flag, compared with only 10 per cent under the Swedish.

As for trade in the eastern Baltic, now under Swedish hegemony, that through Riga, in Livonia, also increased significantly. Whereas

12,000 shipping pounds of hemp, necessary for the navy, had made its way from what is today Belarus through Riga and across the Baltic in the decade 1660–9, some 58,700 did so by 1690–9. The amount of hempseed increased even more dramatically: from 2,300 shipping pounds in the first period, to 123,300 in the latter. As a result, in times of famine – by no means infrequent in the second of half of the seventeenth century – Riga was Sweden's lifeline for the import of grain from the Russian and Belarusian hinterland.

Despite Sweden's vast coastline, the only cities permitted international trade at this time were Stockholm, Kalmar, Gothenburg, Gävle and Turku. However, Gävle was prohibited from trading further south than Stockholm. Also of importance was Karlskrona, principal seat of the Swedish navy. It was an important shipbuilding site as well, and many of the country's naval vessels were built in its docks during the late seventeenth and early eighteenth centuries. This production was facilitated by the English shipbuilder Charles Sheldon who, among other activities, assisted in the construction of seven large naval ships there.

Forestry also remained an important export activity for Sweden, even if, by the sixteenth century, at the latest, the primeval forest of the more southerly provinces had largely disappeared. In Finland, by contrast, much of the land had never been brought into cultivation and primeval forest, swamp and scrubland continued to abound. Moreover, unlike the situation in much of Sweden – excluding Gotland, Dalecarlia and Norrland – some 90 per cent of the land which had been cultivated in Finland was in the hands of yeomen farmers, rather than those of the crown or aristocracy. This is, in part, to be accounted for by the fact that the nobility of Finland was very small: only 215 households in the early sixteenth century. However, their position had strengthened over the following century, as the nobility on both sides of the Gulf of Bothnia was aided by the growing centralisation of government and the removal of onerous obligations for them to bear arms on behalf of the king. That said, in sparsely populated Finland, where even the environs of its administrative capital and principal city, Turku, had few habitations, the power of the nobility remained limited vis-à-vis that exercised in the rest of the Swedish realm.

THE ESTABLISHMENT OF NEW SWEDEN IN DELAWARE

Sweden's growth on its geographical peripheries bore witness to its interest in expanding its economic powers, but its most dramatic, if hardly long-lasting, initiative was the establishment of a colony in North America. In 1637, the New Sweden Company was founded in Sweden for this purpose, under the initiative of two Dutchmen, Samuel Blommaert and Peter Minuit. It enabled the establishment of the first Swedish colony in the Americas at Fort Kristina (now Wilmington), in what is today the state of Delaware, the following year. Few volunteered to emigrate, however, so that, in 1641, the Swedish government decided to transport prisoners there. Military deserters, soldiers court-martialled, as well as poachers, vagabonds, and one man accused of cutting down six apple trees in the royal orchard at Varnhem Monastery, soon arrived to populate the new colony, in the company of their families.

Its first governor was Johan Printz (1592–1663), later appointed governor of the province of Jönköping, after his return to Sweden. During his period of administration, the cultivation and export of tobacco to Sweden became the primary source of income, though the fur trade also developed and beaver skins became a significant export.

Security was and remained a constant problem. As the vulnerability of Fort Kristina to military assault became apparent, the need for a new capital became a necessity. Therefore, in 1643, the seat of government was re-established at the better protected site of New Gothenburg further up the Delaware River. Even then the colony proved indefensible: when, in 1655, the Dutch, under Peter Stuyvesant, captured Fort Kristina, they re-established the colony as one of their own. Yet the Swedish presence left a lasting legacy, not least the construction of log cabins in the Swedish style. Moreover, most of the several hundred Swedes and Finns who had settled there remained. More ominously, so too did the legacy of slavery: an African had been imported for that purpose in 1639 and that 'peculiar institution' would be maintained for more than two and a quarter centuries in the ex-Swedish colony.

The Lutheran Church was also established in New Sweden during that period. The first church was erected on Tinicum Island, in the

Delaware River, with Lars Lock appointed its first priest from 1648 to 1654. His presence greatly disturbed previously established residents nearby, not native Americans but Dutch adherents of the Reformed Church, which followed Calvinist tenets. The colony's governor, Printz, abhorred Calvinism and sought to crush its rival presence. However, it was towards the religion of the native Americans that he was most hostile. Indeed, he advocated the extermination of those who refused to accept Christianity, a threat he was unable to carry out through lack of military might. After his departure, though, the colony's administrators became more tolerant and soon not only Dissenters but even Jews were allowed to settle there, a rare example of religious toleration of that time, though not unusual in other Protestant North American colonies. As for the Swedish Lutheran Church itself, with its series of resident priests, it continued to function for more than a century, long after the Swedes relinquished sovereignty.

Despite the debacle of New Sweden, other Swedish colonial initiatives were also undertaken. Indeed, with an eye to capturing some of the slave trade, as well as providing a useful port of call on the west African coast, the Swedes captured the fortress of Carolusburg, on what is now the coast of Ghana, from the Dutch, who had built it in 1637. However, it was soon taken, in turn, by the Danes during the First Northern War, in 1659. Several years of native occupation then followed, but it was returned to Sweden in 1666, only to come under English sovereignty two years later. Only later in the early eighteenth century were new initiatives for a revival of Swedish colonial endeavours once again undertaken.

THE ESTATES

Sweden in the seventeenth century was a highly hierarchical society, politically and socially. In 1626, the estates of Sweden, the corporate political bodies into which the principal strata of Swedish society were organised, finally coalesced into a rigid officially sanctioned hierarchy. The First Estate was formally organised that year as a corporation, itself composed of three different bodies: those possessed of county or baronial titles, those within families who had served on the State Council and those of noble backgrounds but without the higher titles. The Second Estate represented the Church, under the leadership of the Archbishop of Uppsala, supported by his assisting bishops. The Third Estate supported the interests of the merchant class, especially that of Stockholm, which chose one of its members as its leading representative. Finally, there was the Fourth Estate, which served the interests of the peasants, whose leader was chosen from their number. The king himself chose the Land Marshal, who oversaw all of its functions. As such, together with the Council of State, it formed the national government of Sweden. Therefore, in Sweden, in contrast to the situation in almost all of the rest of Europe, all major segments of the population enjoyed their own political representation, at least to some degree.

THE RE-ESTABLISHMENT OF UNIVERSITY LIFE AND THE GROWTH OF INTELLECTUAL THOUGHT

With such a centralised form of government, the education of its future members in Sweden became an imperative, and so an initiative was taken in 1621 to re-establish Uppsala University, first founded in 1477, again in 1595. It is now the oldest functioning university in the Nordic countries. The king himself provided a considerable amount of the money required for its re-establishment, so as to contain, as it was put at the time, an excess 'of fascination for all things foreign and a concomitant failure to value native resources ...' Many of the university's most valuable books, nonetheless, came from Germany, where, fortuitously, they had just been seized as booty from plundered libraries of Habsburg Bohemia during the course of the Thirty Years War.

Other universities soon joined it. Dorpat (Tartu) University, in what is now Estonia, was founded in 1632, that of Turku in 1640 and that of Lund, in newly conquered Scania, in 1668. Greifswald, in the newly won territories of north Germany, already had its ancient university founded in 1456, so the territories of the Swedish dominions now boasted five such seats of learning. All of these served Swedish political needs, in that they helped to form a cultural and literary milieu and value system able to unite its alumni in a common Swedish cultural inheritance, while at the same time integrating them into a wider pan-European intellectual world. It also encouraged the establishment of a more unified legal jurisdiction, while bringing church organisation throughout the realm into greater uniformity. This was made clear by the promulgation of the Form of Government of 1634, in which Lutheran church structures were assimilated and control tightened over previously autonomous local communities. The new social order, based on conformity and homogeneity under the law, as opposed to a growing liberalism and individuality, served to undermine the older forms of feudal order, with many of their former local and regional characteristics and distinctions, divisive to a centralising and military state. In its stead, a new order was fostered, one which looked back to a mythic Gothic ancestry, which glorified Swedes as a warrior people, destined to dominate Europe. Propagated by both Church and state, this lasted as an ideology of state propaganda for more than a century, until the ideals of the French Revolution swept them away.

Sweden was now deeply enmeshed in the political and economic affairs of the Holy Roman Empire, a state of affairs which severely overtaxed the country's material resources. On an intellectual plane, however, it was highly fruitful. For during the course of the seventeenth century, with its now flourishing universities and close links with continental Europe, Swedish intellectual life blossomed. Among the most prominent intellectuals of this period was Johannes Rudbeckius (1581–1646), a professor of both mathematics and Hebrew, who was invested as Bishop of Västerås in 1619 and spent many years as personal chaplain to King Gustaf Adolph. His son, Olof Rudbeck (1630–1702), is also of note, not least for his famed literary work *Atlantica*, a poetical fantasy in which Sweden's hegemonic role in world history is glorified, a vision suited to the king's war-like and centralising policies. He was also an important scientist at Uppsala University where he focused upon the lymph glands and their function within the human body. He assisted, too, in the revision of the academic curriculum in which much of the nobility of Sweden was educated. Of especial note is his establishment of a botanical garden in Uppsala, which would be taken over in the following century by the great Swedish botanist Carl von Linné (Linnaeus, 1707–78) and still exists today.

Yet another important figure was Georg Stiernhielm (1598–1672), author of the hexametrical poem *Hercules*, published in

1658. A career in the judiciary notwithstanding, he carried out considered research into the philological origins of the Nordic languages and was also keenly interested in mathematical and scientific issues.

Literary life also flourished on a more popular level at this time and Sweden's first newspaper, *Ordinari Post Tijdender*, began publication in 1645. It continues in publication even now. Many of its articles focused upon news from the Thirty Years War, their distribution facilitated by the recent foundation of an efficient postal system which had come to serve the whole of country.

In Finland, literacy became widespread through the activities of the Lutheran Church in the late seventeenth and early eighteenth centuries. Students in higher education tended to come from the west and south of the province where society was most hierarchically stratified. That said, during the years between 1640 and 1700, 10 per cent of its university students came from more humble farming backgrounds. Among the wider population, nonetheless, writing, if not reading, remained a rare skill until well into the nineteenth century. However, the publication of Queen Kristina's *Finnish Bible* in 1642, and the Finnish hymn book some fifty years later, did much to spread literacy widely.

Even in Lapland, education made inroads during the course of the seventeenth century. A school for the education of young Saami children, for example, was established at Lycksele as early as 1632. The privy councillor and tutor of Gustaf Adolph, Johan Skytte (1577–1645), was significant in this regard, fostering as he did higher education in Lapland, since he assisted in the provision of funding for four Saami students each year to attend Uppsala University during the following century. In political terms, though, it was his role as tutor to the young Gustaf Adolph which was to prove of the greatest importance. Having been granted the barony of Duderhoff, in recently conquered Livonia, he was, in 1629, appointed governor-general of it, along with the provinces of Ingria and Karelia. Then, in 1632, he became rector of the newly established University of Dorpat. Later, in 1634, early in the reign of Queen Kristina, he was appointed president of the Göta appellate court. His contributions to Swedish natural philosophy are also of note and he was especially influential in moulding the powerful intellect of the young Queen Kristina.

QUEEN KRISTINA

Queen Kristina was a woman keenly interested in both the sciences and arts, gifted with a fluency in a wide range of languages, including German, Dutch, French and Latin. Highly self-willed, during the 1640s she increasingly attempted to assert her independence from her long-established advisers, in particular Axel Oxenstierna, Lord High Chancellor of Sweden at the time. That said, she increasingly came to rely on the help of others, in particular the diplomat Johan Adler Salvius (1590–1652), who was, for many years, Swedish Resident in Hamburg, in consequence of which he was admitted to the Council of State. She even managed to lure the French philosopher René Descartes to Stockholm, to serve as her tutor, though he died there of pneumonia not long thereafter. Later, she would maintain, it was Descartes who motivated her to accept Catholicism. Forbidden by Swedish law, this act, so unpalatable to the Lutheran Church and state, was to force her abdication, making way for her cousin Karl X to assume the throne.

Her reign was, therefore, brief but she effected many changes in government, not least in the composition of the Noble Estate, which she greatly increased in size. The higher nobility, which had altogether been composed of only thirteen county and baronial families at the beginning of her reign, at its end encompassed a further eighteen county families and fifty new baronial ones. Their privileges were also augmented, including the right to name provincial governors and found new towns. Her reforms encompassed the lower nobility, as well, which was enlarged to an even greater degree, its membership being doubled from three hundred to six hundred. However, these actions inhibited the strengthening of the Third Estate, by placing its members at a numerical disadvantage vis-à-vis the others. The construction of the House of the Nobility in Stockholm, carried out from 1642 to 1672 by the father and son French architects Simon (1590–1642) and Jean de la Vallée, with the assistance of the German H. Wilhelm, the Dutchman J. Vingboons and the Swede A. V. Edelsvärd, served as confirmation in the heart of the capital of the considerable power of the Noble Estate. It continued to serve as the seat of the nobility until 1866, when the four estates themselves were abolished as the country's parliament, and it remains one of the most imposing monuments of the High Baroque in the country.

Despite the international successes gained by Sweden through the Thirty Years War, Kristina's reign was plagued by serious problems at home. In 1650, when her cousin Karl X was chosen as her heir apparent, famine plagued the country, the result of both a poor harvest and an epidemic among domestic livestock. External pressures on Sweden also were taking their toll. In 1654, the First Bremen War broke out, over the right of that city, formally a part of the Holy Roman Empire, to continue under Swedish administration imposed in consequence of the Thirty Years War. Denmark also renewed its menaces, bolstered by the increased support of Holland, which now wished to suppress the burgeoning growth of Sweden maritime power. The marriage of King Karl X to Hedvig Eleonora, daughter of Frederik, Duke of Holstein-Gottorp, further exacerbated the problem, by heightening Denmark's feeling of vulnerability to the south.

Ex-Queen Kristina had, meanwhile, been forced into official exile by reason of her conversion to Catholicism. She travelled first to Brussels, where she was formally received into the Catholic Church, and then, the following year, she retired to Rome, having taken many royal treasures abroad with her, a good number of which were sold to help pay her expenses. Upon her arrival in the papal capital, Pope Alexander VII received her with great pomp and ceremony. Establishing herself in the fifteenth-century Palazzo Riario, in the Lungara, she lived in the city until her death in 1689, making occasional informal private trips back to Sweden. Although her religious reputation was soon tarnished there by a variety of political intrigues and scandalous personal liaisons, her financial sacrifices for the benefit of the Balkan wars against the Ottoman Turks, as well as her generosity towards the Jews of Rome, provided some compensation. In any case, after her death from erysipelas, she was buried in St Peter's Basilica in the Vatican, where Pope Innocent XII commissioned the artists G. Theudon and L. Ottani to erect a bronze and marble monument in her honour. This was completed in 1702 and shows Kristina in an allegory of queenly virtue relinquishing her throne for the sake of true religion.

RAPID DECLINE OF SWEDEN AS A GREAT POWER

Despite Sweden's military successes in the second quarter of the seventeenth century, it soon became apparent that the country, still underdeveloped economically, was in rapid decline as a major military power. Already in the 1650s, the Swedish west African colony of Cape Corso, just recently established, was captured by the Dutch. Then, in 1666, during the regency of young Karl XI (1655–97), Sweden became involved in the debilitating Second Bremen War. This was followed, in 1674, by yet another war between Sweden, on the one hand, and both Denmark and Brandenburg-Prussia, on the other, which proved even more unfortunate. As a result of the Battle of Fehrbellin in 1675, fought between Sweden and Brandenburg, Sweden was left isolated, abandoned by its former French ally, and was successfully repelled. Making matters worse, the Danes, under Christian V, invaded Scania via Helsingborg in 1676, assisted by the *Statholder* (viceroy) of Norway, Ulrik-Frederik Gyldenløve, who threatened Gothenburg from the north. At the Battle of Halmstad the invaders were rebuffed, but at the battles of Öland, that same year, and Køge Bay, the following, Sweden's de facto sovereignty over the Baltic Sea was brought to an abrupt end. The Danes and Dutch were now undisputed joint masters of its waters. A lull in hostilities during the winter in between those battles did, it is true, enable Karl XI to assemble sufficient forces from around Sweden to push them back, as well as to crush that local support which the Danes had acquired. Yet when the war was finally concluded in 1679, Sweden, though able to enjoy peace for more than a generation, remained sadly diminished from its former great power status. Henceforth, under Karl XI, the country maintained a largely defensive, rather than actively aggressive, military stance.

Nonetheless, with Sweden's mainland boundaries now secured, King Karl was able to strengthen his autocratic stance and, with the Council of State reduced to a subservient role, could now address other problematical issues, many of an internal nature. In Scania, for example, in 1681, he saw to it that Swedish law was introduced and the Swedish language made obligatory in both schools and churches. He also granted permission for the dowager queen, Hedvig Eleonora (1636–1715), to commission the building of the summer palace of Drottningholm, Sweden's ambitious attempt to emulate Versailles in the countryside outside Stockholm, on the site of an earlier humbler edifice first commissioned by King Johan III for his Queen Katarina Jagellonica. Nicodemus Tessin the Elder, by now Karl XI's court architect, was granted the commission in the years 1662–86, and his success in the enterprise still astonishes today: it is the largest summer palace ever built in any Nordic country and its architectural merits, highlights of the Swedish Baroque, are still praised.

A new political and military settlement demanded new alliances, and powerful ones now came to be forged with England and Holland, in particular. These served, once again, to strengthen Sweden as a naval power. The old alliance with France, however, was on the wane. This was especially true after France's role diminished in consequence of Karl XI's endeavour to eliminate Sweden's financial and political dependency on that country. This independence required a major reorganisation of Sweden's finances, which led to the controversial introduction of the so-called Reduction, an initiative which returned vast tracts of land to the crown and which was placed under the direct authority of the king, by virtue of powers officially granted him in the *Riksdag* of 1682.

REDUCTION

The reduction of estates exempted from taxation had become a necessity because of the dire economic straits in which the Swedish crown found itself after highly costly wars. In consequence, desperate measures were taken to ensure that money accrued to the royal coffers as quickly as possible. The economic import of reduction was, thus, dramatic and swift. As a result of its implementation, by the end of the seventeenth century, some 80 per cent of the estates transferred to the nobility had been returned to the crown, either in the form of the land itself or taxes. These included all specifically baronial and county estates. King Karl XI was assisted in this by his trusted courtier, Count Johan Gyllenstierna (1635–80). Together they proved so successful that the crown was provided with an income per year of at least 2 million *dalers* in silver, the overwhelming majority of which – 1.3 million – came from the overseas Baltic provinces. It also deprived the nobility of half its landed property, undermining its political power base in the process.

This was further diminished dramatically when the centuries-old Council of State was itself abolished and, in 1682, an emasculated

Royal Council was set up in its stead. Royal absolutism was, thus, secured. As such, it reflected similar political trends elsewhere in Europe, but in Sweden, its growing dependence on support from a wide national consensus drawn from all segments of society was specific. Seven years later, Karl XI was granted the further privilege of levying taxes directly in times of war. This strengthened the royal prerogative to such a degree that, in 1693, the king was finally declared an absolute monarch by the *Riksdag* itself. Countless farms were also dispersed to soldiers returned from the wars, while prosperous yeomanry was freed from taxation, in return for the 'voluntary' provision of horses to the military. Many, also, took the option of avoiding conscription for their sons, by participating in the new organisation and allotment of land which made this possible.

DESTRUCTION OF THE OLD ROYAL PALACE OF TRE KRONOR

Karl XI died four years later in 1697 and, as if forming a theatrical backdrop to the end of his era, the royal palace of Tre Kronor (Three Crowns), in which he lay in state, itself went up in flames. This symbolic event then opened the way, both politically and architecturally, for his son and heir, the fourteen-year-old Karl XII (1681–1718), to endeavour to establish, with few encumbrances, the hallmarks of his own reign. To begin with, he saw this event as an opportunity to build a far greater palace, one more worthy and representational of the status of one of Europe's mightiest kings, which he would so vainly endeavour to acquire. In his attempt, he drew upon the talents of the architect Nicodemus Tessin the Younger (1654–1728), who had studied in Paris during the years 1678–80 and who had succeeded his father as court architect to Karl XI in 1681. Having been deeply inspired by the allusion – said to have originally been made by Cardinal Richelieu – that, if the King of France was the Sun King, the King of Sweden was the North Star, Tessin incorporated this motif as central to the decorative symbolism of much of his royal architecture. He was also able to draw upon his experiences and impressions of Paris, to which he had returned for further studies in 1687. In that year, he submitted to a competition there his own proposals for new works at the Palace of Versailles. Although these were not chosen, they were exhibited in France alongside others by such architectural luminaries as Bernini, Le Vaus and Perrault, earning the young Swedish architect international repute. Tessin the Younger was, thus, the architect most suited in Sweden to fulfil Karl's intention of making Stockholm a Paris of the north. He also contemplated constructing a new summer palace, which would dwarf Drottningholm, as well as a vast church on the scale of Les Invalides, which could be used for great military ceremonials. However, their realisation, like that of so many grandiose Swedish plans, was prevented by a lack of funds. Indeed, even the construction of the Royal Palace itself was much delayed for that reason. That said, there were more pressing, if equally unrealistic, matters to be dealt with, and the king's attention to his architectural projects was turned aside in favour of his military ones.

KARL XII

Upon the death of Karl XI, a regency had been quickly set up in April 1697, under the Dowager Queen Hedvig Eleonora and five royal counsellors. However, it lasted little more than six months and in November that same year Karl XII was declared king and crowned the following month, an amazingly speedy coronation compared with others of the seventeenth century. This had been made necessary because the political and military noose with which Russia was threatening Sweden became tighter and the authority of the country's leader had to be bolstered by all means possible. Already in less than two years, he would be confronted by an alarming alliance of Denmark, Poland-Saxony and Russia, all now united in a pact against Sweden. Therefore, seeking allies himself in January 1700, as his father had done before him, the king allied himself with England and Holland.

His principal efforts now went to strengthen his military forces. Soon, as a result of his efforts, an effective standing army came into being, trained in yearly manoeuvres. By 1700, on the eve of war, Sweden's military forces boasted a total of some 90,000 men, most of whom were mercenaries, but 36,000 native soldiers. The country could also rely for support on its ally Holstein-Gottorp, an implacable foe of Denmark under the rival Oldenburg dynasty, as well as England and Holland, on the sea. Nonetheless, Sweden's enemies, Denmark, Poland-Saxony and Russia, were formidable when united, especially so since each now proceeded to attack Swedish forces on a different front.

Poland-Saxony was the first to invade Swedish territory, attacking Riga in February 1700. Denmark then invaded Holstein-Gottorp in March. In response, Sweden invaded Denmark in July, assisted by the combined naval forces of England and Holland, which led, shortly thereafter, to the conclusion of hostilities by the Peace of Traventhal.

However, in August of that year, Russia, under its great western-looking Tsar Peter the Great, took the initiative, by attacking Swedish forces first in Estonia and then in Ingria the following month. Karl II, returning from Denmark, immediately reacted by taking concerted action against Russia, delivering it a serious blow by forcing the retreat of Peter the Great and his forces at the Battle of Narva, on 20 November 1700. He failed, though, to consolidate this gain, turning instead the following year to deal with the Poles in a protracted campaign which lasted until 1707. At first, he was successful, defeating the latter at a major battle by the Duena River, in Courland, in 1701. Then, in 1702, he conquered not only Warsaw, but Klissow and Krakow. The following year, Danzig and Thorn (Torun in Polish) were also captured. Swedish influence in Poland was also extended because Karl succeeded in having his ally Stanislav elected as king of Poland, in place of the hostile Augustus II. These actions ensured that the military alliance with Russia and Denmark would now be dissolved.

Nonetheless, the military campaign in Poland and forbearance towards Russia were not successful. On the contrary, they proved disastrous, for they enabled Peter the Great to regroup and reinforce his troops. These actions made it possible for the Tsar to seize the mouth of the Neva River and the Swedish fortress Nyen situated there. He then wasted no time in founding his new city of St Petersburg in 1703, which, in an act of calculated bravura, he made his new Russian capital. He also recaptured Narva, on the borders of Estland, in November of the following year. True, Sweden then took Lvov and its military forces, under Lewenhaupt, seized

Gemäuterhof, in Courland, in 1705, but these were hardly major compensations for Sweden's losses to Russia.

That same year in which Sweden was able to conclude a short-term peace with Poland, Mazepa, hetman of the Cossacks (later immortalised in Tchaikovsky's eponymous opera), undertook a series of negotiations with Karl XII in the hope of fulfilling his own political ambitions which stood in opposition to those of Peter. In 1706, though, war again broke out between Sweden and Poland-Saxony, where Augustus had once again assumed the kingship. In this instance, Sweden proved victorious at the Battle of Fraustadt, enabling Karl II then to attack Saxony later in that year and to secure once again the abdication of Augustus II, through the Treaty of Altranstädt. However, Russia remained the principal threat and the Swedish king therefore confronted it head on.

Karl XII, with troops in excess of 56,000 men, invaded Russia in the summer of 1708, their destination being Moscow. The Russians retreated, but not before implementing a scorched earth policy, which destroyed crops and other resources which could have benefited the invaders, in what proved to be an unusually cold winter, a brutal tactic which would be used again in the course of history when invaders threatened Russia. This obliged the Swedes to take a more southerly course. However, Peter the Great's success in crushing Mazepa's rebellion eliminated Karl XII's principal ally. When, by the late spring of 1709, the Swedes had reached the environs of Poltava, an important city overlooking the River Dnepr, in the heart of the Ukraine, the situation became precarious, for, laying siege to it in May, Karl soon found himself confronted by 40,000 Russian troops under Peter. The conclusive battle was fought on 28 June 1709: the king himself was wounded and, under the command of Carl Gustaf Rehnskiöld (1651–1722) and Adam Ludvig Lewenhaupt (1659–1719), the Swedes were utterly devastated. Karl himself took flight, escaping into the Ottoman Empire, where he set up camp at Bender, in neighbouring Bessarabia, in what is now Moldova, in the company of 4,000 Swedish soldiers. Rehnskiöld and Lewenhaupt, on the other hand, were both taken into Russian captivity.

Meanwhile, in Poland and other parts of the southern Baltic littoral, Karl's absence left a vacuum, quickly filled by his enemies.

Augustus regained his Polish throne and Denmark attacked Scania, in 1710, in an attempt to regain its former province, as well as Sweden's overseas territories in Pomerania. The former was effectively resisted by Karl's skilful commander Magnus Stenbock (1664–1717), at the Battle of Helsingborg, in February of that year, but the Russians captured Riga and Tallinn. Although, two years later, Stenbock was victorious in his campaign against the Danes in north Germany, thereby preserving the country's possessions in the region, he was taken prisoner by them the following May, at the Battle of Tönningen, and remained in their custody until his death in 1717. Sweden had therefore lost one of its most able military leaders.

Russia also took advantage of the Swedish king's absence by attacking Finland and rapidly occupied this province after the Battle of Storkyro, forcing the Finnish General Armfelt to flee to Sweden. In reaction, Karl, from his camp at Bender, increasingly involved himself in the high politics of the Sultan's Porte, encouraging the Ottomans to attack Russia by all means at his disposal. This they did on a number of occasions, but the overall effect was of small benefit for the Swedish war effort and Karl's attempts to raise further troops in Sweden in order to regain Finland proved of limited success. In any case, his machinations in Ottoman politics brought him many enemies with different political and military agendas. As a result, the so-called *Kalabaliken* hostilities erupted against him in 1713, an uproar in which he only narrowly survived by escaping to nearby Demotika.

Waiting for an appropriate and safe opportunity to effect his return to Sweden, the king finally departed from the Ottoman Empire, arriving overland in the Swedish Pomeranian city of Stralsund in November 1714. Yet a year passed before, in December 1715, he finally set foot in Swedish Scania. Immediately, he set to work with various other military adventures and the following year, in desperate need of money for reviving his military activities, Karl XII enlisted the support of the German diplomat and administrator Georg Heinrich von Görtz (1668–1719). Görtz was given leave to attempt the reorganisation of Sweden's finances to this end, through the implementation of compulsory loans and a debasement of the currency, both of which led to considerable discontent at home. As for the king, though, he never to returned to Stockholm. Instead, the following year, he undertook a campaign against Danish-ruled Norway, with some 22,000 men. It was to be his final misadventure. His attempt to capture the fortress of Akershus by Christiania (now Oslo) failed, and he himself was shot – whether accidentally or deliberately is still not clear – by one of his own troops, at Fredrikshald, during the Battle for Fredkriksten's Fortress, on 30 November 1718. He died immediately thereafter. With his death, any hopes that Sweden would regain its superpower status in Europe, so arduously won in the Thirty Years War but without the economic basis to support it in any long-term way, were gone forever, even if vain hopes to re-establish it would survive for almost a century.

HEALTH AND HYGIENE

If the end of the seventeenth century and beginning of the eighteenth were disastrous for Sweden in military terms, they were no less so in terms of health and hygiene. The final decade of the seventeenth century was a demographic catastrophe, as severe climatic conditions led to mass famine and devastating epidemics during this period. Especially debilitating was the severe outbreak of famine in 1695, the result of crop failure throughout the Swedish heartlands. That in Finland towards the end of the 1690s was also destructive, carrying off about a third of the entire population of the province. Climate change had played a major role. Indeed, modern research has shown that the growth of Arctic pack ice that year, with concomitant colder sea waters in summer, had helped to drive North Atlantic depressions further south. These circumstances had led to summer frosts and major crop failure. Yet it was not so much starvation, as diseases such as typhus to which many undernourished people were vulnerable, which caused the greatest mortality. Young and old died equally, as people scavenging in the countryside for food brought disease from one village to the next.

Even worse was to follow, for during the period 1710–12, plague devastated Sweden. Stockholm and Helsinki were particularly affected; a third of their populations succumbed. Fortunately thereafter the threat of plague did recede, for reasons not fully understood, though possibly aided by the improved implementation of strict quarantine regulations. In any case, Swedish territory was never again visited by an epidemic of the disease.

Smallpox, however, remained a serious scourge. Queen Kristina herself had been badly scarred by the disease, which attacked rich and poor in equal measure. Another age-old disease, on the other hand, visited the country in the seventeenth century with less severity than had previously been the case: leprosy. It was dramatically on the decline at this time, in the south and the centre of the country, if not yet in Hälsingland and in Finland. Care for its victims was also improving and suitable accommodation now came to be provided for sufferers, according to the standards of the time. The leper hospital at Enköping, in the centre of the country, was the largest of its kind in Sweden, with some twenty inmates treated on a regular basis. As the numbers affected by the disease declined further, this and many other leprosaria were given over to the containment, if not treatment, of the mentally ill.

It was also during this period that the first hospital associated with industrial ailments opened its doors: in 1695, an infirmary was set up by the mouth of the Falun mines, in Dalecarlia, to deal with those injured in the copper mines there, with accommodation for sixteen miners.

ORPHANAGES

During the early seventeenth century, the government strengthened its social infrastructure, compensating for those foundations previously supported by the Church which had been wiped away by the Reformation. Social welfare, like so much else in Sweden at the time, now came into the increasing remit of the state. In 1638, an orphanage for children was established in Norrmalm, in Stockholm, insalubriously sited next to the House of Correction for adults. It accommodated some 150 children. Sharp distinctions were made there between the legitimate and illegitimate inmates. Whereas the former were groomed for a variety of skilled trades, the latter were trained for domestic service or similarly menial work. Baths, as well as religious education by a local parish priest, were provided twice a month.

With respect to the poor, the quality of welfare provided was closely related to both the social background and respectability of those bereft of the financial means to look after themselves. For example, impoverished aristocratic ladies and their gentrified cousins were catered for by special foundations, financed by wealthy private benefactors. One such was the Queen's House, overlooking the churchyard of the St Johannes Church in Stockholm, which was built in 1689 by Mathias Spihler, to accommodate the widows and daughters of officers, priests and the gentry. Similarly, impoverished elderly gentlemen in Stockholm were housed in their own independent establishment, the Home for Old Gentlemen.

CRIMINALITY

During the seventeenth century, magisterial authority was exercised not only by aristocratic landowners, but, after a new law in 1671, by yeoman farmers, in their extended households. This served to bring the arm of Swedish law to a grass-roots level, making it thereby more effective. Punishments for servants and labourers included fines, beatings and imprisonment on bread and water for up to a month. Four years later, however, because of the discontent of all but the noble estate, this law was repealed. Nonetheless, this regimen continued in practice well into the following century. Transportation to the colonies was also a penalty, to Delaware specifically during the few years Sweden had sovereignty over the colony. The opposite also occurred, for in one instance, a Swedish gunner, Sven Vass, who stood accused of arson against the settlement of New Gothenburg there, was repatriated to Sweden itself for judgment, after a makeshift local trial.

Most crimes in Sweden, then as now, were committed by men, especially assault, often perpetrated under the influence of alcohol. Alcohol-fuelled crimes of violence were especially frequent among loggers and in the sawmill industry. Gang fights among youths were also common, in particular in the coastal fishing villages of Halland where, it was said, the young members were goaded on by their elders. Street fighting was also not unusual, especially in the largest cities, Stockholm and Gothenburg. In Lapland, it tended to occur in conjunction with fairs and markets. By contrast, crimes against property such as burglary and theft were infrequent in Sweden (as they remained until the middle of the twentieth century), the punishment, for the convicted, being long years of penal servitude. Smuggling in spirits and highly taxed commodities was, on the other hand, frequent, even though the penalty was higher – death by hanging; yet many took the risk, for the rewards could be high. Most serious crimes incurred the death penalty, so that the scaffold remained a familiar site throughout Sweden well into the nineteenth century. Lesser criminals could expect incarceration.

There were many small gaols but Karlsten Fortress, by Marstrand, on Sweden's west coast, long remained one of Sweden's most notorious prisons. Up to twenty men were locked up in individual stone-vaulted chambers, constructed with walls some four metres thick, and during the daylight hours set to work on a variety of menial tasks.

Vagabonds and petty thieves received lighter penalties. In Stockholm, they were sent for short periods of time to the House of Correction, where they were set to work in the penal smithy. Nearby was the so-called state Rose Chamber, in use until 1850, in which serious political offenders were imprisoned and sometimes tortured. One such prisoner was the Finnish priest Lars Ulstadius who was incarcerated within its walls for more than forty years, because of his radical Pietistic beliefs which spilled over into the political sphere.

As for the crime of sodomy, that is, homosexual activity and bestiality, it was strictly condemned by the appendix added to the State Law Codex of 1608 and the penalties were severe. Nonetheless, arrests were rarely made and prosecutions were even fewer.

WITCHCRAFT

The existence of witchcraft, as elsewhere in Europe, had long been accepted by many Swedish people not only as a genuine threat to public wellbeing but as undermining the state itself. Indeed, Olaus Magnus had published an image of a woman being carried off by the devil in his *History of the Nordic People* in 1555, as an illustrative admonishment. However, it was between 1668 and 1675 that a major series of judicial proceedings against witches took place in Sweden which became notorious. These were predominantly based on accusations of pacts made with the devil. Although Lapland, with its many shamans hostile to Christianity, was perceived by many

Swedes as a hotbed of witchcraft – one shaman was burnt at the stake for attacking a Lutheran priest who had confiscated his drums – the majority of trials were carried out in the heartland of Sweden, in Dalecarlia and even in Stockholm. The most infamous of these, the so-called Blåkulla trials, focused upon a small island situated off Sweden's south-eastern coast, during the years 1668–75, and involved some 856 people, many of whom were children. In the end, more than three hundred people, mostly women, but some men, were executed during this period, the majority condemned by the denunciations of children, who had accused them of bringing them 'into the devil's service'. Finland, too, suffered from such trials. In Ostrobothnia, 152 people were prosecuted, of whom 28 were put to death. By the closing years of the seventeenth century, however, a backlash ensued, in part motivated by a growing awareness of the role private vendettas and self-interest played in the accusations, in part through the efforts of such men of science as the Swedish physician and mineralogist Urban Hiärne (1641–1724). In part, too, it was motivated by profound shifts in religious concep- tions of vice and virtue, fostered by a new religious focus within Lutheranism, which in the seventeenth century continued to place strong emphasis upon the strictures of the Old Testament, with its imagery of a highly exacting God, models suitable, also, in the political sphere for a state like Sweden, extremely centralised, bureaucratic and in an aggressive state of military expansion throughout the period.

LAPLAND

While Sweden was attempting to expand southwards and eastwards by military means, a more peaceful expansion was also taking place northwards into Lapland, undertaken in large measure by church- men rather than the military. Already at the beginning of the seven- teenth century, in the wake of the Reformation in Sweden, Karl IX had taken an initiative to spread Lutheranism in Lapland, within which the state borders of Sweden, Danish-ruled Norway and Russia continued to shift back and forth until the eighteenth century. To this end he commissioned Daniel Hjort, in 1605, to find suitable loca- tions for the construction of new churches. In consequence, new churches were erected in Arvidsjaur, Jokkomokk, Jukkasjärvi and

Enontekiö. Their purpose was not only religious; they were seen as useful tools for furthering the integration of Lapland and the Saami people into wider Swedish society and body politic, while extending the country's northern boundaries. The Treaty of Knäred, nonetheless, obliged the king to relinquish all claims to Norwegian Lapland, and to content himself with what remained.

Yet if Lapland had ceased to attract military attention by the turn of the eighteenth century, it did draw literary and scientific notice. By then, its notoriety for shamanism had become a draw, its very exoticism beginning to exert its own wild and romantic allure, so that the great old man of Swedish literature, Olof Rudbeck, even published a lyrical ode to the region in his *Lapponia illustrata*, in 1701. When, then, an eccentric Swedish confidence man, Nicolaus Örn, appeared at Versailles in 1706, laying claim to be the Prince of Lapland, a fascination with the subject became an international rage, but one which soon took the form of serious intellectual initiatives: scientific expeditions to the region later in the century would capture the learned world's attention, altering the study of biology and botany, especially after the botanist Carl von Linné appeared upon the scene.

As for the Saami people themselves, some had now come to amass considerable wealth through a form of inheritance known as ultimogeniture, according to which the youngest son inherited all. This was at odds with the primogeniture which held sway in the rest of Sweden at that time. One prosperous Saami man proved so successful that he was appointed governor of the province of Västerbothnia in the late seventeenth century. Far more numerous, though, were those others who suffered economic hardship, not least from the growing competition for land and other resources which had been occasioned by the rise in immigration from the rest of Sweden. Many of these new arrivals had sought to benefit from the tax relief offered to new settlers, as a means of encouraging agricultural development. As a result, large farms began to spread out from the river basins of the far north, such as that of the River Torne. Quite isolated one from another, they tended to be composed of rectangular log cabins, with a minimum of decoration, organised around a central courtyard, and pierced by few windows. As such, they were particularly suited for the severe climatic conditions of the region, which continued to limit large-scale immigration until well into the nineteenth century. Yet such northern settlements, however modest, were just part and parcel of a wider multifaceted movement which sought to consolidate and expand Swedish political, economic and social hegemony in all directions during the long seventeenth century which ended with Karl XII. By the time of his death, though, the illusion of Sweden as a major self-sustaining European power had become all too obvious.

5

The collapse of absolutism and the Age of Freedom

Karl XII's sudden death in battle against Norway was disastrous for Sweden. In its immediate aftermath, the country's military campaign collapsed and Sweden's vulnerability, militarily, economically and politically, was laid bare. Bohuslän, in the west, was set upon by the Norwegians under Peder Tordenskjold, while funds earmarked for the campaign disappeared in the confusion. Russia's sudden attack upon Sweden's largely undefended east coast in 1719 added further devastation. Södertälje was burnt to the ground and other cities, as far north as Umeå, suffered badly. In Finland, many men were carted off to Russia as prisoners of war, conscripted into Russian military service or set to work as serfs. Many of those who escaped capture fled to Sweden, where they settled new homesteads, never to return to their native land. Stockholm, it is true, under Rutger Fuchs (1682–1753) successfully resisted the Russian invasion, but the country was in no position to resist for long. In consequence, Sweden was obliged to accept very severe impositions, not least the loss of much of the German territory it had acquired in the course of the Thirty Years War, in particular Bremen and Verden to Hanover, though some financial compensation for them was provided. Wollin and Usedom, among other pieces of land in Hinter Pomerania, were ceded to Prussia. Only that part of the province to the west of the River Peene remained in Swedish hands.

There were financial disabilities as well, for the recently won freedom from Danish customs duties for ships passing through the Sound was also now abolished. Most severe, though, were the demands made upon Sweden by Russia, by the 1721 Treaty of Nystad, which confirmed not only the permanent secession to Russia of Ingria, in any case already in Russian hands for a generation, but that of Estonia, Livonia, Karelia and Kexholm.

THE NEW POLITICAL ORDER

In this new order, the status of the monarchy itself also suffered. When therefore Ulrika Eleonora (1688–1741) in 1719 accepted the regency of Sweden after the death of her brother Karl XII, she was also obliged to accept the end of royal absolutism in order to secure the throne. For that reason the period which followed, until 1772, has traditionally been known in Sweden as the 'Age of Freedom'. Only after a lapse of more than fifty years would royal absolutism once again be introduced, by her grandson Gustaf III (1746–92).

One year after her accession to the throne, Ulrika Eleonora abdicated on behalf of her husband, Count Fredrik of Hesse (1676–1751), who reigned for more than three decades as Fredrik I. In this new settlement, it was the *Riksdag*, in particular the higher of the four estates – nobility, Church and burghers – which benefited most, becoming more parliamentary in its functioning, even if the estate of the peasants was often excluded from the most important decision making. This was generally the case, since most important decisions were made by the so-called Secret Committee, composed of fifty noblemen and a further twenty-five priests and burghers, respectively. According to the *Riksdag*'s promulgation of 1723, the powers of law making and taxation were, henceforth, to be invested in it, rather than in the monarch, and its convocation was to take place every three years. Sweden's new legal code of 1734 was also of considerable significance in that it streamlined legal proceedings, relative to the old one.

THE HATS VERSUS THE CAPS

In this new era, State Councillor Arvid Horn (1664–1742) came to play a major role, especially in his office as President of the

Chancellery, one of the most important positions in the state bureaucracy. A moderate mercantilist, he was keen to encourage domestic industry, in particular the production of textiles. He also strove to keep Sweden out of military entanglements. For some, however, his measures were too half-hearted. These more ardent mercantilists, often young military officers, bureaucrats and merchants, nicknamed the Hats, became increasingly well organised in their opposition to Horn and his rather more elderly, aristocratic supporters, who had now come to be known as the Caps. When the former succeeded in dominating the *Riksdag* of 1738–9, Horn was obliged to retire from his offices. Carl Gyllenborg (1679–1746), a leading Cap, now came to the fore, succeeding as President of the Chancellery. Henceforth, until Gustaf III's *coup d'état* in 1772, Sweden enjoyed what was for most practical intents and purposes a parliamentary system of government. While Horn had been a dove with respect to military adventures, Gyllenborg was an unequivocal hawk, determined at all costs to regain those territories lost to Russia, when circumstances seemed favourable. After the military debacle of the renewed war with Russia following which, in 1743, South Karelia was lost, Gyllenborg retired from politics, taking up instead a position not altogether less stressful, involving university administration.

THE HOUSE OF ESTATES

In the political system of government which had evolved, all Swedish subjects were politically represented by one of the four estates. That of the nobility, decimated by the previous wars in which Sweden had been engaged, comprised by now only 5 per cent of the population. The priestly estate formed 9 per cent, and the burghers and the peasantry the overwhelming majority. The first estate, relative to those in many other European countries of the period, was quite porous. The nobility was by no means a closed caste and some of the most prominent burghers who rose through the military and state bureaucracy eventually joined its ranks.

The greatest political power was invested in the crown and nobility, but that of the Church was also of significance, influential in both rural and urban areas, in secular as well as ecclesiastical affairs. Its leader in the House of Estates was invariably the Archbishop of Uppsala, the Swedish primate, whose authority remained limited in scope, subject to the authority of the state.

DOMINATION OF THE HATS

In June 1741, war, popularly supported, once again erupted with Russia. Subsidies from France had been expected, but these did not prove forthcoming. Poorly funded and with inadequate planning, Swedish forces under General Charles Emil Lewenhaupt (1691–1743), with the assistance of Lieutenant General Henrik Magnus von Buddenbrock (1685–1743), were rapidly defeated. Villmanstrand fell to the Russians in August, despite the arrival of fresh Swedish troops. A brief truce provided a respite, after the accession of the Empress Elisabeth to the Russian throne, but hostilities again erupted the following spring when Russia, once again, attempted to seize Finland. Its military might rapidly debilitated, Sweden's forces surrendered in August 1742, but at a terrible cost: Finland was now altogether ceded to Russia. Lewenhaupt and Buddenbrock were made the scapegoats and, after a summary trial, executed. However, the lasting consequences proved less harsh than anticipated and, after the negotiations which followed, most of Finland was given back to Sweden. In return, the childless Swedish king, Fredrik I, agreed to accept, as his heir to the throne, Adolph Fredrik (1710–71), a relation of Elisabeth from the House of Holstein-Gottorp which was friendly to Russia, and his wife Lovisa Ulrika (1720–82), a sister of the Prussian king Frederick the Great. Not content with this choice – they preferred a Danish contender and his consort – some 4,500 otherwise disgruntled farmers and soldiers from Dalecarlia used this as an excuse to organise themselves in a strident protest, arriving in Stockholm in June 1743 for that purpose. Known as the *Stora daldansen* or Great Dalecarlian Dance, it was rigorously crushed by the military and its leaders executed or imprisoned. This aroused the ire of Denmark, and, fearing an attack from the west, Sweden was constrained to invite its erstwhile enemy Russia to send troops to protect the Swedish coast. Hostilities were avoided, but Russian influence in the region increased enormously in consequence. Russia could, thus, afford to be magnanimous and so, when the official peace treaty was signed in August 1743, only

South Karelia was lost by Sweden to Russia. Russian forces in Sweden then departed the following summer.

Sweden immediately turned its attention to the fortification of its regained Finnish territories. To protect Helsinki, still a small fishing village, against future Russian assaults, the construction of the fortress of Sveaborg (formerly Viapori, in Finnish, but Suomenlinna today) was commenced, in 1747, under Augustin Ehrensvärd (1710–72), who became its first commandant. One of its most prominent features was Galär Dock, built in the 1760s, which cost some sixty-seven tonnes of gold. It was a vast project for its time, with no fewer than 6,750 labourers contributing to the fortress's construction. The Swedish government was spared its cost, since French subsidies, recently renewed, paid for it. Seeming to herald a new age of military security for the south of Finland, it was fittingly commemorated in a famous painting of 1765 by the noted Swedish artist Elias Martin (1739–1818). Yet the west coast areas of Finland also needed to be secured, their trade encouraged, and so a number of ports and harbours on the Gulf of Bothnia were also developed at this time.

By now Carl Gustaf Tessin (1695–1770), whose grandfather and father had both been court architects, was coming to the fore, albeit in politics rather than in architecture, as an important Hat leader. However, the strength of the political constellation in which he was central was weakened by the growing interference of Russia in Swedish internal politics, which tainted both the reputation and popularity of his party. It was his opponent, Anders Johan von Höpkin (1712–89), who formulated this resentment. At the meeting of the *Riksdag* in 1746–7, he issued a 'National Explanation', criticising Tessin, while censuring Russia for its intrusions into the Swedish political arena. Yet the Hats continued to dominate the political debate and ties with both Russia and Prussia continued to strengthen.

Adolph Fredrik and Lovisa Ulrika shared, however, in the growing wave of political discontent and, feeling their control over the state diminishing, formed their own political coterie, in which the demands forced upon the king by the Hats to relinquish any claims to Holstein-Gottorp, in 1749, were actively resisted. This led, in 1756, to an attempted coup, which, royal support notwithstanding, proved to be a dismal failure: its non-royal leaders were executed and the royal couple themselves were consequently thoroughly isolated. The Hats remained in power and were able to use the excuse of the failed coup as a stick with which to beat their enemies into submission.

THE POMERANIAN WAR AND ITS AFTERMATH

France, too, was now beginning to obtrude more prominently upon the Baltic scene. In 1757, the Pomeranian War broke out against Prussia, in part the result of Sweden's alliance with France, now engaged in the Seven Years War, which had begun the previous year. Sweden's persistent desire to regain its lost German territories dovetailed nicely with the French agenda. However, subsidies from France were not forthcoming on this occasion and Sweden's military might was no match for the troops of Frederick the Great. Therefore, the *status quo ante* in Germany remained in place when, in 1762, the war was concluded by a treaty in Hamburg. The domestic political scenario, though, had by now changed significantly, for with the economy debilitated and spiralling inflation, the Hats were clearly on the defensive. In consequence, the Caps once again gained the upper hand in the *Riksdag* of 1765–6.

They now began to distance Sweden from France, forging closer links not only with Russia but with Britain, as well. The country's finances were reorganised along anti-mercantilist principles, as advocated by such economy-minded notables as Anders Bachmanson Nordencrantz (1697–1772) and Anders Chydenius (1729–1803). Bureaucratic expenditure was reduced, with the loss of many jobs, restrictions were imposed on the import, production and consumption of luxuries, especially coffee, chocolate, wine and costly fabrics. The navy was strengthened and, in 1763, Sweden's first dry dock was built at Karlskrona. New bank loans were, in large measure, prohibited, debts called in. Deflation of the economy resulted. A greater openness was encouraged in politics, as a result of which assemblies of all four estates increasingly supplanted the political activities of the Secret Commission, which had previously excluded, as we have seen, representatives of the peasants. When, in 1766, political censorship was abolished, Sweden could boast of being, along with Britain, one of Europe's most liberal, unautocratic, countries, but at a heavy price, that of political chaos.

ADOLPH FREDRIK THREATENS
ABDICATION – RETURN OF THE HATS

The Swedish economy was also in a poor and stagnant state, with general discontent reigning among large segments of the population. When the king insisted, under threat of abdication, upon a revocation of the *Riksdag*, supported by the Hats, fearful of judicial proceedings by the Caps against them and by whom he expected to have his prerogatives strengthened, the Hats were returned to power. However, they were unable to provide the king with a return of those royal prerogatives he had been promised. Nor were they able to accommodate those seeking greater rights for the rising professional and bureaucratic classes who resented the privileges of the nobility which they could not attain. In consequence, counter-revolution followed.

The death of Adolph Fredrik in February 1771 helped to create the circumstances in which his son, Gustaf III, on the return leg of his Grand Tour at the time, could foment a *coup d'état*. Arriving in Stockholm the following May, having stopped in Prussia to visit his uncle Frederick the Great for political discussions, he was aware that the Caps, supported by subsidies from Russia, had regained the ascendancy in the *Riksdag* convoked after the death of his father. General discontent, aggravated by crop failure, had, nonetheless, prevented the Caps from consolidating their position. Gustaf took advantage of this chaotic state of affairs, with his own support from France. On 19 August 1772, the king and his supporters carried out a bloodless coup, re-establishing royal absolutism, after a lapse of more than half a century.

ECONOMIC LIFE

The Great Nordic War in the beginning of the century had proved disastrous for Sweden economically and so, after its conclusion, many of the innovations that had been introduced by von Görtz under Karl XII were rapidly put aside. Von Görtz himself was tried and executed, the currency devalued.

Population displacements, which proved to be permanent, also affected the economy. Many Finns who had fled to Sweden eventually acquired their own homesteads there and never returned to their native land. Their abandoned holdings, therefore, often came to be taken over by others who had remained or by those who had returned from Russian captivity. This served particularly to benefit those of the Finnish nobility and yeomanry who remained in the province, along with the crown itself, which also received a substantial share of the abandoned land.

Mining continued to be the country's principal industrial undertaking, for iron was, by now, an extremely important export commodity, amounting to some 75 per cent of total exports during much of the early eighteenth century. The establishment of the *Jernkontor* (Iron Office), in 1747, was also important in that it helped to regulate the price of Swedish iron efficiently. Thus, iron had come to supersede copper as Sweden's most lucrative commodity. Indeed, it contributed more than 85 per cent of all its exports by the middle of the eighteenth century, half of this quantity going to England alone. Afterwards, the development of a native British iron industry made Swedish iron redundant there. However, Russia and the Mediterranean countries rapidly bought up the Swedish iron. In Bordeaux, in France, viniculturalists were especially eager to import the metal from their country's ally for use as bands to hold together their casks of wine. New economic undertakings, international in scope, were also initiated. Taking its cue from other northern European countries, Sweden developed new lines of international trade, among the most novel and lucrative of which was the trade to China.

THE SWEDISH EAST INDIA COMPANY

In 1731, the Swedish East India Company was established, linking Gothenburg, by way of India, to Canton, in China, the following year. Its headquarters were impressive, designed by Carl Hårleman (1700–53), who also carried out work on the new Royal Palace in Stockholm.

The expeditions of the company were financed by public subscription and, though the risks were high, so were the profits. These were based on the import to Europe not only of tea and porcelain from China, but of spices, including ginger, cinnamon and arak. This last was especially popular in Sweden where it was used in the production of punch, a beverage still popular in academic circles in Uppsala today. Other imported commodities included fabrics, lacquer goods and ivory. On the other hand, endeavours to balance these with suitable exports to China, which would have been beneficial for the Swedish economy as a whole, proved largely unsuccessful. Therefore, the flow of money to the east proved, in many respects, a debilitating drain on the economy as a whole, the rewards which accrued to specific individuals and shareholders notwithstanding. As for the India trade which the company's name implied, this was but a minor adjunct: only eight of its ships ever sailed there as a point of final destination. Moreover, the brief Swedish initiative to establish a colony at Porto Novo, on India's south-eastern coast, foundered before it could be fully realised, scuppered by concerted British and French hostility to any possible competition.

SOCIAL DEMOGRAPHY

In 1720, Sweden remained a sparsely populated country, even if, excluding Scania and other areas conquered the previous century from Denmark, its population had risen to 1.12 million. That said, its population was increasing, following similar demographic trends to those in the rest of Europe, despite the vagaries of wars and epidemics. Indeed, by 1750, the population had burgeoned to some 1.8 million. The cities were also increasing in size, especially Stockholm, the population of which had risen to 85,000 by that time. This increase was predominately through immigration from rural areas, since mortality rates in the unhygienic capital were so high that the city was unable to reproduce itself. Sweden's other major cities were far smaller in size. Gothenburg and Karlskrona, the latter Sweden's principal naval seat, had a population of approximately 10,000 each. Finland's largest city, Turku, was slightly smaller, with 9,000 residents, but its population, too, was growing dramatically after the demographic devastation caused by famine and disease in the late seventeenth and early eighteenth centuries: from 1754 to 1769, its population grew by more than a third. Swedish Pomerania, too, contributed significantly to the population under Swedish sovereignty, for its territory was more densely populated than anywhere else in the Swedish realms. Highly urbanised, despite its small geographic size compared with the rest of Sweden, Swedish Pomerania's population was in excess of 100,000 in the second quarter of the eighteenth century.

Despite the demographic increase, health and hygiene in early and mid eighteenth-century Sweden remained poor. Medical services were few and far between, especially in the countryside. In the northern half of the country they hardly existed: as Linné put it at the time, the apothecary shop and resident doctor of Gävle, in Gästrikland, not far north of Stockholm, were the last to be found south of the North Pole.

Life expectancy in Stockholm and other cities, where living conditions were in general cramped and unhygienic, was low, but in the countryside it was considerably higher. In the capital, a quarter of all babies died before they reached their first birthday. In rural areas, on the other hand, six out of seven survived their first year. Mortality rates then fell the older the child grew. In cities, 60 per cent reached the age of twenty-five, in the countryside, 70 per cent, throughout most of the eighteenth century. Among illegitimate children, whether urban or rural, the rates were less favourable: almost a third did not see their first birthday. This high mortality rate was not always unwelcome to the parents, for, as an Uppsala general practitioner put it at the time, 'The grinding poverty which afflicts the greater part of crofters and agricultural labourers, makes parents more grateful for the demise of a child than their arrival into the world.' With poor conditions of hygiene holding sway and little understanding of the way infections are transmitted, many infants fell prey to epidemic diseases. Whooping cough alone was especially lethal, carrying off more than 40,000 children in Sweden between 1749 and 1764. The situation was also further undermined by poor diet. That said, the introduction of potatoes as a staple crop in the middle of the eighteenth century proved a boon to farmers, providing the poor, as it did, with a substantial part of their diet with relatively little effort compared with that demanded by the cultivation of other crops. They could be grown in poor soil and were, moreover, more likely to survive bad summers than was grain.

Smallpox

Among acute diseases, none was more devastating in Sweden during the early and mid eighteenth century than smallpox. A severely disfiguring scourge, it afflicted the country in periodic waves of epidemics. It was especially devastating in Lapland, since, unlike in many other parts of Sweden, it visited the population rarely and therefore few had developed a resistance to the disease, which made its way upriver from coastal towns and settlements, reaping a harrowing harvest. Its destructive inroads in Lapland evoked particular horror among the population. By contrast with the fatalistic stance with which it was met in the rest of the country, as Linné noted on his visit there in the 1730s, the Saami fled to the hills, abandoning both relations and possessions in the panic to avoid the contagion. The epidemic of 1740 in the north was particularly severe, afflicting the old more than the young, the inverse of its usual effects elsewhere in Sweden and Europe as a whole.

Fortunately, inroads against its devastation were made in 1756, when inoculation against the disease was introduced, offering at least a modicum of protection. Gustaf III and his siblings were inoculated in 1769 by the Prussian David Schultz von Schultzenheim (1732–1823), ennobled because of his services in this regard to the crown, as well as to many members of the court and the prosperous middle classes. Nonetheless, over the following decades, smallpox continued to account for a quarter of the total mortality rate for Sweden. Its effects were especially lethal for children in the south and centre of the country, whose deaths from it during epidemics accounted for three quarters of the mortality rates altogether. As for the more isolated north of the country, inoculation remained virtually unknown.

Even where the benefits of inoculation were known, its risks not infrequently made those in positions of authority hesitate to implement it. Sometimes inoculation itself led to epidemics among those not inoculated and, not infrequently, victims also died from the effects of the inoculation itself or from other infections, like syphilis, spread through its unhygienic practice. Serious epidemics of smallpox broke out in Sweden at regular intervals, in 1754, 1763 and 1771. For those who survived the disease there were often social consequences, as well as physical ones: victims who recovered tended to marry one another, since the characteristic scarring which usually followed in its wake left them less desirable on the marriage market than would otherwise have been the case.

Hospital care

Leprosy had dramatically diminished in Sweden by this period, but in the early years of the eighteenth century its presence in Finland was more persistent. There a leprosarium had been constructed at Seili, in the archipelago of Turku, but, like those elsewhere in Sweden, it was eventually given over to the care of the mentally ill. That said, specific new hospitals to contain the mentally ill now also came to be established. One such example was Danvik's Mental Asylum, near Stockholm, constructed between 1719 and 1725 by the architect Göran Josua Adelcrantz (1668–1739), and one of the largest institutional buildings in Sweden at that time. It was built with large, wide windows to facilitate ventilation and let in light, in accordance with the latest principles of treatment of that period. In Finland, Kronoby Hospital, situated between Pietarsaari (Jakobstad) and Kokkola (Gamla Karleby), had its leprosarium, established in the 1670s, given over in 1743 for the containment of the mentally ill. Less influenced by 'Enlightenment values', its most severely afflicted patients were locked in cells, or cages, as they were known, only 1.8 metres by 2.4 metres in size and made of wooden gratings. Not infrequently, inmates were chained. Elsewhere, in Kronoby Hospital, there was additional accommodation for the chronically ill, blind and lame. Orphans were also accommodated, in scattered cottages on its surrounding land which they cultivated to provide food for themselves and the other inmates. It thus formed a relatively self-sufficient community for those living within it and limited the community and the state's financial burden.

Veteran hospitals were also erected during this period, especially at the end of the Thirty Years War, which left so many human disabilities in its wake. That built at Vadstena, within the premises of the old monastery which had been dissolved in 1595, became the most important for the accommodation of invalids at this time. It continued to function until 1783, undergoing a series of renovations, as growing numbers of inmates and new regimens of treatment demanded. It housed not only the invalids themselves, but also their families and dependants.

Another important hospital built during this period was the Seraphim Infirmary in Stockholm, which opened its doors in 1752. It provided accommodation for thirty-six of the urban poor, unable otherwise to look after themselves. Considerable attention was paid to hygiene, unusual at the time, and its floors were strewn with spruce or juniper branches to hinder the spread of infection. Funding originally came from lotteries, the tobacco tax and charitable donations, but, after 1783, the government funded it directly.

ORPHANAGES AND POOR HOUSES

By the middle of the eighteenth century, the social infrastructure, to a large degree established in the early seventeenth century to deal with orphans and the poor, was under strain. By 1756, the orphanage at Norrmalm, in Stockholm, had doubled its population of inmates to more than three hundred. To alleviate this overcrowding and to provide, as the French philosopher Jean Jacques Rousseau had exhorted, more salubrious rural environs in which the children could grow up, a reform was introduced through which the orphans – excluding infants and the sick – were farmed out to foster parents in the countryside round about the capital. It also reduced the costs of their upkeep.

For the poor of humble background in the capital, a new foundation was established in 1752, the Sabbatsberg Poor House. It accommodated some three hundred inmates and continued to be the principal urban refuge for the poor until the 1870s. Elsewhere in Sweden, it had already become the rule, in 1734, for each parish to provide a refuge for the local poor or homeless. As a result, by the middle of the century, there were no fewer than 1,400 poor houses scattered throughout the country. They continued to function until well into the twentieth century, sometimes funded by the parish, sometimes by a prosperous landowner. Their inmates were overwhelmingly women, since impoverished men were expected to become *cottars*, in exchange for occasional labour. Thus, a well-to-do landowner would typically have about two dozen suitable homesteads on his land, which could accommodate a similar number of such men, sometimes with their family members as well.

ARCHITECTURAL DEVELOPMENTS

A number of grand architectural projects initiated in the days of Karl XII still remained to be completed, and a number proceeded slowly, hampered by Sweden's difficult financial straits, the vagaries of war and the country's reduced political status. The most important of these was the completion of the new Royal Palace in Stockholm. Work had proceeded very slowly, especially after 1709, but under Karl XII's successor, Fredrik I, the pace of its construction was quickened. This was made possible in 1727 by a special tax levied by the *Riksdag* for its completion. Unfortunately, the following year, the architect, Nicodemus Tessin the Younger, himself died, so the project was entrusted to his son Carl Gustaf Tessin, now a courtier and later tutor to King Gustaf III. Much of the supervision and design of the actual work came to be relegated to the famous Swedish

6 Eighteenth-century view of the Royal Palace in Stockholm, by Jean Eric Rehn. The construction of a new Royal Palace in Stockholm was commenced by the architect Nicodemus Tessin the Younger (1654–1728) who had studied in Paris for several years before succeeding his father as court architect. Though only completed much later in the eighteenth century, its size and grandeur in the heart of Stockholm belied the impoverishment of the Swedish crown and general state of the economy at the time. Photo: The Nationalmuseum, Stockholm.

architect Hårleman. A keen Francophile, he decorated the interiors in an elaborate Rococo style, popular in Paris at the time, with French workmen imported for that purpose in 1732. Nine years later Hårleman was put in charge of the whole project and soon became the country's most sought-after architect, designing another royal palace at Svarstjö, in 1735, as well as grand houses for wealthier members of the aristocracy. In consequence, the rural areas of south and central Sweden were gradually adorned by splendid residences which could vie with those rising up in England and France at the same time.

During the reign of Adolph Fredrik and Lovisa Ulrika, the arts of the Rococo flourished at the Swedish court, in both art and architecture, bearers, as they were, of the symbolism of political power. Yet in one respect, the most lasting influence on the arts in Europe was not that of the court but of the Swedish East India Company. For this enabled William Chambers (1726–96), a young architect of Scottish parentage but a native of Gothenburg, to journey to China, where he became deeply influenced by its architecture and garden design. Knighted by the Swedish king and later, after his settlement in England, architectural tutor to the future King George III there, he proceeded to propagate his ideas throughout the western world by means of his great illustrated work, *Designs of Chinese Buildings*, published in 1757. The pagoda which he designed for the English Princess Augusta, second daughter of George III, at Kew Gardens, near London, became the consummate realisation of these imported values. In Sweden itself, they also found expression, albeit through his influence on other Swedish architects, especially at the Royal Park of Drottningholm, Haga and country houses, in particular Forsmark, north of Stockholm. Aside from the elements of Chinese exoticism that he introduced, there was a new and informal intimacy which came to be incorporated in his designs and those of his followers, which maintained elegance while yet appealing to the Rococo playfulness of the age.

Not all, however, were happy with the introduction of such foreign influences. The great botanist Linné, though keen to augment his collection, as well as Swedish agriculture itself, with specimens and crops from abroad, considered the interest in things foreign, as well as the superficiality of the modern fashions, debilitating to

Swedish society, industry and culture. The pietistic flank of the Church of Sweden also had its objections, seeing the Chinese trade in both aesthetic and economic terms as one serving to introduce wasteful luxury, thereby exerting a corrupting influence on Swedish morality and spiritual values. These moral issues preoccupied many of the intellectual circles of Sweden at this time, not least in government, for pietistic values, provided they remained embedded within the established Church, also served a useful purpose: cementing the joint interests of Church and state. Indeed, after 1766, royal proclamations were regularly read out from the pulpit, throughout Sweden, along with religious exhortations, thereby making churchmen the voice of the state. In the new dioceses of the north, such as Härnosand, in Norrland, the churchmen were especially important, the unofficial arms of the crown in areas in which governmental administration was limited in scope. That said, they could foster a considerable local autonomy, in consequence, even if they proved a somewhat debilitating drain in terms of the expenses they entailed.

Despite the remoteness and sparse population of much of the interior of Sweden, the priests of the Church of Sweden who resided there were by no means provincial in mentality or parochial in their worldly horizons. On the contrary, many clergymen were highly educated and widely travelled. Gustaf Fredrik Hjortberg (1724–76), for example, from the village of Släps, in Halland, was a member of the Academy of Science in Stockholm and had travelled as ship's chaplain to China three times. Yet knowledge of the world and a well-trained mind did not necessarily imply open-mindedness to other religions. Indeed, Enlightenment values notwithstanding, religious toleration remained an alien concept in eighteenth-century Sweden. One noted courtier, Count Nils Bielke (1706–65), was obliged, after his conversion to Catholicism, to go into exile and so he fled to Rome. This was hardly an onerous punishment though, for, once established there, he was made a papal courtier and Roman senator, and served as an agent facilitating commerce between the Papal States and Sweden. He also became an indispensable *cicerone* for aristocratic young Swedes on their Italian Grand Tours. Indeed, upon his death he was buried in the Church of St Brigitta in Rome, eminently respected both there and in Sweden.

Drottningholm in the 1760s

At court, as we have seen, King Adolph Fredrik and Queen Lovisa Ulrika had been constrained by the failure of their attempted coup in 1756 to reinstate absolutism from engaging in all but a limited degree of political activity. However, the royal couple refused to be intimidated in other aspects of their life at court and therefore carried on the torch of high culture in an especially determined fashion.

In particular, they undertook major architectural initiatives at Drottningholm Palace during the 1760s. The palace had been given to the queen as a wedding gift by the king in 1744, but its most famous architectural feature now came to be the Chinese Palace, designed by Carl Fredrik Adelcrantz (1716–96), the most elaborate example of Rococo flamboyance in Scandinavia. Also of note is the Court Theatre he built there in 1766, on the stage of which Gustaf III himself performed, both as crown prince and later king, and where much of the palace's historic theatrical machinery can, in fact, still be seen. Drottningholm assumed considerable importance in Sweden during this period, not only because of its architectural and garden attractions but because of the liveliness of the intellectual and cultural elite who gathered there, especially the members of the Royal Academy of History and Antiquities, which had been founded in 1753, and such scientists as Linné. For, in a country like Sweden, shorn of much territory and with only two traditional universities left and the state not always able to provide alternative possibilities, it was these academies which increasingly provided the intellectual venues for the exchange of ideas by the country's most learned personages, a role they, in some respects, still fulfil today.

SCIENTIFIC DEVELOPMENTS AND LAPLAND

Linné was, without doubt, Sweden's greatest man of science, leaving a lasting mark which still informs the biological sciences even in our own day. When, during the first half of the eighteenth century, a fashionable interest in Lapland focused attention on Scandinavia's most northerly region, he was one of the first to arrive there in pursuit of scientific exploration and discovery. He travelled to Lapland in 1732 on a scientific expedition which resulted in the

7 *Portrait of Carl von Linné in Lapp Costume Carrying a Saami (Lapp)
Drum* (1737), by Martin Hoffman, oil on canvas. Carl von Linné (1707–78)
was Sweden's most famous scientist, sometimes known as the Father of
Biology, because of his contributions to the nomenclature of the subject, still
the basis of our modern differentiation of the various biological species. He
was also one of the first men of learning to explore Lapland, of which the far
north of Sweden forms a part, home of the Saami people, in whom he took
great anthropological interest. Photo: Sören Hallgren. The Linnémuseet
Museum, Uppsala.

publication of his famous *Flora Lapponica*, in 1732. Richly illustrated, it presented not only enthralling images of the botanical life to be found in Lapland, but idealised depictions of the Saami people themselves, portrayed as natural denizens of the wilderness, unspoilt by civilisation and carrying out a nomadic existence, much as they had for centuries.

Yet the reality of Saami life was somewhat different from that romanticised by Linné and other visitors, their empirical approach notwithstanding: while one or two members of a family might be exclusively occupied with reindeer herding – on average some two hundred to the herd – the livelihood imagined by many to be the principal occupation of the Saami people – the reality was somewhat different. For many Saami were by now engaged in fishing or farming, among other more mundane sedentary work activities. That said, after the right to cross state borders freely was granted to the Saami by the territorial states concerned in 1757, herding did dramatically increase in scope, especially in the late spring and early autumn. Since reindeer herding was a highly seasonal occupation, many Saami herders travelled from Sweden and Finland as far afield as the coast of Norway towards the end of April, in order to fish and hunt, providing lucrative taxation to the Danish customs officers who, for that reason, welcomed their arrival.

Yet even at home in Sweden, the Saami were engaged in a variety of activities other than reindeer herding: the making and selling of brandy and other spirits, though usually illegal, was, nonetheless, highly profitable, while the trapping of foxes and preparation of reindeer hides and antler for a whole range of purposes was also lucrative. These were sold at the large annual Saami markets, the most important of which was held, for ten days, in the middle of February, in Karesuando on the Finnish–Swedish–Norwegian border. The flax, wool and hemp woven by Saami women were also marketed there, along with useful items such as skis, sledges, cradles and domestic implements.

In 1736–7, Pierre-Louis Moreau de Maupertuis followed in the footsteps of Linné, but used his sojourn in Lapland to measure the length of a degree along the meridian, with great implications for maritime travel and land surveyance. Linné, meanwhile, went on to leave a lasting imprint on the study of botany, biology and

8 *Saami in Front of their Summer Tents*, by Pehr Hilleström the Elder
(late eighteenth century), oil on canvas. The Saami (or Lapp) people, long
indigenous in the far north of Sweden, were the last of the inhabitants of
Sweden to be Christianised. Historically living predominantly from reindeer
herding and, to a lesser degree, fishing, they were frequently marginalised
politically and economically throughout the country's history because their
nomadic existence often came into conflict with the needs of more sedentary
farmers. Hallwylska Museet, Stockholm.

even physics, far beyond the geographical scope of Lapland, with
numerous publications. Appointed professor in Uppsala in 1741, he
wrote a series of books, including *Philosophia botanica* (1751) and
Species plantarum (1753), in which he began to establish a nomenclature for the classification of many types of fauna and flora known
at the time. Their groupings were organised under Latin names
according to observations based on the appearance of their sexual
organs. This 'shocking' method of discrimination led the eighteenth-
century English naturalist William Goodenough to ejaculate his
horror over the Swede's 'disgusting names, his nomenclatural wan-
tonness, vulgar lasciviousness, and the gross prurience of his mind'.

Nonetheless, the system he founded went on to become the basis of modern botanical and biological analysis. By no means an 'ivory tower' scientist, Linné also sought to introduce the cultivation of valuable commodities, such as coffee, sugar cane and ginger, into Sweden, by 'acclimatising' them to such cold climes, cognisant of the economic benefits which might thereby accrue, but in this, of course, he failed. Still, Linné had helped to open a new scientific age, not only in Sweden but in the wider world. The introduction, in 1753, of the Gregorian Calendar in Sweden, which led in that year to 1 March following 17 February, though totally unconnected with Linné, in retrospect seems to symbolise the dawn of this new era which has continued to make Sweden, even in our own day, a country famed for its scientific research.

Linné was by no means the only Swedish scientist of his age to win international acclaim. The astronomer Anders Celsius (1701–44) is another famous example. He provided a scientific explanation of the aurora borealis (northern lights), while leaving a permanent legacy for the world in scientific terms in his creation of the centigrade thermometer. Other signficant figures included the mathematician and physicist Samuel Klingenstierna (1698–1765), a professor at Uppsala University who assisted in the invention of the achromatic telescope, and the astronomer and statistician Pehr Wargentin (1717–83). With the establishment in 1739 of the Swedish Academy of Science, where Wargentin was later secretary, an important focal point for discussions of the development of scientific research and the exchange of ideas emanating from it came into being. Still another important scientific figure of the time was the chemist Johan Gottschalk Wallerius (1709–85). He devoted his attention to the way in which chemicals affect agriculture, the subject of his major work *Agriculturae fundamenta chemica*, which brought him international fame after it was published in 1761.

AGRICULTURAL DEVELOPMENTS

The new scientific insights notwithstanding, Sweden remained a largely rural country throughout the period, with almost half the population engaged in traditional farming, but the agricultural methods now used were themselves in a state of flux. In Scania, where some of the richest land and largest estates of the nobility were to be found, physiocratic ideals of agriculture were gaining acceptance, as the great landowners increasingly let their land to tenant farmers in exchange for goods or money. Of greatest import, though, was the major overhaul of agricultural organisation, which the government began to implement in order to increase productivity. Here, too, as in industry, England provided the model but, in Sweden, it was based specifically on the Enlightenment philosophy propagated in such books as *Svenska landtbrukets hinder och hjälp* (The Obstacles and Aids of Swedish Agriculture) published in 1746 by the Swedish land economist Jakob Faggot (1699–1777). It was in this context that *Storskiftet* (The Great Change) was initiated, now seen not only as a Swedish phenomenon but as part and parcel of the wider enclosure movement which was occurring throughout northern Europe at this time.

First implemented in 1757, *Storskiftet* continued in various stages for well over a century and profoundly altered rural life throughout the country. For it obliged the wider farming population to leave their villages and re-establish themselves in new homesteads, on sites located in the midst of the land being cultivated, thereby making them more efficient. Widely unpopular within the small landholding population itself, it was, nonetheless, implemented by various means of non-violent coercion. Its goal, moreover, was achieved: the expansion and improved efficiency of arable land. With greater prosperity, a growing number of farmers were then able to purchase their own land, albeit not from those noble landholders the sale of whose estates to commoners remained prohibited until 1864. That said, not all farming people benefited from the new system, for many cottagers, who had been granted their homes and pasturage without charge, were henceforth obliged to pay for them and frequently became more impoverished in the process.

LITERATURE AND EDUCATION

Despite the economic difficulties which plagued Sweden in the first half of the eighteenth century, its literature flowered, in growing contact with the French and British Enlightenment. One leading early figure, especially prominent in introducing Enlightenment values into Sweden at this time, was Olof von Dalin (1708–63), who had been educated at Lund University. His weekly periodical, *Den Svenska Argus* (The Swedish Argus), took inspiration from the initiatives of Joseph Addison who, together with Richard Steele, had founded *The Spectator* in London in 1711. Through his satires of life in Stockholm, where he had come to reside, he was able to popularise the British and French literary fashion for scepticism and reason. In his *Sagan om hästen* (The Story of the Horse), published in 1740, an allegorical dimension was added to the satire, which serves to mock those serious ones which had gone before. He also produced plays, such as *Den Svenska sprätthöken* (The Swedish Fop), which appeared in 1740, a comedy by Count Carl Gyllenborg. However, his fame today rests on his historical writings, in particular his three-volume *History of Sweden*, published between 1747 and 1762, a commission from the Swedish House of Estates.

As the eighteenth century wore on, the influence of Rousseau, rather than the pragmatic values of British scepticism, began to dominate the Swedish literary scene. This is apparent in the writings of another leading figure of the period, Hedvig Charlotta Nordenflycht (1718–63). An autodidact, she drew upon her pietistic beliefs to produce such poetry as *Den sörjande turturduvan* (The Mourning Turtledove), which appeared in 1743, written under the shadows of the recent deaths of both a fiancé and then her husband. Later, in the 1750s, she helped to form a literary society, the so-called *Tankarbyggarorden* (Order of the Thought Builders), together with the men of letters Gustaf Philip Creutz (1731–85) and Gustaf Fredrik Gyllenborg (1731–1808). The former is best known for his poem *Sommar-qväde* (The Summer Song) of 1756, though *Daphne* and *Atis och Camilla* (Atis and Camilla), both from 1762, were equally well received. Creutz later largely abandoned poetry and went on to become a prominent diplomat in the service of Gustaf III. Gyllenborg followed a similar course. Having written his poems *Verldsföraktaren* (The Misanthrope) and *Menniskans elände* (Misery of Man), which takes a cynical view of mankind, in 1762, he too went on to an official career in the civil service. However, before that, all three collaborated on joint anthologies, including *Våra försök* (Our Attempts), published from 1753 to 1756, and *Witterhetsarbeten* (Literary Works), from 1759 to 1762.

As scientific interest grew among an educated elite in Sweden during the course of the eighteenth century, the French language was, in every sense of the term, the lingua franca of communication with the rest of Europe. Among the nobility, French had, by now, become a second language which, while never achieving the ubiquity among the nobility which it had achieved in Russia during the course of the mid- and late eighteenth century, did enable the aristocracy to communicate fluently with others of their social background both in Sweden and abroad. Many governesses were French and, for the royal family, as well as many other aristocratic ones, it was used at home in both speech and literary correspondence, not least for the reason that it heightened privacy in a world where servants were unlikely to understand it. Its use also enabled access to a wide range of European literature, so important in a country where long winters gave reading added significance as a means of entertainment. Noble families like the De Geers of Leufsta Bruk, in Uppland, the Armfelts of Åminne Gård, to the east of Helsinki, in Finland, and that of L. H. von Nicolay, at Montrepos, near Viborg in Karelia, amassed vast libraries, with many books in French, though those in a variety of other languages also found their place.

Some works were in Swedish translation. The most famous and influential of these was the translation of McPherson's *Ossian* into Swedish in 1765, for it became a major catalyst in encouraging an interest in ancient Nordic mythology, which dovetailed with Gustaf III's grandiose imperial fantasies, yet would eventually reach its full blossoming in the following century during the reign of the warrior king Karl Johan.

Since learned visitors from France and elsewhere attending court were usually invited to lecture to avid audiences of Swedes eager for knowledge of the world abroad, such venues became important occasions for the dissemination of information from the British Isles, continental Europe and beyond.

For the bulk of the literate population, however, unconnected to court life as they were, it was the Bible which was and remained the principal source of reading. That said, as education broadened during the course of the eighteenth century, so did literary horizons and tastes. Already, in the 1760s, general elementary schooling was established in Sweden, with reading, writing and arithmetic the subjects taught. Teaching had by now largely come to be in the hands of the Lutheran clergy, many of whom were Pietists and for whom much literature from abroad was considered theologically and morally suspect for their parishioners, even if they themselves might be curious to read it. For that reason the propagation of the French language itself found little favour among them, until the arrival of the French Marshal Jean Bernadotte upon the Swedish throne in the following century provided a more potent and patriotic justification for its acquisition.

MUSICAL DEVELOPMENTS

Along with education and an extension of literacy, an interest in classical music as emanating from a central European tradition was becoming increasingly appreciated not only by the court but by an ever widening public. So along with art, architecture and science, music, too, began to flourish during the middle decades of the eighteenth century. This development was to a large degree due to one man, the composer of German origin Johan Helmich Roman (1694–1758), which has earned him the sobriquet 'the father of Swedish music'. Appointed Kapellmeister at the Swedish court in 1727, he was a skilled violinist and oboist, but he is most noted for his occasional musical compositions for court ceremonials and his sacred music. This includes two church symphonies, numerous sonatas, as well as a setting of the Swedish Lutheran liturgy and scores of sacred songs. Much of his work was inspired by George Frederick Handel, with whose compositions he had become acquainted during his five-year sojourn between 1716 and 1721 in England. The public concerts he organised during the 1730s, in the House of the Nobility in Stockholm, did much to influence musical life in the capital. His election to the Swedish Academy of Science in 1740 was an indication of the importance of his role in the cultural life of Sweden at that time. The height of his career, though, was reached with *Drottningholmsmusik*, a work composed to celebrate the wedding of Adolph Fredrik of Hesse, while still crown prince, with Lovisa Ulrika in 1744.

Yet another musical figure of note was Ferdinand Zellbell the Elder (1689–1765) who served at the Royal Chapel as organist and composer from 1715 to 1751, and at the Great Church in Stockholm from 1718/19 as organist, until 1753 when his son Ferdinand the younger took over the post. He published a number of collections of choral works, but he is best known for his *Bassoon Concerto in A Minor* and *Five Organ Preludes*. Yet if the latter composer was acceptable, with his ecclesiastical music, the former was not, since, for many within the Lutheran Church of Sweden, the lavish balls and other 'vanities' accompanied by music which were so fashionable at this period throughout Europe provided just another sign of the moral degeneracy of the times imported from abroad. Many of these individuals were finding a spiritual home within the established Church, in a movement which became known as Pietism.

PIETISM

Although the origins of Pietism were foreign, these in no way hindered its establishment in Swedish soil by the second quarter of the eighteenth century. In particular, its roots were in Germany, where its teachings had been propagated at the universities of Halle and Greifswald by Lutheran scholars such as August Hermann Francke. A social activist, Francke had taken the initiative to write to the Swedish crown prince himself, convinced that 'a sound foundation in the fear of God, as a result of which the powers that be may expect loyal subjects and faithful servants among all the estates', was the most solid basis for a successful state. While government leaders frequently concurred, Pietism's spread was further encouraged by the fact that many of the Swedish officers captured by the Russians during the Great Northern War had themselves come to be influenced by its ideals, while held as prisoners of war in Moscow and Tobolsk.

After Francke's death in 1727, Julius Hecker carried on his teachings, which rapidly spread beyond the borders of Germany and the countries of eastern Europe, assisted by the proselytising of Johann Konrad Dippel. Although speaking in tongues and other such elements sometimes played a prominent role in individual gatherings, Pietism in Sweden, nonetheless, remained a highly rationalistic movement, which dovetailed well with a growing interest in Enlightenment values.

In its later mid-eighteenth-century expression, Pietism in Sweden was predominantly influenced by another German, Count Nikolaus Ludwig von Zinzendorf (1700–60), who had established a community at Herrnhut, in Moravia. This branch of Pietism, therefore, came to be known as Moravianism and found a wide following within the Lutheran Church from 1732. Its ethic was, on the one hand, communitarian and based on hard work, but on the other, based on subservience to the state and those appointed to carry out its dictates. Although public convocations of Pietists, as such, had been forbidden already in 1726, the sect grew from strength to strength among the aristocracy, particularly in Stockholm and Gothenburg. It also left a lasting cultural imprint, even obvious in the late twentieth century in such a film as *Fanny och Alexander* (Fanny and Alexander) by Ingmar Bergman, in which the dichotomy between such religious values and a more sensual and 'artistic' approach to life form the theme, reflective of a personal struggle which the famed playwright and film director himself underwent in childhood and his life beyond.

While Pietism remained embedded within the established Swedish Church, numerous other sects increasingly began to break away from mainstream Lutheranism. The cult fostered by Emanuel Swedberg (1688–1772), who was generally known as Swedenborg after his ennoblement in 1711, is among the most prominent of these from this period and provided a mystical alternative to the state Church itself. Swedenborg's father had been a professor of theology at Uppsala University. However, Swedenborg himself was more interested in mechanics and metallurgy, only turning his attention to religious matters after a spiritual crisis in the early 1740s. Thereafter, he devoted himself to the literary exposition of a new theological system. His eight-volume work *Arcana coelestia* (Heavenly Arcana), published between 1749 and 1756, and later *De coelo et inferno* (On Heaven and its Wonders and on Hell), from 1758, expound a belief in the unity of the spiritual and temporal world, with a plethora of arcane elements, both rational and mystical. Rapidly gaining adherents to his new world view, he established the Church of New Jerusalem, which exerted considerable appeal within intellectual, often aristocratic, circles, not only in Sweden, but in London, too, where he eventually died. Indeed, it was one of his students, Carl Bernard Wadström (1746–99), who became a prime advocate of Sweden's endeavour to establish a colony in Sierra Leone, in west Africa, while at the same time expressing the moral necessity of ending Sweden's involvement with the slave trade there. The first goal was never realised, the second only in the course of the following century.

6

Royal absolutism restored

In 1771, during the final year of his father King Fredrik Adolph's reign, when Gustaf III was in Paris, carrying out important negotiations relating to Swedish–French relations, the political situation in Sweden had become increasingly chaotic. But Gustaf had already been laying his own plans to deal with this state of affairs upon his return, so he utilised his time at the court of King Louis XV associating with a wide range of French and foreign intellectuals there, who could bolster his intellectual pretensions to benevolent autocratic rule when the situation permitted. Their conversations, however, frequently left him disappointed. As he himself wrote to his mother, Queen Lovisa Ulrika, at home, 'I have become acquainted with almost all the philosophers here: Marmontel, Grimm, Thomas, the Abbé Morellet and Helvétius. It is much more amusing to read them than to meet them.' So, when the sudden death of his father made him king, he eagerly returned to Sweden, where he finally put into action the plan which had long preoccupied him. For he had single-mindedly determined to succeed where his parents had failed, in refashioning Sweden into an absolute monarchy. The *coup d'état* carried out on 19 August 1772 by the king and his supporters was bloodless, yet it proved successful in re-establishing royal absolutism after a lapse of more than half a century. Whereas, in 1720, the four estates of Sweden – the nobility, Church, burghers and peasants – had together taken over the role of the absolute monarch,

Gustaf III now reclaimed that role from them. At the same time, he increasingly allied himself with the peasants, an arrangement which worked to the detriment of the interests of the nobility, in particular, since he made it possible for peasants with sufficient means to purchase at least some of the land that had previously been inalienable from the aristocracy. He also saw to it that, henceforth, only through his own initiative could the *Riksdag* be summoned. In celebration of his new autocratic order, he had the great history painting *The Coronation of Gustaf III*, commissioned from the famed Swedish portrait painter Carl Gustaf Pilo (1711–93), composed in such a way that the figure of the monarch was isolated as if divine, the king's ascension to the throne appearing a veritable apotheosis. But the situation was less sublime for Gustaf than a reading of the painting would seem to support.

In reality, this autocracy had a number of significant limitations: the initiation of an offensive war required the *Riksdag*'s agreement, laws had to be promulgated by both king and *Riksdag*, and, most importantly, only the latter could levy taxes. That said, the royal prerogatives had been increased and Gustaf could turn his attentions not only to politics but to the arts, which he adored for reasons of aesthetics but which, more importantly, could serve to symbolise and bolster his newly won autocracy. In consequence, the worlds of politics, art and architecture now became intermeshed in Sweden to a degree never achieved before or since.

JOHAN TOBIAS SERGEL

Gustaf III was encouraged in his artistic interests by a coterie of highly gifted artists, deeply infused by the neo-classical values which had come to hold sway in Paris and Rome. Of these, the sculptor Johan Tobias Sergel (1740–1814) achieved the greatest fame, both at home and abroad. Having won a stipend from the Swedish Parliament Sergel was enabled to travel to Rome in 1767, where he became deeply imbued with the aesthetic values propagated by the German Johann Joachim Winckelmann, Prefect of Papal Antiquities there, who, in 1764, had published his seminal work *Die Geschichte der Kunst des Altertums* (The History of the Art of Antiquity). Taking a keen interest in Greek and Roman archaeological ruins, as well as the eccentric and fantastical designs of Giambattista Piranesi, he came to reject the sensuous curves of the Rococo, in favour of a more robust, geometric and linear style, based on antique prototypes. When Gustaf III's brother Fredrik Adolph visited Rome in 1776, he was taken to visit Sergel and became his patron. Shortly thereafter, Gustaf III himself purchased from Sergel *Eros and Psyche*, a sculpture originally commissioned by Madame du Barry, former mistress of the late French king, Louis XV. This was the first of many the Swedish monarch would order from Sergel and was intended to be placed in a vast temple folly in the gardens of Haga, outside Stockholm, just one element in a vast new palace scheme envisioned by Gustaf with increasingly megalomaniacal dimensions. Like many of his architectural schemes – and military ones, as well – this was never carried out. Nonetheless, in 1778, Sergel was appointed court sculptor, succeeding the previous French incumbent, Pierre Hubert L'Archevêque (1721–78), and returned from Italy to Sweden, taking up a position as professor of the Swedish Royal Academy of Art, founded by the king early in his reign in 1773.

TRAVELS IN ITALY

In 1782, Gustaf's plans to attack Denmark-Norway the following year to further his territorial ambitions – despite his marriage to a Danish princess, Sophie Magdalene – were abandoned after discussions with the Russian empress, Catherine the Great, who opposed such an action. However, the king had other plans: an extended Grand Tour to Italy, for both political and cultural purposes. Gustaf had intended to visit Italy for many years, indeed, even before the death of his father, but only in 1782 did he feel the time was finally appropriate to do so. Sergel, with his wide artistic knowledge, was now commanded to return to Italy as the king's personal companion. Along with Sergel, Karl August Ehrensvärd (1745–1800), son of the architect of the Sveaborg Fortress outside Helsinki, recently appointed Chancellor of the Swedish Royal Academy of Art, also joined the entourage.

Thus, while Gustaf's travels to Italy were explained to the Swedish public as a cure for a minor injury, sustained during a campaign in Finland, it is undeniable that they had artistic and aesthetic dimensions. Yet the king loved power even more than art and so it was the political dimensions which were ultimately paramount on the journey: in particular, Gustaf wanted to win the support of the Bourbon powers of France, Spain, Naples and Parma for an alliance against Denmark and Russia, and this his presence at the courts of Italy might enable him to do. Their support was in many respects imperative, since he intended war against both Russia and Denmark, at some later date, in the hopes of regaining much, if not all, of those territories lost by Karl XII. For Gustaf's weaknesses as a warrior not withstanding, his imperial megalomaniacal visions continued to inform his long-term strategy.

Therefore, he and his entourage set forth across Europe, travelling incognito as the Count of Haga – this ruse was expected to fool no one but enabled him to avoid undesirable protocol – travelling first to Venice, Verona and Vicenza, in the north, then Mantua and Padua, before heading south to the *Mezzogiorno*, to Naples and Sicily. There the ancient ruins and temples at Pompeii and Herculaneum, near the former, and Agrigento, in the latter, made an overwhelming impression upon him. Yet most important of all was Rome: Sergel and the French artist Louis-Adrien Masreliez (1748–1810), long resident in Sweden, smoothed his path there, introducing him to a plethora of artists, architects and antique dealers. Gustaf also became acquainted with Pope Pius VI and attended high papal mass in St Peter's, on both Christmas 1783 and Easter 1784.

Unfortunately for Gustaf and his plans for a grandiose renewal of Sweden's Baltic hegemony, the Russian Crown Prince Paul (later Emperor Paul I) and his consort also travelled to Italy at this time, assuming, in his turn, a false identity, that of the Count of the North. Although the reasons for his journey were, in part, a response to domestic politics at home in St Petersburg, the visit also served as a means of undermining Gustaf's negotiations, contrary as they were to the interests of Russia.

LOUIS-JEAN DESPREZ

Gustaf saw architecture and the arts as powerful tools with which to propagate his imperial visions through symbolical forms, capable of reinforcing his political and military machinations. To accomplish this, he needed to employ a retinue of individuals whose knowledge of the art world and artistic skills had already won them accolades. So in Rome, Gustaf chose the Frenchman Louis-Jean Desprez (*c.*1743–1804) to spearhead his wide-ranging plans for the architectural and artistic embellishment of his capital, after his return to Sweden. Desprez had studied under the French artist Charles-Nicholas Cochin, but it was the theatre designer Charles de Wailly who provided him with the extravagant fantasies which so appealed to the king. In Italy, Desprez had assisted the acclaimed Abbé de Saint-Non in his great architectural work, *Voyage pittoresque ou Description des Royaumes de Naples et de Sicile* (Picturesque Voyage, or a Description of the Kingdoms of Naples and Sicily), with some 136 illustrations of extraordinary charm. So, after Gustaf III had brought him back to Sweden, he wanted Stockholm refashioned in a similarly grandiose neo-classical fashion.

The architectural jewel in the crown for the king was to be the new palace of Haga. Its central feature was to be a rotunda, joined by two projecting wings, containing altogether no fewer than sixty-two window bays, and adorned by an enormous Corinthian colonnade of sixty columns on its southern façade. An imposing interior salon was also planned, beneath a central cupola, supported by sixteen columns of Siberian malachite. Work commenced and a large granite hill was blown up in order to lay the foundations of the palace which was then constructed. Its completion was at first envisioned for 1797, but Gustaf had failed to take into account one insurmountable flaw in this, as in so many of his plans: there were insufficient funds in the royal coffers to achieve it. In consequence, this vast palace complex, along with the intended Victory Column and other embellishments the king had planned, was never realised. The impoverished royal treasury and draining war with Russia, waged from 1789 to 1790, put an end not only to this but to all such lavish undertakings, which included, among numerous others, the erection of an imposing Greek temple folly at Drottningholm. In a manner completely contrary to what Gustaf had desired, his architecture and art did, indeed, symbolise his politics and military undertakings, for the failure of their realisation mirrored that of the Swedish–Russian war itself: Gustaf's vision of the Baltic as a Swedish lake was as much bankrupt and in ruins as the aesthetic visions of the antique he was so keen to recreate in Sweden.

Yet, while Desprez's grand visions were never brought to fruition, others far more modest in scale by some of his Swedish students were: one pupil, Carl Christoffer Gjörwell (1766–1837), designed the principal building of the Åbo Academy, in Turku (Åbo in Swedish), Finland's only university at that time, in a style which derived inspiration not only from Vitruvius and Palladio, but from early Roman basilicas as well, and in which the Swedish monarch was depicted as Apollo, the god of the arts and music, in its rich architectural embellishments.

SWEDEN'S CARIBBEAN COLONY

While Gustaf's attention was predominantly focused north and eastwards, in glorious, if futile, obsession, developments to the south and west also caught his attention. Ironically, it was these, rather than his more grandiose visions, which had the most practical benefits. In Paris, in 1784, negotiations were undertaken by Gustaf III for a new secret alliance with France, as well as for the Swedish acquisition of the French island colonies of St Barthélemy and St Martin, along with the provision of French subsidies, in return for France's right to use Gothenburg as an entrepôt. These were successfully completed and, on 7 March 1785, Sweden assumed full sovereignty over these Caribbean islands. They were hardly a major windfall, though, with a meagre population, in 1787, of only 739. Of these, 458 were of European background, 115 of whom were Swedes. The remainder were French, English and Dutch. A further 281 were of African descent. With limited agriculture and long periods of drought semi-annually, the new Swedish colony was unlikely to offer rich pickings in terms of natural resources. Indeed, its total production of sugar and cotton hardly exceeded more than four shiploads per year, while supplies of fish, lime and animal husbandry only covered the needs of the inhabitants. That said, its harbour, Le Carénage, was splendid, while its location in the eastern Caribbean was conveniently near both the British and French colonies of the Leeward and Windward

Islands, as well as the Spanish Main. It, therefore, had the potential of becoming a very successful transit port. At first, this potential seemed to be fulfilled. Trade thrived and within a year the colony had doubled its population. In consequence, Sweden established the Swedish West India Company to administer the new colony, with its capital established at Gustavia, St Barthélemy's only real town, named in honour of the king, and with its fortress, Fort Gustaf.

The advent of the Napoleonic Wars proved a particular blessing to the colony, since much Caribbean trade now came to pass through it, as the major European powers, including at times the new United States, waged war with one another. By 1800, its population had grown to five thousand, putting it on a par with Uppsala in terms of size. With such a diverse ethnic and linguistic population, Swedish, French and English were all accepted as official languages in the colony and religious toleration was complete. In this it stood in sharp contrast to the situation which reigned in Sweden itself at that time. There conversion to Catholicism, for example, remained a serious crime and those who embraced that faith found their property confiscated and they themselves forced into exile.

Not everything, of course, during the course of the Napoleonic Wars went well for Sweden in the Caribbean. In 1801, for example, the colony was briefly seized by the British but the following year, restitutions were paid and it was returned to Swedish administration. Thereafter, it continued to profit and, in 1804, with wealth abounding, a theatre was established in the capital and concerts were frequently held, with musicians both local and imported. Two years later, by virtue of the opening of free trade to all Swedes, the colony enjoyed its greatest boom time. In 1811 alone, some 1,800 ships visited St Barthélemy. Moreover, during the hostilities which followed between Britain and the United States, no less than 20 per cent of American exports passed through the colony during the period October 1813 to September 1814. Although St Barthélemy's poor agricultural hinterland derived but scant benefit from this activity, many merchants also now profited from the fact that runaway slaves from elsewhere in the Caribbean who had sought sanctuary on the islands were auctioned off to slavers for the benefit of the Swedish crown.

AFRICAN COLONIAL VENTURES

Along with the establishment of a Swedish Caribbean colony, ventures were once again undertaken on Africa's west coast in this period. Inspired by the voyage of the *Chevalier des Marchais*, undertaken on behalf of the French government, a Swedish society for the colonisation of west Africa was organised at Nyköping. Supported by the Swedish Secretary of State, Baron Johan Liljencrantz (1730–1815), a charter was granted to forty families from manufacturing and mercantile backgrounds for their African resettlement. They set sail from Sweden not long thereafter, boarding vessels of the French Senegal Company at Havre de Grâce, in transit for the African coast. Initially, the society had hoped to create a settlement near Cape Verde, but in the end they sought to establish themselves further south, in what is today Sierra Leone, where rich agricultural lands seemed to beckon them. Ingenious, if utopian, plans to build elaborate tree houses, suitable to the geography and climate, were made, incorporating classical balustrades for the dwellings, by C. B. Wadström, one of their number. However, the climate, disease and hostile natives conspired together rapidly to undermine Sweden's African colony and effect its complete ruination, and further initiatives were abandoned.

GUSTAF III'S FALTERING REGIME

If the foundations of the Swedish colonial venture in Africa were in a state of collapse, the stability of Gustaf III's faltering regime in Sweden was also severely undermined, not least by renewed war with Russia, undertaken in July 1788, with little financial resources and poor planning. A Swedish assault on the Russian navy by the island of Högland in the Gulf of Finland brought few benefits. No decisive military gains were won and discontent among officers grew to such a degree that, in August 1788, a conspiracy was fomented at the country estate of Anjala, in which 113 officers took part. It failed, powerless to oblige the king to end the disastrous war he had so recklessly undertaken. Gustaf crushed it and, while many of its members escaped with minor penalties, its leader Colonel J. H. Hästesko was executed.

True, the Battle of Svensksund, on 9–10 July 1790, was a great naval victory for Sweden, but it belied the overall unhappy military realities of the wider conflict. Increasingly aware of this, Gustaf III initiated negotiations and concluded peace with Russia at Värälä, in August 1790. The ultimate military debacle was thereby avoided. Yet opposition to Gustaf III remained strong, especially among those opposed to the king's autocratic rule at the expense of the aristocracy, and this was to prove the king's final undoing.

ASSASSINATION OF GUSTAF III

On 16 March 1792, Gustaf III was shot by a disaffected nobleman, Captain Jacob Johan Anckarström (1762–92), with the support of other discontented figures, at a masked ball at the Royal Opera House, a building for which the king himself had contributed architectural designs and which had been built by the architect Carl Fredrik Adelcrantz in 1782. As such, in character with the theatrical frameworks he himself loved to design, he had succeeded in architecturally framing his own demise. Ever since, the theatricality of the event has fascinated millions, both in Sweden and abroad. Indeed, it was later commemorated, albeit in much fictionalised form, by Giuseppi Verdi in his opera *Un ballo in maschera* of 1859, which he rewrote with references rich in import for the Italian *Risorgimento*. Still, the reality of the event was melodramatic in itself. Mortally wounded, the king lingered on for days, only succumbing on 29 March. Anckarström was apprehended and executed, his fellow conspirators imprisoned or exiled. The status quo remained and his son Gustaf IV Adolph (1778–1837), under a regency, succeeded to the throne. Nonetheless, change was in the offing, mediated by events far beyond the frontiers of Sweden: the Napoleonic Wars.

RELIGIOUS TRENDS

During the later eighteenth century, Swedish society was informed by a remarkable degree of internal stability and consensus. This was, to a considerable extent, informed by the established Church of Sweden, which, unlike the monarchy itself, remained one of country's most dominant and stable institutions, imposing religious obligations on almost all Swedes. The most prominent of these was the duty to attend church regularly and to take Holy Communion, at least several times a year, depending upon the communicant's residential distance from a church and other such practical circumstances. Adherence to other Christian churches was strictly prohibited.

In the Caribbean, however, where more colonists were foreign and adhered to other faiths, a de facto toleration had come into practice. In St Barthélemy and St Martin, non-Swedes enjoyed complete religious toleration, to a degree only realised in Sweden itself more than seventy years later, although Swedes themselves in the colony were still obliged to adhere to the established religion.

A Swedish Lutheran church was founded in Gustavia, the colony's capital, in 1787, named after the queen, Sophie Magdalene, but, since the colony had only twenty-one Lutheran residents at this time, it also provided the venue for residents of other denominations. These included 234 Methodists, 149 Anglicans and 60 members of other Protestant communities, including the Calvinist-inspired Reformed Church. There were also more than 519 Catholics, many of whom were from the nearby French colonial possessions. So important were the latter for the prosperity of the colony that the island's governor, Rosenstein, was exhorted by the Swedish government itself to financially remunerate the Catholic priest, Father Épiphane, who, despite residing on St Martin, served the community twice monthly. Their services were held at the little stone chapel at the village of L'Orient.

Back in Sweden itself, however, the old rigid Lutheran order persisted, leading many, especially those who tended towards less orthodox views, to lament the Church's 'mummified state'.

ECONOMIC DEVELOPMENTS

Despite the pride taken in joining the ranks of colonial states, Sweden's colonial ventures proved to have little lasting impact on its economy as a whole. Rather it was such traditional industries as mining, metallurgy, forestry and agriculture that remained of paramount importance. During the later eighteenth century, forestry, in particular, was significant, despite the fact that the southern and central provinces had lost much of their vast forests to cultivation, but in Finland little had changed over the previous centuries and forest growth remained luxuriant. That said, 'colonial' settlement in the provinces of the east and north, Karelia, Savo and Kajani, grew considerably as agriculture was extended. The availability of land for yeoman farmers and landless farm labourers was an especial attraction, for in these areas very few of the nobility came to settle. This was in sharp contrast to the long-settled rural areas in the south-west of Finland, around Turku, where, in 1805, some 14 per cent of the population were of noble background. The use of the slash-and-burn method of bringing virgin land into cultivation enabled quick returns, encouraging many farmers to abandon old homesteads in the south, which brought in limited returns, and seek out new ones in these recently settled provinces. From 1789, peasant farmers were allowed to purchase both crown land and land free from taxation belonging to the nobility, without constraints, and this reform further served to increase and spread the ownership of land among a wider section of the population than had previously been the case. Sweden was, thus, clearly on the way to becoming a modern state, one in which the individual, through his own practical efforts and the accumulation of capital, could make his way up the socio-economic ladder.

The production in the south-west of Finland and in Ostrobothnia of almost all Europe's tar and pitch, so necessary for the maintenance of Europe's many navies, was also a great allure to many in need of employment. The production of these commodities came to provide alternative sources of income for many in those areas and improved the general prosperity. On the other hand, in those regions cut off from the sea, the state of the economy remained poor, since the absence of suitable transport meant those who lived there were isolated, with little employment other than that its meagre agriculture and forestry provided. For this reason, as elsewhere in the western world, canals began to be built to alleviate the problem. One of the first, the Trollhätte Canal, was completed in 1800, enabling sailing vessels to travel from Lake Vänern to the Göta River and thence to the sea. Integrated with the Göta Canal, in a network which linked the North and Baltic seas, Sweden's transport system was soon in a position to facilitate the rapid movement of trade throughout much of the country.

Maritime trade to Asia, on the other hand, as filtered through the Swedish East India Company, was dwindling in profitability. Still, its economic returns had been considerable over the years, permitting some of its shareholders to amass substantial wealth. Indeed, they made it possible for the Grill family to accumulate enough capital to diversify into the iron industry, enabling them to set up the famous Österby Works, near Uppsala. However, by 1807, the Swedish East India Company had fallen into a state of collapse and ceased to trade. Nonetheless, it left a memorable record, for during the more than seventy years in which it had functioned, some 132 voyages under its auspices had been made to the Orient from Gothenburg, many to Canton, where it established a factory, and it left a lasting legacy both economically and culturally, in both Sweden and in China.

Mining and metallurgy

Mining and metallurgy continued to be bulwarks of the Swedish economy, and, though the share of iron and later steel grew, copper continued to be a major commodity. The great copper mines of Dalecarlia, though less important in a pan-European context than they had previously been, were still productive, and contributed no less than 12 per cent of all Swedish exports. When Gustaf III visited the Great Copper Mountain Mine, its significance was underscored by the commissioning of a famous painting by the noted Swedish artist Pehr Hilleström the Elder (1733–1816) to commemorate the event, when a great banquet was held in one of the mine shafts, elaborately decorated for the festive occasion.

Economic returns in the industry were considerable but working conditions for the miners were difficult and insalubrious. As Carl von Linné put it, when he himself visited the mine on a less festive occasion than the king, 'The *damned*, as they were called, were naked to the waist and wore woollen cloths over their mouths, in order, hopefully, to hinder breathing in the smoke and soot. It was virtually impossible to take a clean breath of air and sweat ran down their bodies like water out of a pouch.' Those in administrative positions in the industry, however, were more interested in its financial returns and these were significant, indeed. Proprietary ironmasters working in Gästrikland, for example, frequently built neo-classical country houses, set in extensive parkland adjacent to their forges, decorated with furniture in the latest neo-classical style.

The workmen in the forges themselves, living nearby with their families in rows of tiny two-room cottages, were paid according to the quantity of iron bars they produced. This income they could supplement by the production of pig-iron and charcoal. However, once the Lancashire method of forging was introduced to Sweden, the industry changed significantly and with it the lifestyle of the workers. The men who laboured in the forges then became increasingly itinerant, travelling without their families and residing in dormitories at the various sites in which they took up temporary work.

9 *The Walloon Forge at the Gimo Works* (1838), by Fritz von Dardel (1817–1901). The mining industry has for centuries been highly important in Sweden, producing the country's most important export commodities, first copper from the mines of Falun, in the province of Dalecarlia, and then iron. Much of its success depended upon the skills of Protestant religious refugees who had arrived in the sixteenth and seventeenth centuries from the Walloon region of Belgium, where they had suffered persecution from its Spanish Catholic administration. (*Interiör av vallonsmedja vid Gimo bruk 1838*, Akvarell (nr=38) av Fritz von Dardel.) Inv nr=67483. Uppland, Olands härad, Skäfthammars socken, Gimobruk. Nordiska Museet, Stockholm.

The Mining College, which had the ultimate administrative and judicial control, ran the industry, but subdivided it administratively into twelve separate units, together encompassing not only the province of Dalecarlia, the ancient centre of Sweden's most important mining ventures, but more recent ones in Uppland, Närke and Västmanland as well. International partners were also changing. While Britain no longer required Swedish iron as it had done previously, because of its own developing industry, the nascent United States did, especially during the American War of Independence when it could no longer import any from its mother country. Yet Britain played a different role with respect to the Swedish mining industry even so, which was equally significant: it provided men with the know-how on how to develop the industry. One such leading individual was John Jennings (1729–73), who settled in Sweden after a sojourn in Paris, becoming a leading member of the Swedish Academy of Science. Based at his estate, Forsmark, in Uppland, where he introduced the latest technical innovations, he became the country's largest single exporter of iron.

SCIENTIFIC DEVELOPMENTS

If the earlier eighteenth century was important in Sweden for the botanic discoveries, research and systemisation carried out during that period, the latter eighteenth century was similarly notable for chemistry. Particularly important was the chemist and mineralogist Torbern Bergman (1735–84). His insights into both subjects enabled him to formulate a classification system for minerals, which was based on both their chemical composition and appearance. His *Physisk Beskrifning öfver Jordklotet* (Physical Description of the Earth), published in 1766, earned him wide acclaim not only in Sweden, but elsewhere in Scandinavia and beyond in Germany and Russia. He is also noted for his ability to produce carbonated water out of chalk, through the action of sulphuric acid, even if its artificial production had first been achieved by Joseph Priestly in 1767. This processed soda-water went on to become popular world-wide as a health inducing beverage. Also significantly, Bergman provided considerable financial support for another leading Swedish chemist of that time, Wilhelm Scheele (1742–86), who is noteworthy for his discovery of oxygen in 1771, though he failed to publish anything at the time on this discovery, thereby enabling Joseph Priestly, who discovered it independently in 1774, to publish the information first. In 1774, Scheele also noted, for the first time, the existence of another substance, chlorine, though its presence as an element did not suggest itself to him at the time. Other experiments by him took note of the effects of light on silver compounds, the results of which were later useful for the invention of photography in the following century.

Gottlieb Gahn (1745–1818) was another leading scientific figure of this period, who combined knowledge of both mineralogy and crystallography. His insights in these areas enabled him to discover the element manganese in 1774. With Scheele, Gahn also helped in the discovery of phosphoric acid as a component in bones. Although publishing little, he was nonetheless very active in his experiments, inventing improved processes for copper smelting which were of considerable utility for the mining industry. In consequence, he was appointed assessor of mining in Stockholm in 1784.

Yet another important figure in Sweden at this time was the botanist Carl Peter Thunberg (1743–1828), who studied under Linné at Uppsala University. Later travelling abroad, he carried out extensive research at the Dutch Cape of Good Hope colony in South Africa, before proceeding to Japan, which at that time, otherwise, admitted only Dutchmen to its shores. There he was based on the island of Dejima, in the Bay of Nagasaki, where he was only rarely permitted to go ashore. When he did so, though, he made a thorough study of Japanese flora, before departing the country in 1776. After his return to Europe, he further benefited from making the highly useful acquaintance of Sir Joseph Banks, the British explorer and naturalist, in London, and was able to examine the splendid seventeenth-century Japanese botanical collection of the German Engelbert Kaempfer who had also resided on Dejima, many years before him, as well as the new botanical specimens brought back from Captain Cook's second Pacific expedition. Arriving back in Sweden in 1779, Thunberg eventually produced his great and wide-ranging work *Flora Japonica*, which was published in 1784. Other publications followed, including that which described his various travels within Japan, one of which took him to the court of the Shogun himself in the Japanese capital, Edo.

When, in 1786, Gustaf III founded the Swedish Academy, the country could boast of a rich and varied scientific elite and a new foundation, which henceforth provided a focal point for the exchange of scientific ideas on the highest level, a function it continues to carry out to this day.

EDUCATION

As scientific research and industrial technology developed, so a more general education of the wider population was developing in tandem, in which skills in reading, writing and arithmetic were becoming fairly widespread. This trend was assisted by religious education, which prepared the young for confirmation, an important custom, if not sacrament, in the Lutheran Church of Sweden. As a result, literacy had become general and reading skills went hand in hand with the propagation of Lutheran religious values. In some regions of Sweden, special catechists, who lived in the family of the local parish priest, were paid by the Church to go out into rural areas, to disseminate literary skills together with Christian knowledge. This was, for example, the case in Lapland, though visits to the Saami in their nomadic encampments were paid for by the Saami themselves, rather than by the Church.

Once the basic tenets of Christian belief had been inculcated, the provision of books for further knowledge became a prerequisite. Since books were expensive, the idea of establishing subscription libraries had taken root in the later eighteenth century, imported from the fledgling United States, under the initiative of the new nation's international roving ambassador Benjamin Franklin and its second president, Thomas Jefferson. Already by the 1780s, such lending libraries had been established in Norrköping and Karlskrona, and numerous discussion groups had been founded in their wake. These allowed the reading public access to a wide range of books, which the majority of them would not have had the means to purchase. In Vasa, in Finland, members of the Court of Appeal established their own library society, 'for their own amusement and diversion', and it provided a prototype for others which later sprang up in various parts of Finland.

MUSIC

Gustaf III was a man of music, as well as art and the theatre, and music in Sweden during his reign blossomed in consequence. The establishment by the king, in 1771, of the Royal Swedish Academy of Music helped to turn his court into a highly cultivated musical milieu, in which such famous musicians as Carl Michael Bellman (1740–95) were able to thrive. Bellman was the most genial musician of his time in Sweden, composing musical settings for his poetic songs, often accompanied by the zither, which have remained highly acclaimed from his day to ours, despite the vagaries of musical fashion. A sceptical man of the Enlightenment, his drinking songs and biblical parodies were highly popular among all segments of the Swedish population, from the king down to his lowliest servants. His *Fredmans epistlar* (Fredman's Epistles), begun in 1765 but first published in 1790, is a collection based on earlier compositions, which utilise reinterpretations of fashionable dances, like the *minuet* and *contredanse*, but in an idiosyncratic way which is clearly inspired by such fashionable French writers of the time as Jean-Joseph Vadé. A second collection appeared in 1791, entitled *Fredmans sånger* (Fredman's Songs), which focuses more on drink and conviviality, rather than the Bible. He also was a prolific writer of plays but these were only published after his death.

GUSTAF III'S REFORMS

With scepticism and Enlightenment values coming to the fore in other realms than just the musical, Gustaf III took the initiative to rid the country of laws promulgated in what he considered to be a more superstitious age. In 1779, he repealed those laws relating to witchcraft and in other ways sought to temper the religious intolerance of the age, but only in so far as public opinion and the clergy of the Church of Sweden would allow. The practice of Catholicism remained forbidden to Swedes, but Catholic immigrants whose labour the country needed were now allowed to do so. In 1782, Jews, too, were finally permitted to come and settle in Sweden, where henceforth they were allowed to practise their religion privately. They were permitted to settle in Stockholm,

Gothenburg, Norrköping and Karlskrona but this only applied to those Jews with the means and skills deemed sufficient to carry out trade and industry productively. Moreover, their rights were circumscribed: membership of craft guilds, the ownership of landed property and intermarriage remained prohibited to them. Poorer unskilled Jewish labour continued to be unwelcome until the middle of the nineteenth century.

Gustaf was also interested in prison reform. The English prison reformer John Howard's notable work *The State of the Prisons in England and Wales*, published in 1777, was especially influential in encouraging this initiative. It also inspired David Schultz von Schultzenheim, the Prussian who had introduced smallpox inoculation into Sweden in the 1750s, to advocate a range of improvements for dealing with prisoners and their reform. Nearer to home, local Swedish initiatives with respect to prison reform were also influential. In particular, a new model prison designed by the famous Swedish architect Gustaf af Sillén (1762–1825) won wide approval for its reformist vision, a three-storey edifice, in which hardened and lesser criminals were separated from one another, with a chapel situated between the two principal wings, the only venue in the complex in which all were permitted to assemble.

Most acclaimed at the time, at least by Enlightenment thinkers abroad, was Gustaf's abolition of the use of torture, enacted during the early years of his reign. This won him the approbation of Voltaire and, among many of the *philosophes* of the Englightenment, Gustaf III came to be lauded as a true philosopher-king, joining the ranks of such 'benevolent autocrats' as Catherine the Great of Russia and Frederick the Great of Prussia.

SOCIAL WELFARE AND GENDER

Yet the enlightened reforms of Gustaf III on a variety of levels notwithstanding, social welfare in Sweden during the Gustavian period remained limited. Family and marriage remained the dominant social institutions on which most people depended in times of need. Recourse to the aid of the community or government was usually a last resort. Husbands had conjugal rights, not only over the persons of their wives but over their physical property as well.

Since the overwhelming majority of women in Sweden in the late eighteenth and early nineteenth centuries married, this meant that most women, by virtue of their gender, looked to their husbands or children for care. For the remaining 10 per cent of women, by 1800, who never married, those of sufficient means looked after their own interests, but those less fortunate continued to depend upon other relations for their support in times of need. Only in the most extreme cases of need, usually involving the so-called virtuous poor, did people look to the local community itself for assistance and this, when rendered, was minimal. As for beggars, of all ages, strict provisions were made, with these 'unworthy poor' sent to so-called 'spinning houses', where they were set to work in producing cloth. The spinning house built by the architect Carl Fredrik Adelcrantz (1716–96), in Norrköping, became Sweden's most important textile factory in 1784. This had important consequences for the city as a whole, as well as its inmates, since the construction of numerous textile mills and other related industrial enterprises in the years which followed made Norrköping Sweden's textile capital.

Ladies of the higher social circles who fell into poverty generally fared better than their more humbly born sisters. The long-established Queen's House in Stockholm continued to serve the needs of impoverished ladies of rank throughout the period, providing a reasonable modicum of comfort and security. It proved a highly sought-after refuge and demands upon its services grew to such a degree that, in 1775, a third floor – also by Adelcrantz – was added to the central elevation, providing sufficient space for the ever greater number of inmates it now came to accommodate.

HEALTH AND HYGIENE

The greatest innovation of the time, though, was not in the realm of an improved social welfare infrastructure, but in measures taken for illness prevention, above all, the introduction of vaccinations against smallpox in 1801. Five years previously, the English doctor Edward Jenner had discovered that a vaccine from cowpox could offer almost total immunity against the disease, at least for several years. As a result, after the introduction and extension of the use of vaccination during the following decade, incidents of smallpox in Sweden dropped dramatically.

Venereal infections, on the other hand, remained a serious health problem throughout the period. Syphilis had been introduced to the country already in the early sixteenth century and by the late seventeenth century had become endemic. In the late eighteenth century, the Swedish College of Medicine declared the state itself to be in peril but to little effect as no decisive measures were undertaken to contain it. Therefore, the disease continued to take its toll throughout Sweden in all segments of society, especially after the return of troops from war, along with a plethora of fevers and other ailments introduced from abroad. Only in the later decades of the nineteenth century did health and hygiene begin significantly to improve, largely as a result of improved sanitation, as well as a better diet. Yet a beginning had been made and, at least in the short term, as the wider world later noted, in the years which followed the Napoleonic settlement, 'the peace, the vaccine and the potatoes' brought undeniable benefits in their wake.

7

Constitutional Sweden

During the decades which followed the assassination of Gustaf III, Sweden followed a path increasingly informed by consitutionalism. However, its journey on that path was extremely uneven. When Gustaf IV Adolph (1778–1837), still a child, succeeded to the throne, Sweden's political future seemed highly volatile. Although the old king's brother Duke Karl (1748–1818) became official regent, political power actually was vested in the hands of Baron Gustaf Adolph Reuterholm (1756–1813), a statesman who had been briefly imprisoned under Gustaf III because of political opposition, but was now supported by powerful allies. This took place against a backdrop of the French Revolution, which had led to a general military conflagration in Europe, a conflict in which Sweden was obliged to take a stand.

At first, the country was able to maintain its 'armed neutrality', in alliance with its erstwhile enemy Denmark. However, the flourishing trade that it was now enjoying led to confrontation with its old ally Great Britain, attempting to isolate and economically strangle France through a naval blockade. With the naval port of Karlskrona threatened by the British navy in 1801, Sweden relented. Yet an internal confrontation between Gustaf IV Adolph, a committed autocrat who, upon coming of age, had succeeded to the throne in 1796, and disgruntled members of the nobility, some of whom sympathised with revolutionary ideas, led to a conflict in government and international political repercussions which could not be easily resolved. The tumultuous *Riksdag* convoked at Norrköping in 1800 demonstrated to the king his lack of support. So he refused any further convocations, and hostility to his reign increased among wide segments of the population. With the king and the *Riksdag* in stalemate, the situation was aggravated further by the deterioration, once again, of relations with Russia. This had major consequences for Finland.

THE WAR OVER FINLAND

For centuries, Finland had been an integral part of the Swedish kingdom. Although it was seen by many, both in Sweden and abroad, as a rather primitive land, its staunch Lutheranism and hostile eastern frontier with Russia gave it a centrality in Sweden's aggressive military strategy. Its Finnish-speaking population, moreover, was a source of growing fascination for linguists and historians, intrigued by the Finno-Ugric roots of the language and their perceived exoticism. In 1777, the German historian August Ludwig Schözer had written in his book *Algemeine Nordische Geschichte* (General Nordic History) about the 'Aborigines' of Finland, stating, 'If the Finns are neither Scythians, nor Samoyeds, nor Huns, nor Hebrews, who then are they? Well, they are just Finns, and that is where I have to stop, my family tree for them does not go any further, and between the Finn and Noah, I do not know of any ancestral links.' Yet at the same time, Finland was described by others as 'Europe's Canada', a frontier land rich in economic opportunities for its burgeoning population. As in the young United States, European colonists could be contrasted with native, 'wild' 'Indians', so Professor Henrik Gabriel Porthan (1739–1804) of the Åbo Academy could maintain, in 1789, that 'the Russians are really Asians, while the Scandinavians, on the other hand, are Europeans'. Not surprisingly, therefore, it was in Finland that the decisive confrontation between Russia and Sweden came to be resolved.

Sweden, of course, had other enemies too now, for by 1805 the country had been drawn into military confrontation with Napoleon's France, in Pomerania, under irresistible pressure from both Russia and England. True, Sweden itself escaped the French occupation which devastated so much of the rest of continental Europe, but, when the Treaty of Tilsit was signed in 1807, Russia suddenly switched sides and allied itself with France. Suddenly isolated to the south and east, Sweden was powerless to prevent Pomerania from being rapidly occupied by Napoleonic troops. Even worse, Russia took advantage of the situation in February 1808, when some 24,000 Russian soldiers under the Livonian General Friedrich Wilhelm von Buxhoevden invaded it. Swedish forces, only 16,000 in strength, resisted under Wilhelm Maurtiz Klingspor (1744–1814), but to little avail, as the arrival of reinforcements was hindered by the frozen seas of the Baltic. While Sweden still avoided occupation by French troops, an attack by Denmark, allied with France, on Sweden's southern and western flanks, in Scania and along the Norwegian frontier, was highly threatening and few reinforcements could be spared. Although the British navy provided assistance, enabling Swedish troops in Finland to retire north-westwards to Ostrobothnia, to await the spring and a renewed southern offensive, an unexpected disaster occurred: the Sveaborg Fortress, in which 7,000 men under the command of Carl Olof Cronstedt (1756–1820) were stationed to protect Helsinki, suddenly capitulated. This was a major blow and, despite Swedish victories at Lappo, in Ostrobothnia, and Virta Bro, in Savo, the Russians gained the upper hand in Finland. The situation worsened further in early 1809, when the southern coastal areas of Finland were also attacked. With a military victory in the offing, Russia's Tsar Alexander I then compelled a convocation of the Finnish estates at Porvoo (Borgå in Swedish) in March of that year. There, they were obliged to accept him as their grand duke, albeit with the proviso that he would respect the grand duchy's internal autonomy. The peace treaty was signed in Hamina (Fredrikshamn in Swedish) on 17 September 1809 and the cession of Finland to Russia by Sweden became an irreversible *fait accompli*. While vast tracts of territory were thereby lost, the age-old friction along the eastern frontier, which had made Russia Sweden's hereditary enemy for centuries, was also now vastly lessened and no further wars were waged by Sweden with its erstwhile enemy.

At the time, however, traumatised by the debacle through which one third of Swedish territory was now suddenly lost and already at odds with the king, a number of Swedish military officers came together to foment a *coup d'état*, with Colonel Carl Johan Adlercreutz (1759–1815), a native of Nyland, in Finland, at their helm. They arrested Gustaf IV Adolph and declared him deposed. His uncle Duke Karl then resumed the regency of Sweden and, on 6 June 1809, a new political order was established: royal absolutism, as it had been functioning since Gustaf III's *coup-d'état*, was set aside and the old regent was elected as King Karl XIII. Though the new king was confirmed in his right to wage war and make peace, the authority of the Council of State had once again been established and strengthened. Moreover, the *Riksdag*, by formally disinheriting the descendants of the deposed Gustaf IV Adolph – sent off into exile, where he eventually died at St Gallen, in Switzerland – further bolstered the new order. But as for Finland, its loss could not be made good.

Since Karl XIII was by now an elderly man, with no legitimate offspring, the Danish prince Christian August von Augustenborg was adopted by him and chosen as heir apparent. However, this heir's sudden early death in 1810, though of natural causes, was viewed suspiciously by many Swedes, especially in the capital, and led to a popular uproar in Stockholm as his funeral cortège proceeded there. State Marshal Axel von Fersen the Younger (1755–1810), an intimate of Queen Marie Antoinette in his younger days and closely associated with the unpopular and deposed Gustaf IV Adolph, was seized from his carriage while travelling in the funeral cortège and murdered. While the mob was eventually calmed, it became incumbent on the king to select a new heir. This time the choice was the French former Napoleonic marshal Jean Baptiste Bernadotte (1763–1844). Famed as a warrior, it was vainly hoped that he would be in a position to assist in the reconquest of Finland and otherwise improve the country's military status. While peace with Denmark and France was successfully made that year, the reconquest of Finland was never realised. For the new king, seeing Russia as a necessary ally rather than as an enemy, abandoned the grand duchy to the Tsar and focused his sights instead on a future conquest of Norway. A central feature of the so-called 'politics of 1812', which this involved, was the meeting in Turku of Bernadotte with the Russian Tsar Alexander I. In consequence, Sweden became allied with its erstwhile enemy Russia, while confirming Bernadotte's status as heir to the Swedish throne, under the name Karl Johan.

When in 1812, France attacked Russia, Bernadotte broke with France and assisted in the defeat of Napoleon at the Battle of Leipzig. He also marched into the Danish-ruled duchies of Schleswig and Holstein and from that position of strength pressured Denmark to cede Norway to Sweden, an action confirmed by the Treaty of Kiel in 1814. After a series of military campaigns and ensuing negotiations in Norway, which clearly preferred a Danish prince to rule it, the crown of Norway was given to Karl Johan. True, the country was granted its own constitution and domestic political autonomy, in a new loose union with Sweden, but this remained highly unpopular. Yet if the Congress of Vienna, which decided upon the post-war settlement in Europe as a whole, had confirmed this new acquisition, seemingly advantageous to Sweden, it also saw to it that Sweden lost its north German territories and in this new settlement with respect to them Prussia was the winner.

Their transfer to largely Prussian control was deeply lamented by many both at home in the old Swedish realm and abroad, but by none more so than the German artist Caspar David Friedrich (1774–1840), who had been born under Swedish sovereignty. A native of Greifswald, in Swedish Pomerania, he was profoundly influenced by Pietism, which emanated, as we have seen, from both Germany and Sweden, and was more lasting than Sweden's political legacy. Already, in his powerful Tetschen altarpiece, *Cross in the Mountains* (1807), painted during the height of the Napoleonic Wars, Sweden is directly invoked, by its dedication to King Gustaf IV Adolph, and the painting is full of symbolism, rich in Swedish references. In another work, he depicts his own young son Gustaf, named in honour of the Swedish king he so admired, as an ardent Lutheran, waving a Swedish flag. Most noticeably, though, it was the fascination that the Swedish mystic Swedenborg exerted upon him, through his philosophical writings rather than any political message, which was central to Swedish influence upon him. This aspect is most obvious in those of Friedrich's landscape paintings that are infused with a plethora of mystical references. As Friedrich himself wrote, fully aware of this fact, 'The painter should not paint merely what he sees in front of him, but also what he sees within himself. If he sees nothing within, he should not paint what he sees before him . . .' Yet such spiritual overtones as these, while powerful in themselves, had little political resonance. Rather, they were the final vestiges of what now remained of Sweden's almost two-century-long presence in the region.

With the death of Karl XIII in 1818, the dynasty of the Holstein-Gottorps was brought to an end in Sweden. In its place, Jean Baptiste Bernadotte ascended the throne as King Karl XIV Johan. Like Gustaf III before him, the new king also took an interest in the arts and architecture, but in less grandiose terms and in a rather more practical way. For his principal intention, thereby, was to bolster his own new dynasty, by dressing it up in allegorical contexts beneficial to himself, rich in historical symbolism. Like Gustaf III, too, he was taken by the sculptor Sergel. Indeed, already as crown prince, he had visited the aged neo-classicist in his atelier in 1810. Eight years later, though, after his accession to the throne, he altered his stylistic focus. Contributing 10,000 *riksdalers* to the Free Academy of Arts, as the old Academy for Artists and Sculptors had been rechristened shortly after he became king, he now turned to French rather than Italian prototypes. He and his consort, Queen Desideria, were, of course, French and both were deeply imbued with French culture. That said, the European rage for emulating the decorative features of the Palace of Malmaison, the Empress Josephine's residence outside Paris, designed by Charles Percier and Pierre-François-Léonard Fontaine, had now reached Sweden. The richness of its political symbolism and philosophical expressiveness seemed an ideal means for the conveyance of values the new Swedish king wished to stress. Therefore, Karl Johan's new Palace of Rosendal, at the Royal Deer Park just outside Stockholm, built by the Swedish architect Fredrik Blom (1781–1853), took its inspiration from Malmaison when it was built in the years 1824–31. The king took such a keen interest in the building's construction that he supervised many aspects of the work himself. These eventually came to combine neo-classical, Gothic and old Norse elements. Their eclectic mix enabled Karl Johan to associate himself not only with the ancient classical allegories of Greece and Rome, but with native Nordic ones as well. For example, in the library, a sculpture of the Roman Cicero was

10 Sculpture of King Karl Johan as Mars (1816), by Johan Niklas Byström, Skokloster Palace. As the founder of a new dynasty, which still reigns over Sweden today, the former French Napoleonic Marshal Jean Baptise Bernadotte (1763–1844), who as king took the name Karl Johan, was keen to associate himself with the classical and Norse gods and heroes which informed so much of northern European culture at that time. Allegorical allusions in the sculpture, painting and architecture he commissioned provided the means to accomplish this.

placed beside that of the Norse god Heimdal, in his role as the father of humankind. Similarly, the sculptural decorations in the Red Salon included not only Marius and Sulla, founders of the Roman state, but the Norse god Odin, a symbol of militaristic might, and a figure with whom Napoleon's former marshal liked to see himself identified. Sculptors like Johan Niklas Byström, whose mighty sculpture *Karl Johan as Mars* (1816) came to embellish Skokloster Castle, or Bengt Erland Fogelberg, creator of *Odin*, now came to the fore. Both had been deeply influenced by the Swedish poet Erik Gustaf Geijer (1783–1847), a pivotal figure who served as professor of history at Uppsala University, to associate Gothic forms with Norse mythology. In this he was aided by Per Henrik Ling (1776–1839), the so-called 'father of Swedish athletics', whose *Symbols of the Eddas* was another important book which helped to foster a nineteenth-century Scandinavian identity, as distinct from that of the classically inspired Mediterranean world.

Karl Johan also saw to it that Norway, over which he was also now king by virtue of the Napoleonic settlement, was similarly suitably embellished. He commissioned the building of the Royal Palace in the capital Christiania (now Oslo), on a height below which an avenue, appositely christened Karl Johan Street, was laid out during the 1820s. At the same time, in Sweden, he was involved in the construction of Sweden's greatest library, Carolina Rediviva, at Uppsala University, on a site already chosen by the king for that purpose while crown prince in 1812. These remain as important monuments not only to Karl Johan's architectural and aesthetic tastes, but to his own political and social vision. This he was able to marry to the new consciousness of 'Swedishness', as inspired by the literary and artistic fashion of Romanticism, which was something novel at the time, when many of the king's subjects first began to see themselves as citizens, rather than subjects, with an active civic role to play in societal terms and politically.

Karl Johan's most important legacy to Sweden, however, was not in this regard but another: his adoption of political neutrality. This concept had had no basis in international law, as was the case with Switzerland's neutrality confirmed as it was by the Congress of Vienna after 1815, or Belgium's after 1830. Rather it was owing to the king's own initiative and its constant maintenance. Indeed, in 1834, he issued a memorandum confirming the 'strict and independent neutrality' he had laid down for his adopted country on his accession to the throne. His son and successor, Oscar I, later followed by his son, Karl XV, it is true, were less than enamoured by this stance. Yet many members of his government, as well as public opinion, supported him and obliged its maintenance. This was true even then, when the demands of solidarity with the rising tide of Pan-Scandinavianism, a movement popular among students and intellectuals that sought politically to unite the Nordic countries, seemed to auger its demise in the revolutionary years of the late 1840s and beyond. Yet its durability proved long lasting and it has continued in force until our own day.

ECONOMIC DEVELOPMENTS

During the decades following the end of the Napoleonic Wars, Sweden remained an overwhelmingly agricultural society. The revolution in agriculture which had commenced in the middle of the previous century in the country had brought major social upheavals but even these had now largely resolved themselves. In any case, in 1827, new laws, the so-called *laga skifte*, in part motivated by continued overpopulation in rural areas, had concluded the consolidation of disjointed agricultural land into larger units. This required farmers even in remote areas, which had not as yet been encompassed by previous laws, to leave their village homes and to resettle in the midst of the land they cultivated, thereby improving efficiency. In consequence of this and the other changes taking place in the countryside, the old village corporate forms according to which agricultural production had been organised became obsolete, replaced by new capitalist ones.

Efficiency and productivity became the bywords, encouraging those in government circles to investigate and then introduce the latest technological developments, in both agriculture and industry. These, it was felt, would provide keys to the development of Sweden's economy, both rural and urban. In 1801, therefore, the government had sent Abraham Niclas Edelcrantz (1754–1821), civil servant and theatre director, abroad to acquire insights into new technology coming to the fore and into how it might be applied in Sweden. As a result of this initiative, he brought back a new improved optical telegraph, first developed by the Frenchman Claude Choppe, along with four steam engines, invented by the Scot James Watt. These latter were immediately set to practical use: one soon provided energy for a textile mill at Lidingö, a suburb of Stockholm. Two others were used to provide power for distilleries elsewhere in the capital, while the forth produced energy for a mine in Dannemora.

Samuel Owen (1774–1854), also British-born (and a committed Methodist), who had worked with Watt and had recently arrived in Sweden, also provided assistance. Settling in Stockholm, Owen ordered a fifth engine to power a mill on Kungsholmen, in the capital. By the 1830s and 1840s, a plethora of cotton mills powered in this way were thriving in a range of Swedish cities, including Norrköping, Gothenburg and Borås. These depended on cotton, imported until the advent of the Civil War in the United States in 1861, from the slave states of the Deep South.

Wider Jewish immigration now also came to be encouraged, as a means of bringing the requisite wealth and business skills required into the country. Many settled in Norrköping, Gothenburg and Stockholm. Some of the new arrivals were the sons of prosperous Jewish families established in Germany, often from the former Swedish territories in Hither Pomerania, as well as neighbouring Mecklenburg. By 1815, some 800 Jews had become residents in Sweden. Their business and trading acumen, especially in textiles, proved so beneficial to the country's economy that they were gradually granted greater rights and, by 1838, most restrictions on them had been lifted.

The paper industry also enjoyed a period of dramatic development at this time. New industrial machines were introduced in the early nineteenth century, based on those invented by Nicholas-Louis Robert in France in 1799, improving quality, lowering costs and increasing the quantity of production. In consequence, sparsely populated but richly wooded Norrland became a new frontier for the enterprising towards the end of the period, and attracted many people to that industry.

Improvements in transport were also taking place, which exerted a major effect upon the economy. In particular, the construction of canals during this period dramatically facilitated the transport of goods from the Swedish interior to the coast and from one side of the country to the other. The Södertälje Canal, begun in 1806, was completed in 1819, the Hjälmare Canal in 1830 and, most importantly, the Göta Canal, in 1832. The plan of the latter was masterminded by the Scottish civil engineer

11 *The opening of the Göta Canal on 26 September 1832* (1832), by Johan Christian Berger, oil on canvas. The early nineteenth century was the great age of European canal building, and the Göta Canal was a major industrial undertaking which successfully linked Sweden's east and west coasts, thereby opening up the Swedish interior and cutting back more lengthy and costly transport by sea. However, its usefulness was undercut by the long Swedish winter, during which the canal froze, and the arrival of the railway. Nationalmuseum, Stockholm.

Thomas Telford and based upon British prototypes. Linking
Sweden's North Sea coast with the Baltic, along a route running
west to east for some 347 miles, its construction was accomplished by more than 6,500 soldiers, labouring under the direction of Field Marshal Baltzar von Platen (1766–1829), former
governor general of Swedish Pomerania and later governor of
Norway. It took more than forty years to complete and was
only accomplished after von Platen's death. By then, though, it
had proved to be somewhat of a white elephant, for not only did
the fact that its waters were frozen for at least a third of the year
diminish its efficacy, but the arrival of the railways in Sweden not
long thereafter provided a far cheaper and more efficient alternative form of year-round transport.

It was the railways which really served to open up the Swedish
hinterland and the new urban areas which grew up along the
railway developed dramatically. That said, Stockholm proved to
be the principal beneficiary, attracting, as it did, large numbers of
working people from the countryside. Even as early as 1815, some
years before the arrival of the railways, it boasted a population of
some 100,000, making it similar in size to Copenhagen, and thus
one of Scandinavia's two most populous metropolitan areas, as
well as the largest in Sweden. Yet this newly won prominence
depended on good transport to ensure its growth and prosperity
and this relied to a large degree on significant infrastructural
improvements. For without a constant flow of labouring people
to the capital, its population, undermined by the city's poor
hygiene, insalubrious circumstances and poor natality rates,
would not have been able to sustain itself. Yet sustain itself it did
and with its ever growing working population, new problems were
created requiring new solutions. Strains appeared, to a signficant
degree, because of the inability of ancient economic and social
structures to adapt to the new needs and demands of the industrial
era. Thus, not only in the capital, but in many other urban areas,
such age-old socio-economic structures as the craft guilds and
feudal corporations, unable as they were to absorb those who
were now arriving, became obstacles and, in consequence, were
ultimately abolished, leading to the development of a more open
market economy.

HEALTH AND HYGIENE

A similarly methodical approach as that taken to improve transport and technological development was also initiated to enhance public health. As a result of its effectiveness, important inroads now began to be made to reduce the incidence of disease. British treatises on what initiatives were most effective in improving health and hygiene now aroused considerable interest in Sweden, in both administrative and academic circles. In consequence, new measures were now taken based on the latest medical theories. As we have seen, without doubt the most important event in Sweden in this regard at that time had been the introduction of vaccination against smallpox in 1801. Until that time, the fate of many victims was sealed, not only by the deadly effects of the disease itself, but by the fears which it aroused. For example, that same year, a physician practising in Torneå, in Lapland, had written, 'In the beginning of an epidemic, several Saami families move over to Norway, and it is not rare for them to leave the old people at home and drop those relatives infected on the way, abandoning them to their unfortunate destiny.' Indeed, not only were distant relations given over to a certain death but husbands, wives and children as well.

By the second decade of the nineteenth century, though, the implementation of vaccination, which was now legally obligatory, became so widespread that the rates of infection by smallpox fell dramatically. Thus, whereas in the 1790s some 41,000 Swedes had died from the disease during the epidemics of that decade, by the second decade of the nineteenth century the death toll had fallen by more than 90 per cent, according to church records of the time. By the 1820s, in fact, no less than three-quarters of Swedish children had been vaccinated, a remarkable accomplishment in comparison with its implementation in other European countries at the time. That said, not all regions of the country benefited from it in equal measure. In far-flung Lapland, vaccination was introduced first in the 1820s, much later than elsewhere. However, here its inroads were less dramatic, since mortality rates from the disease had been falling over the previous decades even without its implementation, for reasons still not understood.

After the fall of absolutism in 1809, and the emergence of a civil society increasingly founded on citizenship, a wide range of initiatives were taken, many continuing to be based on British models, to improve other aspects of the country's health and medical care. As a result, during the course of the nineteenth century, a plethora of new hospitals came to be built. This trend was in line with the growing centralisation of the Swedish state bureaucracy as a whole, and so new hospital construction encouraged large institutions near major cities, in place of the smaller ones which had previously been dispersed throughout Sweden. Ulleråker Hospital, for example, by Uppsala, from the 1830s took patients from as far away as Västerås and beyond, treating them more efficiently, as well as cost effectively.

Reforms in treatment and care were also being introduced at this time, under the influence of such international reformers as the Frenchman Philippe Pinel, chief physician at the mental asylum of Bicêtre, in France. In particular, his *Traité médico-philosophique de l'aliénation mentale; ou la manie* (Medico-Philosophical Treatise on Mental Alienation or Mania), published in 1801, exerted enormous influence, encouraging as it did the need to cure, rather than merely contain, the mentally ill. As a result of his campaign, sightseers were no longer permitted to visit mental asylums to gawk at the patients as a form of entertainment, and hospitals, such as that at Danvik, by Stockholm, underwent major renovations in the 1820s, so as to provide more space per patient.

New hospitals were also constructed. The garrison hospital at Hantverkargatan, in Stockholm, was built by the highly innovative architect Carl Christoffer Gjörwell the Younger (1766–1837), according to 'rationalist' principles, which placed rooms and wards on either side of a central corridor, tucked behind a façade decorated by a wide central portico of Doric half-pillars. Opening its doors in 1834, it became a model of its time and remained in use until 1969.

If the incidence of smallpox was in sharp decline, other age-old diseases persisted in Sweden. In its marshy coastal districts, in particular its south-eastern marsh-ridden coastland, malaria was endemic from time immemorial, infecting tens of thousands of people each year, often leaving them debilitated when the more obvious symptoms of the disease itself had temporarily abated. Still, its visitations in Sweden were mild compared with its effects relative to the size of population in the Swedish Caribbean colony of St Barthélemy and where mortality from it and other tropical fevers was extraordinarily high. Indeed, of the thirty-three Swedish men who arrived to settle in the colony between 1805 and 1815, twenty-nine had died by the end of that period, largely in consequence of malaria. Even more acute was yellow fever, carried in periodically by ships to the port of its capital, Gustavia, with especially devastating consequences for the inhabitants, in particular those of European background, with little genetic resistance.

The disease also raised fears in Sweden itself. After news of the outbreak of yellow fever in northern ports like Boston, in the United States, reached Gothenburg, measures were taken to prevent a visitation there. A special quarantine station was set up at Känsö, in Gothenburg's archipelago, in 1834, to which ships from the Spanish Main carrying salt for use in curing Swedish herring were diverted when epidemics from there threatened. Fortunately, yellow fever never broke out in Sweden, but an equally serious new contagion did: cholera.

Cholera first arrived in Sweden by ship in 1834. Gothenburg fell victim first, 10 per cent of its population dying of the disease in a matter of months. Stockholm fell victim shortly thereafter, but was more fortunate, with a mortality rate half that of Gothenburg. Remote rural areas were largely spared. Nevertheless, despite the erection of twelve temporary hospitals to deal with the victims, more than 12,000 people died of the contagion during this epidemic in Sweden. Cholera abated in the autumn but in 1850, it once again broke out there, ravaging a spate of port cities, though leaving the countryside, yet again, relatively unaffected. Its presence made clear the need for improved sanitation in urban areas and prompted the widespread construction of sewers, the introduction of piped water supplies from sanitary sources and a general implementation of the water closet in cities and towns. As a result of these improvements, later epidemics, which ravaged Russia and Germany across the Baltic, made no further inroads in Sweden.

Venereal infections were also a major problem in Sweden, especially after the conclusion of the Napoleonic Wars, exacerbated by soldiers and sailors who returned home infected by such diseases. Syphilis, in particular, had become a serious problem and to deal with its long-term effects, many clinics were established throughout the country, financed by a special tax introduced for that purpose in 1815.

That said, improvements in diet in Sweden in the following decades helped to foster better resistance to a wide range of ailments. The potato crop, in particular, proved to be a boon to farmers during this period, providing as it did better nutrition for much of the rural poor than had previously been available, especially during the winter months. During the Napoleonic Wars, potatoes were considered a good substitute for corn, the import of which had been made difficult by the British blockade during the years 1807–14. That alcohol could legally be distilled from them from 1816 was merely an added bonus.

GRADUAL RELAXATION OF RESTRICTIONS ON WOMEN

While increased transport links threatened Sweden with the arrival of epidemic diseases, both old and new to its shores, they also brought new benefits in their wake, not least greater opportunities of employment. Indeed, the freedom of women to direct their own lives and seek gainful labour where they wanted also depended on improved transportation. The introduction of steamboats to Sweden facilitated both travel and migration after the introduction of regular timetables in the 1820s. These were both national and international in scope: in 1836, a regular service was introduced linking Stockholm with other Baltic ports. Significant too was the relaxation of the Poor Laws in the 1840s, which removed restrictions on the changing of residence, which thereby encouraged a massive influx of working people to urban areas where a wide range of job opportunities were available. More specifically, their removal enabled many women to seek work away from home, in domestic service, factory work or even prostitution.

A relaxation of social mores was also taking place, in particular in urban areas and colonial settlements. In St Barthélemy, where European women were a small minority of the population, concubinage, almost invariably involving black or mixed-race women, became the order of the day. The local Catholic priest from the Church of Our Lady of the Assumption, built in 1829 to serve the needs of the now majority Catholic community, opposed this state of affairs but to no avail. As Robert Montgomery, a favourite of Gustaf III who had been exiled there for his part in the Anjala Mutiny, put it in his diary, everyone had advised him of the necessity of taking a Negro woman, to preserve his health in the hot and languid climate. Yet even for those in the colony keen to marry, the logistics of the situation created their own problems, since priests were not always available to perform the services. Indeed, the absence of a priest during the 1820s led many unmarried couples to set up house together notwithstanding and the governor saw fit to introduce a form of civil marriage to compensate for the lack of matrimonial regularity there.

ECONOMIC COLLAPSE IN ST BARTHÉLEMY

With the end of the Napoleonic Wars, the fortuitous circumstances which had enabled Sweden's Caribbean colony to thrive suddenly disappeared. This was to a considerable degree a result of the fact that the British, French and Dutch ports, which had been hampered by the conflict, now resumed their mercantile activities, taking away custom from St Barthélemy. Other problems also beset the colony, for the prices of both sugar and cotton plunged, not only on St Barthélemy but elsewhere in the region as part of a general Caribbean collapse, as new and cheaper markets opened up in other parts of the world. Many slaves starved in the famine of 1817 and, although there was trade with the Spanish colonies of the Caribbean littoral after 1818, the neighbouring Danish colony of St Croix and St Thomas now also succeeded in capturing much of St Barthélemy's former custom.

That said, there were some positive developments in the colony. In the years which followed, for example, a printing press was imported and the regular publication of a newspaper commenced. Nonetheless, continued economic decline led the government in Sweden to contemplate the sale of both St Barthélemy and St Martin, but no significant moves were made to accomplish this and the dwindling of trade continued unabated, especially after the middle of the 1820s: whereas 150 bales of cotton had been exported in 1825, only 80 were exported in 1826. Matters worsened further as epidemics and hurricanes devastated the colony. The great hurricane of 1834 destroyed more than two hundred houses in St Barthélemy alone and killed over forty residents. New economic ventures were also unsuccessful: the establishment of vineyards, with vines imported from Madeira, also proved a failure. In consequence, the colony languished over the following decades, as an ever-increasing torpor, economic, political and social, settled over it.

The organisation of life in St Barthélemy was typical of that else-where in the Caribbean, but radically unlike that in Sweden itself, with its exclusively European ethnic makeup. For in the colony, racial distinctions usually determined an individual's legal status. The principle was simple: anyone of African or mixed descent was considered a slave, unless in possession of special papers declaring him or her free. Therefore, the following notice was typical of the time and place: it concerned one black boy, Richard Crump, who was to be sold by public auction in 1815, 'for the benefit of the King, if not claimed or his freedom legally proved within Three Months from this date'.

THE CHURCH

This 'peculiar institution' of slavery in the Caribbean was accepted by the Lutheran Church of Sweden (as well as the Catholic and Anglican churches) as tolerable, provided it functioned in a morally responsible way, informed by enlightened values. While today this approach seems to be a contradiction of the meaning of enlighten-ment, this was by no means the case at the time. At home in Sweden, during the 1820s, much of the clergy increasingly saw its role in society as one of enlightenment, both spiritual and temporal, but this was not enlightenment in any modern liberal sense. Rather it was a stress on spiritual clarity and a recognition of the obligations this entailed. No clergyman was more central to this mission than Esaias Tegnér (1782–1846). Professor of classics at Lund University, he disdained mysticism, taking instead inspiration from the eighteenth-century German neo-classical theorist and aesthetician Johan Joachim Winckelmann. Made Bishop of Växjö in 1824, he rejected the Gothic as a bleak and superstitious architectural vestige and en-deavoured to ensure that Swedish churches became bright and airy places, with wide windows to let in the light, sometimes, in his zeal, advocating the destruction of ancient churches to make way for what some called 'barns' in the process. Much of his own copious writings reflected his beliefs, but his most renowned work, *Frithiofs saga*, published in 1825, is a romantic epic which draws inspiration from the Icelandic sagas, but is infused with Christian metaphysics.

Many ecclesiastical figures at this time now came to take a more aggressive approach to combat social ills. The reduction of alcoholism, perennially a plague in Sweden and an especially severe problem in Norrland, was high on their agenda and to this end a variety of temperance movements were now initiated. One of the most important of such movements was that led by Lars Levi Læstadius (1800–61), a missionary to the Saami (some of which ancestry he possessed himself) and vicar of Karesuando, on the Muonio River by the Finnish–Swedish border. Læstadius shared many of the values of the more evangelical wing of the Swedish Church and it was this wing which achieved the greatest popularity in the north, especially in conjunction with the advocating of temperance.

In the south, by contrast, a more sacramentally focused 'high church' wing came to the fore, based in the episcopal and university city of Lund. Led by the priest Henrik Schartau (1757–1825), it encouraged a rich ceremonial for services of worship and a more positive re-evaluation of the Catholic roots of the Church than had previously been the case. Yet others sought to find a middle ground, merging aspects of both traditions. In this, Archbishop Johan Olof Wallin (1779–1839), played a major role, using his highly esteemed Psalm Book of 1819 to draw on the strengths of both traditions. Though conflicts between the two wings of the Lutheran Church persisted, with Uppsala the *hochburg* of the evangelical wing and Lund that of the 'high church', the former was increasingly gaining the upper hand. In this they were aided by an increasingly well-organised missionary movement, which sought to spread its gospel-based message, not only throughout a grass-roots Swedish population but to the far-flung corners of the world.

While many Swedish missionaries were now carrying their faith to Africa and China, new religious movements came to Sweden from abroad. Methodism, imported from Great Britain, spread throughout much of the country, introduced during the 1830s by the Scottish preacher George Scott. Its emphasis on temperance made it especially popular among many Swedes, even if local authorities, both spiritual and secular, remained suspicious of it as a divisive force within society.

The Baptist Church, long excluded from Sweden with the other Free Churches, with its emphasis on adult baptism, made its inroads in Sweden through the activities of American missionaries. Perceived as more revolutionary than the Methodist movement, it met with greater hostility on the part of local authorities, many of which sought to prohibit it as inimical to the Swedish state, as well as to the Swedish Church. In response to this perceived persecution, many Swedish Baptists began to emigrate to the United States. One extreme wing of this movement formed by communist evangelicals left Hälsingland for Illinois in 1846 under the fiery evangelist Erik Jansson, and others followed in their wake. Yet the greatest suspicions and hostility of both government and Church remained focused not on the more extreme branches of Protestantism, but on traditional Roman Catholicism. Thus, its practice by native Swedes remained prohibited throughout this period under threat of severe penalties, including exile and confiscation of property.

EDUCATION

After the promulgation of the Swedish Church Law of 1686, literacy had spread widely throughout the country. Britain, in particular, now came to provide a model for the extension of education among the general population. This trend strengthened after 1809, aided by the establishment of numerous societies and associations for its furtherance. That said, much of Swedish education, both formal and informal, remained vested in the hands of Swedish Lutheran clergymen and was usually privately funded. Although limited in scope in the countryside, it increasingly thrived in Stockholm. In fact, altogether there were more than a hundred such schools in the capital, most of which catered for the children of prosperous families. In the state sector, on the other hand, schools were few – only twelve in Stockholm at the same time – and these focused on subjects of a more practical nature than was the case in the private ones. Only in 1842 was state-sponsored education extended in any significant way. Thereafter, however, literacy was rapidly extended throughout the general population.

Even in its overseas colony, St Barthélemy, the development of education was encouraged. A stone school house had already been erected in the capital, Gustavia, in the first decade of the nineteenth century. However, the linguistic heterogeneity of the population, as well as the rigours of the tropical climate, eventually forced its closure and the building began to function as a gaol. Nonetheless, private education continued to be provided by monks and nuns sent to the island by the Bishop of Guadeloupe, members of whose Catholic flock most of the residents were. That said, the newly founded Swedish Missionary Society established its own schools for the children of prosperous Protestant families in the colony, one for boys and one for girls. As for the black and mulatto slave and freemen population, the Methodist Society, based in London, with its emancipationist agenda, came to provide schools for more than a hundred such children. They appear to have been effective, for the island's Governor Norderling praised them for their work, after examining the students in 1824. Nonetheless, for the majority of the population literacy was a rarity and throughout the Swedish period many slaves continued to remain excluded from education, since the acquisition of literacy by a slave, many owners feared, would lead to an increased risk of slave revolt.

LITERATURE

As the skills of reading and writing spread throughout most of the Swedish population, so literature – both histories and *belles lettres* – developed significantly at this time. The three-volume *Svenska Folkets Historia* (History of the Swedish People) (1832–6), by Erik Gustaf Geijer (1783–1847), was of especial note with its national romantic view of the Swedish people, rich in political as well as literary implications. As a young man Geijer had helped in the foundation of the *Götiska Förbundet* (Gothic Society), to the journal of which, *Iduna*, he had made numerous contributions. This sowed the seeds for a new appreciation of Sweden's historical roots.

The poet Per Daniel Amadeus Atterbom (1790–1855) also played a leading role in this new movement. Having first helped to establish

Aurora, a trend-setting society for the arts, in 1807, he became a key figure in other related initiatives, which included publication of the newspapers *Polyfem* (Polyfemus, 1809–12) and *Fosforos* (Phosphorus, 1810–13), both of which propagated the philosophical and aesthetic values of the new Romanticism. Devoting himself in particular to poetry and drama, he produced one of his most lyrical and celebrated works *Lycksalighetens Ö* (The Isle of Bliss), published as an allegory, in 1823. Appointed professor of philosophy at Uppsala University in 1828, and then of aesthetics and literature seven years later, he facilitated the introduction of much German Romantic literature of that period to the younger generation in Sweden.

Arguably, one of the period's greatest poets was Erik Johan Stagnelius (1793–1823), most acclaimed for his poetical work *Liljor i Saron* (Lilies of Sharon), which appeared in 1821, an allegory in which the human soul attempts to break the shackles of its exiled imprisonment in a world full of death and corruption. Much of his work remained unpublished until after his death. Equal in stature was Johan Ludvig Runeberg (1804–77), a Swedish-speaking Finn, who was of enormous importance in Sweden, as well as in Finland, for the idealised imagery of the Swedish-speaking rural population which his poetry from the 1830s evokes. Later, his *Fänrik Ståls Sägner* (The Tales of Ensign Stål) (1848–60), focusing on the Swedish–Russian war of 1808–9, became very popular on both sides of the Gulf of Bothnia, and was instrumental in bolstering a sense of national identity for both Swedes and Finns.

In terms of prose, it is doubtless Carl Jonas Love Almqvist (1793–1866) who achieved the greatest fame – as well as notoriety – in his lifetime as the author of *Amorina* (first published in 1822, but revised in 1839), a lyrical novel which originally focused on his belief that free will was an illusion, but which was toned down in the years that followed to enable a less controversial publication to appear. Ordained a Lutheran priest in 1837, Almqvist was obliged by the Church to relinquish his clerical office in 1841, under the accusation of immorality. Other accusations of an even graver nature surfaced later and, in 1851, he was accused of the murder of a moneylender, to whom he was in debt. In response, he fled the country, emigrating to the United States. He returned to Europe only in 1865, and then to Bremen, in Germany, rather than to Sweden, where he died the following year, having left a legacy to Swedish literature in the new focus on realism which some of his works evince, a novel development which was also encouraged by Runeberg in Finland.

Three female novelists also achieved considerable fame at this time. Among the most noted was Fredrika Bremer (1801–65), a Swedish-Finnish author who resided for most of her life in Stockholm, but journeyed, in 1849, to the United States. There she travelled extensively, even visiting Cuba, then under Spanish sovereignty, in 1851, before returning to Sweden. One of her most noted works is *Hertha eller en själs historia* (Hertha or the Story of a Soul), published in 1856, a pessimistic novel, which laments the restrictions on personal freedom many women of her time were obliged to endure. Sweden's leading women's organisation later adopted the name of the book as their own in honour of her. Another compatriot, Baroness Sophie von Knorring (1797–1848), sought the subjects of her novels in her own experience of life among the aristocracy of Sweden. *Cousinerna* (The Cousins), published in 1832, is an exceptionally insightful example of its type, although some of her later works, like *Torparen och hans omgifning* (The Cottager and his Milieu) which appeared in 1843, focused upon characters from humble backgrounds instead. Emilie Flygare-Carlén (1807–92), in her turn, took the themes of her novels from the archipelago of Bohuslän, where she resided as a child before moving to Stockholm with her family in 1839. They are full of local colour illustrative of life in the fishing villages of Sweden's south-west coast. Her novel *Rosen på Tistelön* (The Rose of the Isle of Tistel), which appeared in 1842, was among the most famous of her works on this subject and helped to make her one of the most popular and prolific authors of her time. As such, they were the first literary fruits of a growing empowerment of women which would eventually lead to their acquisition of ever greater political rights, until their complete emancipation in the early years of the following century and the final triumph of Sweden's struggle for democratic constitutionalism.

8

The industrialisation and capitalisation of Sweden

MILITARY PREPARATIONS

The middle years of the nineteenth century, a period in which the industrialisation and capitalisation of Sweden underwent a dramatic acceleration, occurred against a backdrop of pan-European military confrontation. Thus, the outbreak of the Crimean War in 1853, between Great Britain, France and the Ottoman Empire, on the one hand, and Russia on the other, was the first major test of Swedish neutrality. At first, Sweden declared itself neutral, but soon King Oskar I, with his advisers, began to see the possibility of a reacquisition of Finland in the event of an Allied victory. This was, in essence, an abrupt turning away from the 'politics of 1812', launched by his father, King Karl Johan, and Tsar Alexander I. Therefore, in 1855, Sweden confirmed the November Accord, with Britain and its allies, setting out Sweden's willingness to resist Russia in return for Allied military support. Whether the unwillingness of some members of government to give their consent could have been overcome remains a moot point. In any case, the end of the Crimean War the following year changed the political scenario before Sweden was able to take part. As a result, in 1856 only the demilitarisation of the Finnish-owned Åland (Ahvenanmaa, in Finnish) Islands, already demanded by Britain, was laid down and confirmed by the Treaty of Paris. Sovereignty remained, however, with Finland, and therefore, indirectly, with Russia, popular support on the islands for Swedish rule notwithstanding. This 'Åland Servitude', as it was called, would remain a considerable source of disgruntlement for many years to come, in Sweden as well as on the Åland Islands.

As the nineteenth century wore on, the country's continued neutrality notwithstanding, the government determined to strengthen the armed forces, now considered a defensive precaution in view of the growth in military might of the major European powers, especially Russia and Germany. In this plan, Sweden's land bridge to Finland and the east played a major role. Already, in 1887, a proposal had been made by the Chief of the Swedish General Staff, expressing the need to make Boden, in the province of Norrland, just less than seventy miles south of the Arctic Circle, a fortified bulwark against growing Russian military might in the Baltic, but this initiative was finally approved by the *Riksdag* only in 1900. Work, therefore, commenced in 1901 and the fortress came into service in 1908. Intended to ward off a land attack from the north of Finland, it was Sweden's only 'girdle fortress', that is, one in which several forts were linked together to form a massive fortification. The military was also organised more efficiently. A variety of military reforms had been enacted in 1885, and, in 1901, compulsory universal military service was finally introduced. The old *indelning* (apportionment) system, introduced in the seventeenth century, was also abolished. This had been based on the subdivision of the country into small districts, each of which supported a soldier, who, together with his comrades, formed larger and larger military units within the forces, up to the regimental level, each of which was attached to a specific geographical area.

POLITICAL REFORMS

As in the realm of defence, the later nineteenth and early twentieth century was also a time of major political reforms. Ethnic and religious minorities benefited in particular. During the 1870s, for example, the political rights of Jews in Sweden were increased, even if complete emancipation was only accomplished at the turn of the twentieth century, when they were finally granted full equal rights with other Swedish subjects, including the benefits of poor relief, previously denied those outside the state Church. A closer relationship with Denmark was also fostered in 1873, with the establishment of the Scandinavian Monetary Union, which fixed rates for the two Scandinavian currencies. Yet Sweden remained a highly traditional country in terms of its political structure. Whereas in Denmark, absolutism had been abolished in 1848 in favour of a fully parliamentary system of government, this process advanced far more slowly and gradually in Sweden. Most significant, though, was the appointment in 1876 of Sweden's first prime minister, in the modern sense of the word. He was Baron Louis De Geer (1818–96), a moderate liberal who had been justice minister from 1858 until 1870 and had played a major role in influencing public opinion to opt for governmental change. This had led, in 1867, to the *Riksdag* being re-formed as a modern bicameral parliament. Within it, during the 1870s, the new Farmers' Party rapidly came to play a leading role under the leadership of Count Arvid Posse (1820–1901), Emil Key and Carl Ifvarsson. In 1880, Posse was elected prime minister, succeeded by Carl Johan Thyselius in 1883, then O. Robert Themptander (1844–97) in 1884. However, neither the authority of the Farmers' Party, nor that of its opposition, was to remain uncontested for long.

A new political party was about to enter the political arena, one which would come to play a central role of unparalleled importance in the course of the twentieth century, up to our own day – the Social Democrats.

Its beginnings were modest. In 1885, the newspaper *The Social Democrat* was founded in Stockholm, by a tailor, August Palm, spreading its political and social message to an ever wider public among the general population. Four years later, in 1889, the Social Democratic Party was founded, supported by working men in Sweden who had become acutely aware of their collective political power. Hjalmar Branting (1860–1925), who had become the newspaper's editor-in-chief in 1886, assumed the party's leadership, a position he would continue to hold for decades until his death. The son of Professor Lars Branting, a noted figure in the movement to encourage gymnastics among the general population, Hjalmar Branting had himself studied mathematics and astronomy, before taking up work at the Astronomical Observatory of Stockholm. However, he soon became more interested in the social sciences and devoted himself to journalism, success in which rapidly propelled him to political prominence.

Economic discontent, a product of the rapidly burgeoning capitalisation of the economy, which had taken place in Sweden much later than in Britain or Germany, had served to strengthen the Social Democratic movement. This trend was especially evident in the sawmill strike, declared in Sundsvall in 1879, which served as a catalyst to the party's initial development. That said, it would take another generation before that power could be successfully harnessed in political terms, enabling Branting to be elected to Parliament in 1896. When that occurred, the creation of this unitary mass political organisation began to exert a profound effect on the formation of Swedish social self-identification, a process which led directly to the nascent development of the welfare state in the interwar years.

Divisions within the Farmers' Party had, meanwhile, also been growing, fomented to a considerable degree by the growing need, perceived by many supporters, for the introduction of protective tariffs on imports. These led to a split in the party, with independent pro-tariff supporters establishing themselves as the New Farmers' Party, under the leadership of Erik Gustaf Boström (1842–1907), and those supporting free trade as the Old Farmers' Party, headed by Carl Ifvarsson but encouraged by the king himself. When matters came to a head in Parliament, it was those in support of the tariffs who won. As a result, tariffs were imposed on the import of timber – much of it cheaply exported from Russia and the United States – and some industrial products. In 1895, though, with these matters finally resolved, the two parties remerged into a single Farmers' Party.

Attempts to encourage pan-Nordic co-operation were also failing. The exhortation of the Swedish economist Pontus Fahlbeck, in 1888, that Scandinavians should form a protectionist customs union in order to maintain their collective economic autonomy, fell on increasingly deaf ears. Even the Scandinavian Monetary Union itself was losing its *raison d'être*, as fixed rates of currency exchange became a thing of the past. Now, each of the Nordic countries had its own agenda, one in which their divergent economic interests were propelling them not only away from each other but into the arms of their major economic partners abroad.

Boström himself twice took the prime ministership, in 1891–1900 and then again in 1902–5. Yet by this time, various other political parties were also beginning to coalesce, including the

Liberals, under Karl Staaff (1860–1915), and the conservative Farmers' Alliance, under Admiral Arvid Lindman (1862–1936). In 1906, Lindman was elected prime minister and remained in office until 1911, pursuing a largely conservative agenda. That said, in 1909, voting eligibility was widened in both parliamentary and local elections.

Under the second premiership of Staaff, though, which followed, the growing discontent of wide segments of the Swedish population with the unhappy side-effects of the capitalisation of the Swedish economy led to the introduction of new measures, including the establishment, for the first time in Sweden, of state pensions, in 1913. The clouds of war, however, were now casting their shadows on Sweden, as well as on the other European states, and new issues were coming to the fore. Indeed, Staaff was obliged to resign the following year, in consequence of a hostile reaction to the so-called Farmers' March of 1914, in which many supporters of greater military expenditure, including Sved Hedin (1865–1952), the famed explorer of central Asia, went in procession to the Royal Palace, in support of King Gustaf V, who himself vociferously advocated the need to strengthen Sweden's armed forces at a time when the other major European powers seemed to be preparing themselves for a war footing. That said, militarism as such was kept at bay and the Social Democrats became the largest party in the Lower House.

Germany, the most militarised of the European states, had long been keen to acquire Sweden as an ally. The German Kaiser Wilhelm II had, after all, written in 1895 that 'all my political thoughts are concentrated upon bringing the Germanic people in the world, especially in Europe – closer together, in order to secure ourselves against the Slavic-Czech invasion, which in the highest degree threatens us all . . . Sweden-Norway is one of the principal partners in this union of German peoples.' However, such views found little resonance back in Sweden. Economic activity and transport contacts with Germany, on the other hand, were binding Sweden ever more closely to its southern neighbour. Indeed, in 1909, a regular direct ferry connection was established between the two countries, just one of a number of indications that, at least in non-political spheres, the two countries were becoming increasingly dependent upon one another and that political tensions were best avoided.

UNION CRISIS

Political tensions between the dual kingdoms of Sweden and Norway under one monarch, on the other hand, were unavoidable and increased dramatically during this period. The first serious crisis had occurred in 1884, when a struggle in Norway to achieve greater parliamentarism proceeded apace. It was victorious and, thereafter, parliamentary rule dominated the executive branch of the ministerial government in the country. But for those pursuing increased political autonomy for Norway, this was not enough. In 1891, they saw to it that the viceroyalty itself was abolished and, the following year, Norway demanded independent consular representation abroad, a reform rejected by the Swedish government. While the atmosphere of confrontation heightened in 1895, it was only in 1901 that matters really became tense, in a militaristic sense, when Norway began to fortify its borders with Sweden. For now an armed conflict seemed to loom between the two Scandinavian nations.

Relations with Germany, on the other hand, remained placid. When in 1903 Sweden finally relinquished its *de jure* sovereignty over Wismar, incorporated into Prussia for decades, it caused no stir, as the sovereignty had long ago become a legal conceit and therefore of no consequence. On the other hand, when Norway unilaterally declared its independence in 1905, the same year incidentally that the new Parliament building was opened in Stockholm, a major rift threatened to tear the Scandinavian peninsula apart. On 7 June, the Norwegian Parliament, *Stortinget*, declared Oskar II removed from the throne, in consequence of the fact that he was unable to form a Norwegian government. This action was then confirmed in a national referendum in Norway, in which an overwhelming majority of those who took part voted against the king. War now looked imminent, but the Karlstad Convention, held in September, drew both countries back from the brink. On 1 November, Norway's independence was complete and the Swedish king and government refrained from precipitous action.

Sweden had successfully avoided a military confrontation with Norway. Maintaining its almost century-old stance, it also continued to maintain its strict neutrality, vis-à-vis other European countries. As Prime Minister Boström put it in a speech in 1905, with respect to the country's foreign ministerial agenda, Sweden had 'no policy in any real sense apart from protecting its neutrality'. The capitalisation of Sweden continued uninterrupted: it was business, economic and political, as usual.

The independence of Norway might have opened up a Pandora's box internationally, unsettling the relationships of the northern European countries, especially those of Britain, Germany and Russia. However, on 23 April 1908, they too all signed treaties accepting the status quo. That said, the agreement of 1855, according to which the territorial integrity of Sweden-Norway was to be guaranteed, was set aside. To what degree the integrity of the Sound was to be maintained in times of war also remained unsettled. For it was clear that Russia would continue to agitate for a revision of the status of the Åland Islands, as an unfortified territory within the Russian Empire. This alarmed Germany, which feared that its shipments of iron ore by sea in times of conflict could be impeded when passing the islands, were they newly fortified. Britain, too, did not relish the idea and that same year, Edward VII, who had finally succeeded his mother the late Queen Victoria to the throne, made a state visit to Sweden, in an attempt to strengthen Anglo-Swedish relationships, which were somewhat damaged by Britain's support for Norway during the last Union crisis which had led to that kingdom's independence.

ECONOMIC DEVELOPMENTS

If the political life of Sweden changed dramatically during the course of the nineteenth century and into the twentieth, so, too, did its economic life under the influence of the country's growing capitalisation. In 1846, the guild system was abolished, opening up a broad range of métiers to people previously excluded. While standards of quality became more difficult to maintain, large numbers of people, many newly arrived in Sweden's urban centres, could now be absorbed to carry out a wide range of crafts and artisanal activities from which they previously would have been excluded. It was just one of many measures taken to encourage the capitalised market economy which became the hallmark of the second half of the nineteenth century in Sweden.

Baron Johan August Gripensted (1813–74) was a key figure in Sweden's economic growth during the middle years of the century and spearheaded such developments. A supporter of the plan to abolish the antiquated estates system, which was no longer responsive to the country's political or economic needs, he was appointed minister of finance in 1856. In this position, he encouraged liberal capitalistic economic policies, including free trade and the development of the railways through foreign loans, the latter, in particular, through French financing. Conservative political leaders, such as Leonard Fredrik Rääf (1786–1872) and August von Hartmansdorff (1792–1856), gathered together a staunch opposition, but it was the liberal reformers who prevailed.

By the 1860s, foreign trade was increasing significantly, with 13.6 per cent of GNP provided by exports, as opposed to 13.2 from imports. This upward spiral began to favour imports, though, and, by 1900, the percentages reversed to 17.4 and 23.4, respectively. The majority of both exports and imports went to and from Britain, no less than 56.4 per cent and 30.6 per cent, respectively, in 1874. That said, Denmark also took a significant share of the exports, 14.2 per cent that year, followed by France with 8.9 per cent and Germany with 6.2. With imports, however, Germany took second place after Britain, with 21.2 per cent of all Swedish exports going there. In particular, iron and steel were extremely valuable commodities, necessary for Germany's burgeoning heavy industry in the Ruhr. Denmark's share of this market, 18.2 per cent, was also significant, but France's share was quite modest, a mere 3.6 per cent.

Despite the continued importance of iron and steel, timber, by the 1860s, had become Sweden's most important export commodity. This had come about, in part, through the introduction of steam engines to provide energy for the sawing of wood, first utilised for this purpose at Askesta Sawmills, in Tunadal, near Sundsvall in Norrland. Indeed, timber provided no less than 40.4 per cent of Sweden's foreign trade, between 1881 and 1885. Paper and pulp contributed another 4.6 per cent during this period, but over the following decades their importance increased dramatically, rising to 17.6 per cent in the years 1911–13, while timber exports remained fairly constant.

Agriculture, like industry, was also undergoing a period of growing capitalisation and restructuring during the later decades of the nineteenth century and into the twentieth. Still employing almost half the Swedish workforce as late as 1910, it made a highly significant contribution to the productivity of the economy, with 11.7 per cent accounted for by grain exports alone. Competition from abroad, however, would ultimately prove too strong and, within twenty years, these exports declined dramatically, falling to only 0.4 per cent at the end of that period.

Mining continued to be a major industry, even if copper production had, by now, diminished dramatically. The capital for its support and development, as well as in manufacturing in general, came in large measure from Denmark and Norway, in the years 1895–1914. Iron, as we have seen, continued to be a significant export and no fewer than 75,000 tonnes of it were shipped abroad in the 1840s. Much of the iron industry was still in the hands of the Walloons who had come to Sweden in the seventeenth century, though Germans too had since made inroads in the industry. New technical innovations, introduced by Gustaf Ekman, followed in the 1850s, enabling the Swedish iron industry to develop further, becoming a leader in the manufacture of cast iron cannon balls. However, this was supplanted in the 1880s by the more efficient alternative introduction of steel for that purpose. By the first half of that decade, iron and steel, therefore, accounted for some 16.2 per cent of Sweden's foreign trade. The high-grade phosphoric iron ore fields of Gällivare and Kiruna, in particular, assumed a growing importance, the transport of these commodities made possible by new railway links to Narvik, on the coast of Norway, and Luleå, on the Gulf of Bothnia. The concession was at first undertaken by a British company, but after its liquidation the construction was carried on with financial assistance from the Swedish and Norwegian governments. It was completed in 1903. Through the development of such heavy industry in Norrland, capital intensive and often, at least in part, dependent on investment from abroad, the far north of Sweden began to enjoy an economic boom, attracting immigrants from elsewhere in Sweden and even abroad.

Industrial activity in Sweden's most northerly province provided both economic and social mobility. That said, along with skills relative to his employment, age tended to determine a worker's prospects in the industry. At the age of thirty-six, he generally became eligible to become a foreman and at fifty-six he retired. With respect to this age limit, the metal industry was unusual, since in most other branches of industry an age of retirement was not fixed.

Maritime trade also became less encumbered by traditional regulations and impositions. For example, in 1856, the Sound toll, first levied on shipping in the 1420s, was finally abolished. Swedish shipping could now ply the seas unhindered and by the advent of the First World War, the Swedish-American Shipping Line, newly founded by Dan Brostrøm, had become a serious player in international maritime transport and trade.

A new industrial dynasty now also came to the fore, one which would play a central role in the development of the Swedish economy up to our own day: the Wallenbergs. In 1856, André Oscar Wallenberg (1816–86), son of the Bishop of Linköping, established the *Enskilda Bank*, which, despite many financial vagaries, rapidly became one of Sweden's most important banking houses, a status it continued to maintain under his sons, Knut Agathon Wallenberg (1853–1938) and Marcus Wallenberg (1864–1943). It still thrives today. The Wallenbergs' financial tentacles extended far and wide. Indeed, they provided not only major funding in Sweden, but the lion's share of funding necessary for the development of Norway's hydroelectric industry, in particular, the Norsk Hydro plant at Rjukan, in Telemark, one of the world's largest, producing artificial nitrates.

Another leading industrialist was also achieving fame at home during this period, a figure whose name would ultimately become famous throughout the world: Alfred Nobel (1833–96). He invented dynamite in 1863, one of the eighty-six inventions on which he took a patent. Becoming one of Sweden's wealthiest men of industry, he was also one of the country's greatest financial benefactors. He established the Nobel Prize in order to 'be of the greatest service to humanity' in the realms of physics, chemistry, medicine, literature and peace. It was first awarded in 1901 and now, in expanded scope, Nobel Prizes have become the world's most prestigious and financially valuable awards.

Banking, too, continued to blossom and, in 1871, *Stockholms Handelsbank* was founded, later to be rechristened *Svenska*

12 *The Large Brewery* (1890), by Anders Zorn (1860–1920), oil on canvas.
Zorn was one of Sweden's greatest society portraitists but he also turned his
eye to humbler themes. His own mother had worked as a servant, while his
father was a German brewer, and he took great interest in depicting the
working life of women, thousands of whom found employment in the new
factories of Sweden during this period of burgeoning industrialisation.
Göteborgs Kulturförvaltning, Gothenburg.

Handelsbank in 1919, as its clientele became diversified throughout Sweden. It has since spread throughout the world, but is now
just one of a number of Swedish banks which have achieved global
prominence.

The textile industry also improved in efficiency and quality as new
technological developments changed its methods dramatically. The
introduction of sewing machines by *Husqvarna Viking* to Sweden in
1872 also had major social consequences for workers in the textile
industry, as many women now came to take work at factories as
seamstresses. Traditionally, seamstresses had worked at home, but
with the advent of costly machines, they increasingly carried out their
work in new, large industrial establishments, many of which were
located in Norrköping. This encouraged growing female immigration from country to town.

Sweden rapidly implemented of new technology and devices.
In 1853, gas lighting was introduced in Stockholm and the first

telegraph lines between Stockholm and Uppsala opened for public use at about the same time. In 1856, the country's first railway line, from Örebro by way of Ervalla to Nora, opened for passengers, Parliament now placing the future of the development of a railway network under the authority of a governmental committee set up for that purpose. Six years later, the railway line linking Stockholm with Gothenburg opened.

Lars Magnus Ericsson (1856–1926) founded his eponymous factory in 1876, the same year Alexander Bell was granted a patent for the invention of the telephone. At first, the factory mainly concentrated on items for the repair of the telegraph, but soon it began to produce telephones and related technology as well. Indeed, Ericsson rapidly became the world's largest provider of manual telephone exchanges, both nationally and internationally. The most important orders came from Russia and, in 1916, Ericsson installed an exchange which handled more than sixty thousand telephone lines. However, as automatic exchanges increasingly dominated the world market, Ericsson's share fell into decline.

Another pillar of engineering was Gustaf de Laval (1845–1913), who in 1878 invented the separator used in the skimming of milk, for the processing of which he established a company that same year. In industrial terms, however, it was his invention of the steam turbine engine which proved of greater significance, useful as it proved itself in a plethora of different industrial and transport contexts. In 1892, the first communal electricity works began to provide energy for Stockholm. Stockholm had become a European city of the highest technological rank and, as if symbolic of the new age, Sweden adopted the metric system, by now in use throughout most of continental Europe, as the standard system of measurement.

With the growth of large industrial organisations, unions of working people now formed to further their economic, social and political interests. In 1886, the Typographers' Union was established, the first of such nationwide organisations, and others in a plethora of industries soon thereafter followed suit. At this stage, they maintain a low profile, avoiding the more aggressive and confrontational stance that they would later adopt, though it served to undermine their position in the public eye, after the turn of the century.

By the early years of the twentieth century, new industrial initiatives further swelled the ranks of those employed in large-scale, highly capitalised, industrial complexes. One such new industrial firm was the AGA Company, or *AB Gasacumulator*, the establishment of which was assisted by Gustaf Dalén (1869–1937) in 1904. A man of immense stature in the scientific world of Sweden at this time, Dalén was awarded the Nobel Prize for physics in 1912. Among his major inventions, that of the sun-valve was particularly useful, enabling a beacon to light up automatically at dusk and extinguish itself at dawn, thereby permitting lighthouses to function for a year without the need for personnel on site to run them. His research on acetylene gas and its industrial applications was also of great import, but an accident during one of his experiments in which a gas accumulator exploded left him blinded. Nonetheless, he assumed the direction of AGA in 1909 and continued to lead the company throughout the early decades of the twentieth century until his death in 1937. By then the company had become famous for its low-energy coke-fired stoves – they were first produced in 1929 – which could run for a full day unattended. Today their production has shifted abroad and they are far more popular in Britain and America than in Sweden.

Further initiatives were also undertaken to broader Sweden's range of economic partners abroad. In 1906, for example, the Wallenberg family sent a delegation to Japan to explore new possibilities for trade. Various endeavours were also initiated with China, facilitated by the continuation of its Open Door Policy, which encouraged foreign investment there by granting all countries the same industrial and commercial rights.

Towards the end of the first decade of the new century, the trade unions, now highly politicised and overconfident in their newly won strength, attempted to flex their muscles. This resulted in the Great Strike of 1909, in which a general stoppage organised by the unions attempted to intimidate the Employers' Union. However, it proved a paper tiger, not only in that the action was unable to grasp any further material benefits for union members, but in that it lost the unions a huge number of members, since more than half the previous membership resigned in consequence of its failure. At least in the short term, the trade unions in Sweden suffered severely in the aftermath.

AGRICULTURAL DEVELOPMENTS

In 1864, entail on many noble estates, which had previously pre-cluded their sale to commoners, was finally abolished. This had considerable implications for agriculture and reflected not only deep-seated political changes but a growing impoverishment of rural areas. For, as agricultural produce from North and South America, as well as Asia, flooded the world market, the rural agricultural market, not only in Sweden, but in many other European countries, slumped. In consequence, many landowners departed to Stockholm and other cities, where alternative business opportunities beckoned, as trade and industry in the capital grew in scope.

Crofters remained among the poorest of the agricultural popula-tion and their numbers stayed fairly constant throughout the second half of the nineteenth century and into the twentieth. That said, a major increase in migration from country to town now occurred, as more and more people sought work in urban areas. The painting *The Outskirts of the City* (1899), by the socially conscious Swedish artist Eugène Jansson (1862–1915), was just one of a number of artistic expressions of Sweden's new unsightly tenement blocks, burgeoning like toadstools on the peripheries of old city centres, in which large families, many recently arrived from the countryside, lived in tiny flats into which little air and light penetrated.

MIGRATION

With major changes in agriculture and the growth of railway trans-port, increasingly large numbers of people, both individuals and families, took even greater advantage of the opportunities to migrate internally in Sweden, as well as abroad, than had previously been the case. While Stockholm continued to benefit most, provincial cities and market towns also grew significantly in size. For example, Uppsala, the archiepiscopal and academic seat, grew from about five thousand inhabitants early in the nineteenth century to more than fifteen thousand by 1900.

Much migration within Sweden was seasonal. During the months when agricultural work was at a minimum, many labourers moved to cities and towns, where work was usually available, or became coastal fishermen during these periods. The latter was especially true of the Saami who frequently migrated to the Arctic coast of Norway to work seasonally as fishermen. Sawmills attracted many seasonal labourers, not only Swedes but large numbers of migrant workers from abroad, who were accommodated during their period of employment in huge dormitories, where drink and violence often created their own problems. The most notorious migrant population in Sweden, however, was the gypsies. Poor and with a reputation for violence and theft, they became the focus of new laws passed to restrict their movements and conduct. Yet their labour was often of benefit to the society in which they lived: many assisted with the harvesting of crops, in particular hops, where local labour was scarce. Many also provided useful services as tinkers, while others maintained stalls at spring and winter fairs throughout the country, so that the policies to deal with them were often contradictory in their application.

The vagaries of Sweden's severe climate also extorted a human toll. During the periods of famine it helped to create, and especially in the third quarter of the nineteenth century, many Swedes emigrated abroad, in particular to the United States, where an abundance of land offered to settlers by the American government proved an attraction which many enterprising people, otherwise constrained by more limited opportunities at home, could not resist. Indeed, during the course of the following century, the Swedish population of America would even come to supersede that of Sweden itself.

CHURCH TOWNS

In order better to serve Sweden's burgeoning population and the economic development which fostered it, the Swedish Church during this period also enjoyed a period of expansion, both organisationally and architecturally, as new parishes came to be created and churches built, especially in the north of the country. Already, earlier in the century, church towns had come into being in major cities all along the coast of the Gulf of Bothnia, where worshippers could come and stay the night before services, in special cabins constructed for that purpose. This was in response to the demands the Swedish Church made on its members. Those living within ten kilometres of the church were usually obliged to attend weekly, those between ten and thirty kilometres, every second week, those yet more distant, every third week, as well as feast days. The most important of such towns was Luleå, in Norrland, the origins of which went back to the Middle Ages. Its significance was not only spiritual, but economic and social, as it grew dramatically in size during the course of the nineteenth century. Trade, in particular, flourished there and on Saturdays young parishioners frequently used the occasion as a marriage market. In the middle of the nineteenth century, it was not unusual on the eve of feast days for three hundred young men and women to attend a single dance, held in the town's assembly room or outdoors. So with the population of Luleå burgeoning, further physical expansion became an even greater necessity. Whereas twenty-one new churches had been built in the early nineteenth century in the newly established parish of Övreluleå, which became a veritable suburb to old Luleå, the number had grown to forty by the end of the century and seventy-six some fifty years later.

GROWING ECUMENICISM

Other so-called Free Churches, as distinguished from the established Church of Sweden, also increased their scope. The Baptist Church, long excluded from Sweden with other Free Churches owing to its unorthodox emphasis on adult baptism, finally succeeded in establishing itself there in 1848. In 1876, Methodism also achieved governmental recognition, even if many local leaders in government and the Lutheran Church itself remained aloof. Although George Scott, who had introduced the sect to Sweden, had since returned home, Swedes, like Carl Olof Rosenius (1816–68), now took on his mantle, albeit with an increasingly nationalist component. Rosenius's form of Methodism became especially popular in Norrland, where he went on to establish the *Evangeliska Fosterlandsstiftelse* (Evangelical Fatherland Foundation), within the confines of the Lutheran Church, in the middle years of the century.

The establishment of the *Svenska Missionsförbund* (Swedish Missionary Society) in 1878 was of considerable importance, not only for its missionary ventures in Lapland but for those it undertook overseas, in particular in Africa. It established its first mission at

Mukimbungo, in the Belgian Congo, in 1881 and numerous others followed in its wake. Initiatives were also taken in neighbouring colonies, where the mission at Madzia, in the French Congo, was founded in 1909 and another at Brazzaville in 1911. The human cost was high and of the 133 missionaries who were sent out to these locations in 1910, 53 succumbed to disease, plus all their children who had come out with them. The Society also established various missions in Asia, in particular in Turkestan, India and Japan.

The Salvation Army, first established by William Booth in London in 1865, began its service, in turn, in Sweden in 1882, concerning itself especially with the needs of the urban poor. By now, the Free Church movement had come to thrive in Sweden and nowhere was it more powerful than in Jönköping, in Småland, henceforth popularly known as 'Sweden's Little Jerusalem'. Elsewhere, however, in the country's larger cities, the Lutheran Church remained strong, its profile heightened by the increasing role it gave the laity in religious and social decision making. People were now also beginning to appreciate the idiosyncrasies in their Swedish church traditions, not only in spiritual terms but architecturally as well. For, as a professor of Latin and aesthetics at Uppsala University put it in the 1840s, 'In all of European architecture one can hardly find such an extravagant orientalism, a so pagoda-like and mysterious physiognomy, as in our belfries.'

Yet, if such eastern religious inspired associations exerted a special allure, those of Catholic Europe were still viewed with suspicion. Indeed, Catholicism itself long remained beyond the pale of growing religious toleration in Sweden, despite the fact that King Oskar I's consort, Queen Josephine, was herself a Catholic. For example, two native converts to Catholicism during the 1850s had their property confiscated and were sent into exile from Sweden. Finally, though, in 1860, and despite considerable opposition, a major legal reform was enacted, emancipating the Catholic Church. Jews, too, benefited from this reform, since, henceforth, they could purchase land and stand on an equal civil footing with other Swedes. In consequence, many Jews from eastern Europe, propelled westwards by pogroms and growing economic difficulties, sought refuge in Sweden at this time. Finally, in 1870, all bars to public office were finally removed.

In Sweden's far-flung overseas colony of St Bartélemy, changes with respect to religion were also taking place, which reduced even further the dominance of the Swedish Church. While it is true that a new Lutheran church was built there in the 1850s, the Anglican church constructed in 1855 proved more central to the spiritual needs of the colony. For by now, American and British residents were far more numerous than any others and English had come to be the principal language spoken there. As for the new church, it was funded by a local Englishman, Sir Richard Dinzey, who was eventually made a Knight of the Order of Vasa by King Oskar I, in appreciation of his munificence.

In Sweden itself during the following decades, the Free Church denominations continued to multiply. In 1892, the Baptist Church there split, enabling the establishment of a splinter group, the Örebro Mission Society. The Pentecostal movement also took root in Sweden, becoming especially strong in Småland through the activities of American missionaries who arrived before the First World War. It later augmented its numbers, when the Filadelfia congregation of Baptists, based in Stockholm, joined its fold.

Numerous changes were, in the meantime, now being implemented within the Swedish Church, in response to both the growth of religious diversity among the population and rising secularism. For example, the obligation to attend Holy Communion several times a year was abolished in 1910. In effect, though, it confirmed what was already a dead letter, for by the late nineteenth century, regular participants are reckoned to have formed only 15 per cent of Stockholm's population. The institution of marriage had also suffered, especially in Stockholm, which had a particularly high percentage of unmarried couples with children compared with the rest of the country.

Nonetheless, a wave of new church building commenced after the turn of the century, in particular in Norrland and the burgeoning suburbs of Sweden's major cities. As such, it was part of a general revitalisation of the Church of Sweden. This trend was mirrored, intellectually and spiritually, in the activities of the primate of the Swedish Church, Archbishop Nathan Söderblom (1866–1931). Elevated to his archiepiscopal see in 1914, he was deeply interested in Sweden's literary culture and became a keen supporter of August Strindberg's candidature for the Nobel Prize, never awarded to him because of the playwright's unorthodox stance on a variety of gender and social issues. One of the first great ecumenicists, albeit still wary of Roman Catholicism, Söderblom also turned his attention to the Orthodox Church of Russia and Byzantium, deriving inspiration there, both spiritually and architecturally, for the Church.

The new church of Saltsjöbaden, built by the noted Swedish architect Ferdinand Boberg (1860–1946) in 1913, is clearly inspired by Orthodox Byzantine architecture. Dedicated to the Epiphany of Christ, its funerary chapel was intended eventually to house the remains of the industrialist Knut Wallenberg and his wife, and although the interior architectural detail is also principally Byzantine, many elements of the Arts and Crafts movement of William Morris are evident as well. As such, in its very eclecticism, it is a prime example of the new encompassing vision of the Lutheran Church of Sweden, which sought to engage ever more broadly with a wide spectrum of spiritual, social and cultural issues in the wider world. In this approach, the writings of such German Protestant theologians as Karl Holl and Karl Schwarzlose provided a major source of inspiration. At the same time, the Church attempted to extend its appeal through greater accessibility to its tenets of faith, by undertaking a more accurate and understandable translation of the Bible, a task only completed in 1917.

Söderblom himself was a man of many parts and even posed for a male figure in decoration by the sculptor Gustaf Wickman (1858–1916) which symbolised Norrland's industry and shipping at the Sundsvall branch of the *Enskilda Bank* in 1900–2. That Söderblom always had a special affinity to the north of Sweden should come as no surprise: he himself was born and grew up in the north of the country at Trönö, in Hälsingland, where his father was a Lutheran priest. Yet despite such a parochial background, Söderblom became one of Sweden's most eminent and multifaceted ecclesiastical figures. His contributions were many, not least an addendum to the Swedish Hymn Book, first compiled by Johan Olaf Wallin, in 1819, which, in truly ecumenical fashion, contained hymns emanating from the Free Church tradition, as well as from neighbouring countries.

DECLINE AND TRANSFER OF THE SWEDISH
OVERSEAS COLONIES

As the nineteenth century progressed, Sweden undertook to rid itself of its increasingly impoverished and burdensome colonial possessions, which brought in no significant capital returns. Indeed, already by the early 1840s, St Barthélemy languished in a severe economic decline, aggravated by the fact that the now independent South and Central American colonies of Spain were free to choose whichever trading partners they desired. Trade was at a minimum and agriculture unproductive, new initiatives to ameliorate the situation and administrative reforms notwithstanding. To improve efficiency and cut costs, the old Colonial Office was closed down and the colony was transferred to the administration of the Ministry of Finance.

Most importantly, at long last, matters were taken to resolve the institution of slavery, as the government in Sweden decided to implement a gradual emancipation of slaves, for both moral and economic reasons. Finally, therefore, in 1846, most of the colony's slave population of 1,800 were finally set free – twelve years after their freedom in the British colony of the western hemisphere. The neighbouring Danish colony would follow suit a couple of years later, but those of Spain and Portugal kept the institution until the final decades of the nineteenth century.

Masters were compensated by the government in Stockholm to the amount of 24,699 Spanish dollars, the currency in general use in the Caribbean. By 9 October 1847, the manumission of all slaves was finally completed, including those in the colony belonging, in name, to King Oskar I. Those freed slaves unable to support themselves through illness or old age were thenceforth supported from public funds, rather than by their former masters, as was the case in the Danish Caribbean colony. Despite remuneration for their losses, many of the colony's already impoverished planters went into bankruptcy. This led many to emigrate elsewhere and what remained of St Barthélemy's plantation economy largely collapsed. A further blow came when a devastating fire in Gustavia destroyed some 135 of the town's houses a few years later. While the enfeebled Swedish administration responded as if in paralysis, charitable relief efforts from both London and New York came to the aid of many victims, a significant number of whom were by now, in any case, British and American.

During the early 1860s – while the American Civil War was raging – cotton was briefly cultivated on St Barthélemy, to help compensate for a fall in supply from the now besieged Confederate States of America, but after the Union won the war, it fell out of cultivation, to be partially replaced by pineapple. This rapidly became the colony's leading agricultural product, a million being exported in 1858 alone. Salt, processed from the sea, was also a growing export commodity and lead, first discovered there in 1868, soon joined this list. Still, nothing could resolve the problems of unemployment which continued to plague St Barthélemy and massive emigration persisted. Therefore, the Swedish government, now wishing definitively to rid itself of its colonial burden, in 1868 opened negotiations with the United States for its sale, but with no success. Similar negotiations with Italy the following year also proved fruitless. Finally, then, Sweden turned to France, the colony's previous colonial power, and in 1876 the sale was finally effected. A referendum was then held on St Barthélemy confirming the transfer. On 16 March 1878, France assumed its sovereignty and the colony was transferred to the governmental administration of French Guadeloupe: 320,000 francs were paid by France for the transfer, funds which were used to provide pensions for the colony's now displaced civil servants, as well as an additional 80,000 francs for the construction of a new hospital in Gustavia. Swedish residents were permitted to continue to reside there while maintaining their Swedish nationality. This was hardly a major issue, though: as far back as 1860, there had been only six Swedish speakers still living in the colony. The retreat of Sweden's colonial presence was now complete.

PAN-SCANDINAVIANISM

Yet, if Sweden was turning away from its decades of colonial adventure, in the Nordic world it was attempting to revitalise its pan-Scandinavian links. Already, in 1810, the Danish clergyman, poet and educationalist N. F. S. Grundtvig had written his polemical *Is Unification of the Nordic Region Desirable? A Word to the Swedish*

People, and many Swedish people – at least students – though it had taken them some three decades to heed his words, now responded. After all, the Scandinavian countries shared a common religion, Lutheranism, as well as a shared literary and cultural fondness for Old Norse mythology, something which Grundtvig was also keen to encourage. Another Dane, the dramatist Adam Oehlenschäger, had also focused upon just these themes, in his *Nordic Poems* and epic work *The Gods of the North*, a modernised version of the great Norse *Edda*. When, therefore, these found a resonance with King Karl Johan, he awarded Oehlenschäger a commemorative medal for his labours and Lund University, in formerly Swedish Scania, awarded the bard an honorary doctorate. Soon a plethora of student and other societies began actively to encourage inter-Scandinavia co-operation and, in 1843, a convocation of students at Uppsala University voiced their support for the Pan-Scandinavian movement as such. Two years later, a similar event occurred in Copenhagen, where the arrival of Norwegian and Swedish students was later depicted in a famous painting by the Danish artist Jørgen Sonne. By now, though, the movement had become political, as well as cultural. As such, it bears comparison with the Pan-Slavic movement as emanating from Russia about the same time, in which a brotherhood of the Slavic peoples was encouraged, also with political and cultural overtones. Some intellectuals in Scandinavia now came to advocate a common defence policy and economic co-operation, though few openly spoke out on behalf of political union, even less over which monarch should reign over it. Still, with the Danish crown prince childless and divorced, there were those who envisioned the role of the king of Sweden as a king of all Scandinavia, almost by default.

That said, the roots of the Pan-Scandinavian movement, the romanticised memories of the Kalmar Union notwithstanding, were feeble. In the largely German-speaking duchies of Schleswig and Holstein, long under Danish sovereignty, Pan-Scandinavianism was an irrelevance, and, in any case, the Danish king, Christian VIII, had little sympathy for it. The real test of the movement's viability came when war broke out between Denmark and a territorially expanding Prussia, first in 1848, and then in 1864. In the first conflict, some 4,500 Swedes and Norwegians did volunteer to support their fellow

Scandinavians in battle, but in the second, their assistance was far more limited. The final death knell was sounded in the latter war by the sonorous silence of the Swedish-Norwegian king and his governments, not wishing to antagonise Prussia. His ministers refused any official contribution to the Danish war effort. Not for the last time, as the Second World War would demonstrate, German guns silenced Pan-Scandinavianism, as each of the Nordic countries went its own way. Weak and alone, Denmark lost Schleswig and Holstein to the aggressiveness of its neighbour to the south, with the northern part of the territories only to be returned by referendum after the First World War. But Pan-Scandinavianism had served one purpose successfully: it had brought an awareness of common Scandinavian cultural values to a wide range of the general population. As such, it was just part of a wider movement of education, cultural and civic, during the middle years of the nineteenth century, which spread throughout the country into all segments of the population, helping to mould a more unified ethnic and national identity.

EDUCATION

The 1842 Law on Public Education was an important key to the development of Sweden's first state-financed schools, for it sought to ensure that virtually all children between the ages of seven and thirteen would be provided with a basic education, in reading, writing and arithmetic, as well as in the tenets of the Lutheran faith. St Barthélemy, though, was not affected by this law: there, less than one in twenty of the inhabitants of the Caribbean island could read or write as late as 1866. That said, even in Sweden itself, it was only from the end of the 1850s that the system began fully to function. University education, in any case, remained beyond its scope, catering for a small elite, though scholarships were available for the especially gifted, provided they were male. For women, the possibilities of higher education were extremely limited: while a select few might attend lectures, only in 1873 were they granted the right to sit academic examinations. Yet even then, it was clear to many that the situation was about to change, as children of both sexes and their families increasingly demanded the right to better and further education.

With the rise of a broader middle class in Sweden and in line with developments elsewhere in Europe and America, a new focus on children and their wellbeing came to the fore, along with the need to educate them in terms of not only personal but civic responsibility. In its wake, a new stress on their moral education came to be advocated, as expressed in the publications of such forceful Swedish intellectuals as the writer Ellen Key (1849–1926). In her seminal work *Barnets århundrade* (The Century of the Children), published in 1900, she focused upon the history of education, its moral failings and the role it should take in the future with respect to both the welfare of the child and that of society at large. In particular, she lamented the stress given to aggressive militarism in the international arena, a development she feared with prescience would lead the next generation into a terrible conflagration, in which the basics tenets of civilised life risked destruction. At the same time, she also felt that sexual issues needed to be addressed, in order for the individual to become 'completely enlightened about his or her own nature as a man or a woman, and so acquire a deep feeling of responsibility in relation to one's future duty as a man or a woman'. The practice of 'bundling', that is the custom according to which a young man and woman were allowed to sleep together, fully clothed, with younger siblings sometimes sharing the same bed, forbidden to engage in sexual intercourse but expected to engage in fondling and kissing, had long proved to be useful in a largely rural peasant society, but urban men and women of the modern world, she felt, needed to acquire a more informed understanding of their conjugal responsibilities.

By now, the nuclear family, usually with only three or four members including children, had become the central unit of Swedish life. It was seen by many as the basic tool by which children could be moulded, and so the education of parents became almost as important as that of their children. Poverty, crime, even illicit sexual activities, were increasingly seen as the result of a failure in family life and education. Books such as Dr Ruff's *Illustrated Health Lexicon. A Popular Handbook for All*, published in 1888, were extremely popular, not only for their modern approach to health and hygiene, but for their advice in curbing undesirable and 'destructive' childish habits, especially masturbation. As Ruff admonished parents with respect to any pubescent son, 'He must not sleep alone in a room; one must not be shy of going several times during the night to his bed and removing his blanket without consideration of whether he is asleep or not. Threatened by such visitations a boy given to such an unhealthy habit would not dare to perform his manipulations.' He also warned parents against too warm physical displays of affection towards their children, out of fear that this might encourage sensuality in them later in life.

A wealth of newspapers now also came to flourish during the nineteenth century, often with increasingly 'tendential' articles, that is, those which sought by polemical means to achieve the improvement of the individual and society. *Aftonbladet* had made its appearance in 1830 and in 1864, the daily newpaper *Dagens Nyheter* began publication. It remains Sweden's most popular daily newspaper. A generation later, in 1884, its principal rival today, *Svenska Dagbladet*, was published, and is still thriving in our own time. In them, such events as the success of Adolph Erik Nordenskiöld (1832–1901) in sailing his ship, the *Vega*, through the 'North-east Passage' in 1880 received enormous coverage, in particular the public celebrations which took place when he arrived in Stockholm in April of that year, and helped to form a Swedish national consciousness and pride in its identity.

This trend was further reinforced in 1912, when the Olympic Games were held in Stockholm. The American Indian Jim Thorpe stood out, winning both the pentathlon and the decathlon. After the award ceremony, during which the tennis-playing King Gustaf V is said to have complemented him, saying, 'You, sir, are the greatest athlete in the world,' Thorpe is famously said to have replied with great simplicity but dignity, 'Thanks, King.'

Hannes Kolehmainen, from Finland, still a grand duchy within the Russian Empire but taking part in the Olympics as a nation in its own right, was also a prominent figure, winning three gold medals, in the 5,000 metres, setting a world record at that time, the 10,000 metres, and the 8,000 metre cross-country run. Altogether some two and a half thousand athletes participated, representing some twenty-eight countries. Such an international presence in the Swedish capital did much to foster an awareness of the country internationally and brought considerable pride to many Swedes, as well as a growing awareness of their own national identity.

WOMEN'S RIGHTS

During the later nineteenth century, women's rights in Sweden began to come into sharp focus, as the role of women in the family and workplace took on a new urgency. Domestic corporal punishment of adults within a household was abolished in 1858, the same year that single women over the age of twenty-five were granted property rights. Fredrika Bremer (1801–65) was one of the leaders in the burgeoning movement of bluestockings who sought to encourage this trend and extend the new rights to other groups of women, in particular, those who were married. In 1874, Parliament finally passed laws enabling working married women to administer their income, but only in 1884 were single women reaching the age of twenty-one granted the same general rights as men. Other women in the next generation took inspiration from Bremer, in 1884 establishing the Fredrika Bremer Society, which became a focus for the taking of initiatives, political and social, for the continued furtherance of women's rights, including, ultimately, the acquisition of the vote.

HEALTH AND HYGIENE

As attention came to be focused on the moral and educational development of society, so improvements in health and hygiene became new priorities. Mortality rates declined and in consequence of a variety of prophylactic measures, especially improved hygiene and sanitation, the population of Stockholm was finally able to reproduce itself, without recourse to immigration to augment numbers. It was, though, a slow and uneven process, subject to the vagaries of poor weather and bad harvests, as well as human interventions. Indeed, during the middle years of the nineteenth century, famine once again broke out in Sweden. Now, the potato crop, formerly a boon to the poor in nutritional terms, became a curse: the potato blight which also devastated Ireland attacked crops in Sweden, causing a major failure of the potato crop in the 1850s, at a time when few alternative foodstuffs were available. Rural hardship was great and massive emigration abroad, often to the midwestern United States, followed, as popularised in the famous novel *Utvandrarna* (The Emigrants), written by the Swedish author Vilhelm Moberg

(1898–1973) between 1949 and 1959, and later made into a film
with the award-winning Norwegian actress Liv Ullmann. By the final
decades of the nineteenth century, however, famine in Sweden had
become a thing of the past, as improved transport and better farming
practices made agriculture less precarious.

Some contagious diseases had now virtually disappeared. In 1895,
Sweden became one of the first countries in the world to eradicate
indigenous smallpox. As for leprosy, though, while eliminated in
much of the country, it persisted in various provincial pockets well
into the twentieth century, despite the fact that in most of the rest of
northern Europe it had died out centuries before. More than a hundred people, virtually all of whom had contracted the disease at
home, still suffered from it at the turn of the century in Sweden.
It remained at its most virulent in Siljan and especially Hälsingland,
in southern Norrland, where a leprosarium was built in 1867,
at Järvsö, accommodating some twenty permanent inmates. It was
extended in 1889 for a further twenty-six inmates, by which time the
quarantine of lepers had become slightly less restrictive, with sufferers now permitted to attend the parish church. This greater openness
was in part a result of the better understanding of the disease which
had been introduced to the Nordic countries by the Danish physician
Edvard Ehlers and the Norwegian doctor Armauer Hansen, after
whom the disease came to be renamed in scientific terms, in honour
of dramatic inroads he made into its treatment while working at
Scandinavia's largest leprosarium in Bergen, in the west of Norway.
More than 2,100 lepers were accommodated there and in dependent
lodgings in the surrounding countryside in 1875, but through the
positive implementation of new measures, Hansen was able to
reduce this number to only 300 by the time of his death in 1912.
To a significant degree in consequence of his endeavours, the disease
died out in the decades which followed.

New hospital developments

The growing population of Sweden and the diminution of care in the
home for many of the country's ill, in both body and mind, also
required major new initiatives, in consequence of which the number
of hospitals increased and care within them improved. The Academic

Hospital in Uppsala, designed by the architect Albert Törnqvist (1819–98) and completed in 1867, was one of the most innovative of these new edifices, provided as it was with a complex system of ventilation ducks and internal windows integrated into the building for the provision of fresh air. That of Sabbatsberg attempted in the 1870s to create pavilions in which the maintenance of an antiseptic environment was paramount, under the influence of Emmy Rappe (1835–96), Sweden's first nurse educated in the modern way with strict attention to hygiene. The daughter of a highly philanthropic aristocratic family, she had gone to England to train under Florence Nightingale, with whom she later had a lengthy and lively literary correspondence during the years 1867–70. This new stress on hygiene now reaped its own rewards: whereas 56.1 women per thousand in Swedish maternity wards had died from puerperal fever in the 1860s, their numbers had fallen dramatically to 0.7 by 1896. The next generation of general hospitals in the early twentieth century also focused on hygiene but they additionally paid strict attention to economies of scale. Hospitals increasingly became vast edifices for the treatment of patients from wide geographical areas, the Carolinian and Söder hospitals in Stockholm providing more than a thousand beds each.

New initiatives were also being taken with respect to mental health. More than a thousand people in Sweden were inmates in mental hospitals by the middle of the century and many others still waited for accommodation. New asylums came to be built, such as Konradsberg, in Stockholm, which served the ever growing needs of that city and its burgeoning suburbs. A vast edifice, still functioning today as Rålambshovs Hospital, it was designed by Albert Törnqvist to give a new emphasis to spaciousness, hygiene and ventilation, according to the latest principles. There the psychiatric professor Bror Gadelius (1862–1938) introduced new treatment for the mentally ill during the 1890s, therapeutic elements of which included warm baths for lengthy periods. The American hospital reformer Dorothea Lynde Dix also came to exert considerable influence on hospitals in Sweden, not least on that built at Hisingen, by Gothenburg, in 1872, where the interior arrangement of rooms began to take on a more domestic appearance than had previously been the case. The environs of hospitals, as well as their buildings, now came into focus. In particular, it became common usage to situate them in large parks, full of trees and plants and lawns deemed salubrious for patient recuperation. Some were quite extensive and the park of the asylum in Lund, in Scania, contained no fewer than 37,000 plants. That said, any similarity with idyllic rural life ended there, for in their regimen such institutions bore more resemblance to prisons than hospitals: everyone was under lock and key, including the staff, who were required to obtain permission every time they wished to leave the premises.

Syphilis during this period also remained a major issue – like AIDS today – social as well as medical, not least because it could affect anyone, rich and poor, urban and rural. As a Swedish medical administrator put it in the 1840s, 'one is struck by the fact that only this illness is treated by special and independent hospital care, while the care and treatment of those suffering from other illnesses has been neglected; one is tempted to believe that egoism (fear of infection) has been the primary reason for the way in which health care is organised, rather than a love of humanity.' Condoms, usually made from the guts of goats and sheep, were available but unpopular and unreliable. Thus, they were rarely utilised. The disease had therefore come to be widely spread throughout the country, with victims frequently living for many years with the contagion. This demanded the provision of long-term care, especially for mothers and children afflicted with the disease, many of the latter being born blind in consequence. The Little Home on Kungsholmen, in Stockholm, was one foundation established to accommodate such young victims. For many prospective mothers so afflicted, though, a darker alternative was preferred: abortion. It was a criminal offence, but a concoction of camomile, aloe, saffron and extract of pine needles was thought to induce it, and if that and other home-grown means didn't work, surgically intrusive methods, accompanied by great risks, legal as well as hygienic, were employed to carry it out.

Prostitution and venereal diseases

In order to curb the spread of venereal infections, Sweden, in the 1840s, became one of the first European countries to regulate prostitution and to introduce compulsory medical inspections of prostitutes. Their numbers in Sweden were considerable at the time – perhaps some 0.85 per cent of the whole female population in 1870 – so the task undertaken was considerable. Many of the prostitutes were poor girls from rural areas who had moved to Stockholm or other cities and towns, and not included in these figures were the men who engaged in prostitution, often in areas with high concentrations of soldiers and sailors, perennially under-paid and in need of money. By the 1860s in Stockholm, these regulatory rules had become entrenched in city health statutes, with a special bureau established to deal with the issue and the implementation of methods to contain it. As a result of these and other measures, the majority of prostitutes were undergoing health checks at regular intervals, up to twice a week by the 1890s. As a result, the frequency of venereal disease declined sharply in Sweden from this time. Nonetheless, and despite these successes, a movement was underway to end regulation and inspection for moral reasons, gaining strength after the turn of the century. Modelled on its British counterpart, the Swedish Federation Movement preferred to have prostitution outlawed altogether, rather than merely have it contained. The Swedish Medical Society of Physicians fought this, but to no avail. Regulated prostitution in Sweden was finally abolished in 1918. By this time, venereal clinics had, in any case, been largely absorbed into the general hospitals.

Tuberculosis and other infectious diseases

Another major health scourge of Swedish society during this period was tuberculosis. It affected far greater numbers than syphilis and was even more costly to confront, since victims might survive for decades. All levels of society were afflicted and in the north of the country it reached serious epidemic proportions. For example, in the village of Antnäs, in Nederluleå, one in seven of the inhabitants was afflicted by it. Indeed, in Sweden as a whole during the 1870s, 3.24 per thousand of the population died from the disease. To cope with it, sanatoria, like that at Hålahult, which opened in 1899, were constructed, with strict regimes of treatment imposed, central to which was good nutrition and fresh air, the latter facilitated by the wide open verandas which invariably were built on to them, hall-marks of such institutions.

Other infectious diseases also remained a problem. The incidence of typhoid and typhus continued to abound in Sweden itself, while St Barthélemy, with its tropical climate, remained an especially insalubrious place throughout this period. In 1849 alone, an unspecified fever carried off one third of the colony's entire population, some 350 people. Malaria, too, remained rife there, even if, in Sweden itself, this disease was now declining in its incidence. That said, between 1875 and 1908, no fewer than 60,000 Swedes remained afflicted with malaria, many in the marshy coastal reaches of south-eastern Sweden and along the shores of its great inland lakes, Mälaren and Vänern.

Orphanages and care for the poor

Illegitimacy, too, was a problem throughout the nineteenth century, especially in the burgeoning slums of Stockholm and other industrialised cities. While one in twenty was born out of wedlock in rural areas, one in four was so born during this period in urban areas. In Stockholm, with the lowest percentage of married women in the country, almost half of all births were illegitimate by the end of the century. That said, many unmarried mothers married shortly after the birth of their children. In fact, perhaps as many as one third of all Swedish women at the time were pregnant at their weddings. That said, these rates were by no means consistent throughout the country. In Lapland and some other parts of rural Sweden, illegitimacy rates were very high, while in the southern provinces of Halland, Kronoberg and Jönköping, with their puritanical Free Church traditions, they remained very low.

During the late 1880s, the old orphanage at Norrmalm was finally torn down and new institutions were built along more modern principles, some catering for the criminal young, whose numbers were increasing. The Råby Salvation Institute was one such establishment, designed by the architect Carl Georg Brunius (1792–1869) and built with bricks which had been provided personally by King Karl Johan himself. Its director was the noted zoologist Baron Axel Gustaf Gyllenkrok (1783–1865), whose own son had fled abroad to escape a criminal conviction for theft. Its first inmates were twelve boys aged between eight and thirteen who had previously been accommodated in Malmö Prison. Similar institutions sprang up in its wake all over Sweden.

Each parish in Sweden continued to provide refuges for the poor and homeless throughout the period. However, from the 1860s, the so-called poor farm came into being, such as that in Blekinge, near Karlskrona, where inmates were given gainful employment as farm labourers. Some, such as Ljusnarsberg near Örebro, offered not only residential accommodation but a school for children and an infirmary, as well as an asylum for the mentally handicapped. On occasion, entire families resided on such farms and, so effective were they perceived to be as an alternative to traditional poor houses, their numbers multiplied considerably. These new establishments came to house those now considered the 'worthy poor', that is, those destitute through age, ill health or for reasons beyond their control. However, for those deemed guilty of their own impoverishment, through an unwillingness to work or other moral flaw, the feared workhouse lay in wait. Here the recalcitrant poor were housed in crowded and cramped dormitories, then set to work on such menial tasks as the chopping of wood or washing. The Dillström Workhouse, in Stockholm, was one such notorious establishment. In 1863, it housed some 414 inmates in vast chambers of triple-tiered beds, an ill-ventilated environment in which epidemics were wont to rage with dreadful consequences.

CARE OF THE ELDERLY

The care of the elderly also came into sharpened focus in the course of the nineteenth century. The commonly held view notwithstanding, most families during this period in Sweden did not include elderly family members. Most of these lived on their own, only moving in with willing family members when ill health or a similar calamity intervened.

While there were houses for the poor and elderly before, it was only towards the end of the nineteenth century that residential care in the modern sense came to be established and then only for those of private means. One of the most prominent of these was the Old

People's Home in Gothenburg, designed by the architect Carl Fahlström, which accommodated two occupants per room. Such an establishment, however, was the exception rather than the rule. Most old people continued to live independently, while a minority resided with family members.

FAMILY VALUES

If the extended family was relatively rare as a domestic unit in Sweden during this period, 'family values', nonetheless, now achieved a new lease of life. The appearance of new magazines, such as *Svenska Familj-Journalen* (The Swedish Family Journal) and *Familjens Vänen* (The Family Friend), fostered such values and role models, going as far as to envision the nation itself as one big family. A lithograph of Queen Louise of Sweden in an edition of the latter from 1864 was accompanied by a poem paying homage to her in the role of mother, wife and woman. Virtues such as devotion, duty and 'moral love' were stressed. Sometimes they merged with political ones, as in the magazine *För och Nu* (Before and Now), in which romantic conceptions of Sweden's national past, from both history and mythology, were married together anachronistically as representative of an ideal for the nineteenth century. Animals, too, were given anthropomorphic characteristics, in the tradition of classical Greek and later French fables, so that horses and their foals, dogs and their puppies, became allegorical symbols of the modern Swedish family.

THE MARRIAGE MARKET

For all its attention to family life, however, the middle years of the nineteenth century saw a considerable reduction in the percentage of women entering married life. Indeed, in 1844, some three quarters of all adult women in Stockholm were single and even in the countryside this proportion was as high as two thirds. To a certain degree, this reflected the institution of so-called 'Stockholm marriages', informal arrangements in which men and women lived together without the benefit of marriage. However, it also mirrored the dearth of available men with financial means perceived as suitable to marry and the proportion grew in inverse relationship to the social position of the women concerned. Most strikingly, it was the women of the higher social strata who suffered most in this respect, with some 40 per cent never marrying, for many of their former reservoir of suitors now married women from the rising middle classes who were wealthier, if socially inferior. However, in the final decades of the nineteenth century a reverse trend had set in and these figures declined dramatically, at least in Stockholm, falling to a quarter of all adult females being single by 1900.

By contrast with women, the overwhelming majority of men married. Among farmers, marriage was virtually universal, since rural life necessitated the presence of a woman to carry out the domestic chores, whether milking a cow or spinning thread, necessary for a homestead to survive. Only among the aristocracy and wealthier middle-class families were perennial bachelors to be found in anything but the smallest numbers in the first half of the nineteenth century. However, during the second half of the century these numbers increased dramatically, especially among men of the professional classes and civil service, for whom housekeepers and maids increasingly provided the necessary domestic infrastructure. Among the landed aristocracy, marriage rates fell particularly sharply at this time, possibly a result of the worsening financial situation in which large numbers of landed estate owners found themselves because of falling agricultural prices and the consequential sale of many estates, forcing many of their former owners to move to Stockholm and other major cities.

CRIMINALITY AND PUNISHMENT

With growing urbanisation and migration, criminality became an increasing problem and the prison population swelled, necessitating new accommodation. To deal with this and related issues, a reformist movement took form which continued to make a variety of profound inroads into the prosecution and punishment of criminality over the course of the middle and late nineteenth century. Karlsborg Fortress, designed by the civil engineer and architect Carl Fredrik Meijer (1791–1872) in 1845, became an architectural landmark of its period. A monumental edifice, flanked by round end towers, it practised a strict separation of prisoners according to the seriousness of their crimes, and became a prototype for many other such institutions.

During the middle years of the century, a spate of new prisons were erected throughout Sweden, based on reformist principles. These included the Remand Prison, by the architect Axel Nyström (1793–1868), in 1852, and the Central Prison on Långholmen, by Vilhelm Theodor Ankarsvärd (1816–78), built in Stockholm in the years 1874–80 for the incarceration of long-term prisoners. The latter was especially innovative in that it was modelled on the Eastern Penitentiary in Philadelphia, in the United States, with its innovative arrangement of cells fanning out from a central block and opening upon balconies. Auburn Prison, in New York, also served as a prototype, since the doors of cells there never faced one another directly and so hindered personal contact among the prisoners they contained. With society more strictly regulated, criminality seems to have diminished and, by 1899, the prison population had fallen to a record low, with only 2,293 incarcerated throughout the country. Various measures of legal reform were also enacted, which served, on the one hand, to reduce the number of felonies, but on the other, to create new criminal offences. Thus, a new law of 1864 specifically made homosexual activity a crime, in place of the less specific, if more severely penalised, offence of sodomy. Despite that fact, though, and the growing notoriety at the time of public baths, parks and logging camps as haunts for such activity, prosecutions remained rare.

LITERATURE AND A CHANGING RURAL WORLD

As Sweden's industrial development and capitalisation altered society dramatically, much of its passing rural culture came into focus in a new way for many authors and poets of the time. As if grasping it for a final embrace, they began to describe in imagery and images a world which they recognised, even in their own lifetimes, would be no more. The poet Erik Axel Karlefeldt (1864–1931), for example, focused upon Dalecarlia's natural beauties and the independence of its yeoman farmers in such works as *Vildmarks- och kärleksvisor* (Songs of the Wilderness and Love, 1895) and in *Fridolins visor* (Fridolin's Song, 1898), the central character of which is an alter ego of the poet, a man with one foot in the modern industrial world with all its ferment, the other in the old rural world of small farmers, preoccupied with their crops and the vagaries of the weather. Having refused to be considered for the Nobel Prize for Literature – he felt it inappropriate since he was on its committee – he nonetheless won it posthumously for his literary contributions. In his subject matter, he had drawn inspiration from another Swedish poet, the eccentric and troubled Gustaf Fröding (1860–1911), but, unlike the latter, had infused his works with Christian elements. Fröding, though lyrical in his nostalgic look at country life in his native province of Värmland, was a radical in terms of his poetical forms. He came from a family riddled with mental illness, a condition from which he himself was not immune, and his sometimes tormented fantasies were used to literary benefit to create poetical works such as *Nya dikter* (New Poetry), which appeared in 1894, rich in a mystical imagery that took much inspiration from old Scandinavian legends.

Anecdotal tales about folk culture had by now found a wide resonance among the reading public, and articles popularised them in such magazines as *Allers Familjen-Journal* (Aller's Family Journal). Reconstituted model villages now came to be built in the environs of cities, such as the Skansen, on the outskirts of Stockholm, becoming places of pilgrimage for an increasingly urbanised and industrialised society, fascinated by folk traditions which were becoming a thing of the past. As the Swedish poet Gustaf af Geijerstam (1858–1909) put it at the time, 'It is the primitive, which we city dwellers seek in the summer life of the countryside, its primitive qualities and its peace.' Others, like the writer, critic and museum director Tor Hedberg (1862–1931), saw musical affinities in Swedish nature. As he put it in his novel *På Torpa gård* (At the Torpa Farm, 1888), the roar of a waterfall was not only like the deep tone of an organ, but characteristic of the essence of the farm itself. Yet his novel also stresses the dichotomies brought about by a conflict between the romantic urbanised images of the countryside which looked nostalgically at rural life and the practical aspects of eking a living out of nature: this conflict tears apart the marriage of the two principal characters in the novel, the wife seeking personal salvation through a lyrical integration with nature for spiritual reasons, the husband seeking to dominate and exploit it for material gain.

For Swedes with the resources to make the daily trip, trains, trams, omnibuses and then the arrival of the motor car were the means by which new suburbs in the archipelago of Stockholm and villa towns, such as Saltsjöbaden and Lindingö, came to be developed. Prestigious wooden houses of extraordinary size, with turrets, towers and balconies, rose up on rocky slopes and rugged promontories throughout the country in the vicinity of urban conurbations. Yet even in remoter areas, such developments were not rare, benefiting those newly rich from the rising income forestry was bringing to the provinces. In the far-off village of Skyttmon, in Jämtland, no fewer than ten grandiose villas were constructed between 1874 and 1914, one of which, designed by the architect Elov Frid, had seven balconies embellishing its exterior, more characteristic of an alpine chalet than a traditional Swedish country house.

The most nationalistic expression of the new writings of the period was to be found in the works of the aristocratic author and poet Verner von Heidenstam (1859–1940), winner of the Nobel Prize for Literature in 1916. His country seat, Övralid, built in 1925, became a geographic focus for like-minded figures from the world of culture, artists as well as writers. There Sweden's historic past could be celebrated and, indeed, remains celebrated to this day: it is a yearly venue for the celebration of Swedish national and literary identity. Heidenstam's historical novel *Karolinerna* (Charles's Men), published in 1897–8, focuses upon the final years of Sweden's greatness as a world power under its warrior king Charles XII and was one of a number of works by Heidenstam which glorified such themes of a lost more heroic past.

Other writers, like Ola Hansson (1860–1925), turned away from old historical ideals and focused instead upon the morbid and destructive elements in eroticism and the human psyche. Hansson's collection of stories *Sensitiva Amorosa*, published in 1887, had a great influence on many Swedish intellectuals of the time. The novelist Hjalmar Söderberg (1869–1941) also concentrated upon the mental interiors of his characters, as evinced in one of his most famous works, *Doktor Glas*, published in 1906. Its central character is a medical man who receives confidences which involve a dissatisfied wife, corrupt clergyman and conflicts of adultery. Issues, highly unusual at the time in literature, such as abortion and the rights of women also play a major role in his output.

For all the brilliance of these writers, Sweden's leading literary figure of this period was, without doubt, August Strindberg (1849–1912), who brought a sharp focus to the inequities, even horrors, of 'bourgeois' life, in a tradition which went back several decades to Almqvist and others. Yet his Apollonian stature in the pantheon of Swedish literature notwithstanding, Strindberg never won the Nobel Prize. His unconventional, tortured views on conventional religion and human relationships led him to be perceived as a dangerous outsider by many establishment figures of later nineteenth- and early twentieth-century Sweden, many of whom, therefore, long rejected his works. In much of these writings, the mystical influence of Swedenborg can clearly be traced, though Hinduism, too, exerted an attraction, along with the philosophical ponderings of Schopenhauer as expressed in *Die Welt als Wille und Vorstellung* (The World as Will and Idea, 1819). The physical and philosophical aspects and potential of reality also deeply interested Strindberg, in particular the conception of time and space as illusory, in one sense, but reflective of a deep spiritual reality, on the other. This led him to experiment in alchemy and painting, in all of which he sought to explore spiritual, emotional and physical relationships. Yet, it is in literature that he achieved his greatest fame, examining not only the natural world with the eye of a botanist, but the psychological and emotional world of people in their natural habitat as well. His novel *Hemsöboarna* (The People of Hemsö), published in 1887, focuses upon the life of Swedes living in the archipelago of Stockholm, as much a part of nature as the evergreen trees that rise up from its craggy shores. Other works, like the play *Fröken Julie* (Miss Julie), first performed in 1889, explore the turmoil of his childhood, in a family in which social disjunction – his mother had been a servant, his father an aristocrat plagued by financial difficulties – plays a major role.

THE VISUAL ARTS

The visual arts in Sweden also focused upon similar issues and, as in the world of literature, they experienced a blossoming in the final two decades of the nineteenth century and the first of the twentieth which many have called Sweden's artistic Golden Age. Its two leading proponents – and rivals – were Carl Larsson (1853–1919) and Anders Zorn (1860–1920). Like the poet Karlefeldt, they came to reside in Dalecarlia, enchanted with rural life there and its rich history of folk traditions, including music, dance and crafts.

Larsson's idealised visions of family life became icons of their time, which were deeply loved, and the role models of domesticity they glorified have continued to be emulated even to this day. His *Old Man and New Planting* of 1893, painted in a naturalistic style, focuses upon the life cycle of living things, human beings and nature both subject to the same inexorable progression, with light and shadow, mass and plane, youth and old age forming an inextricable unity. Later works by him, such as *Midwinter Sacrifice*, the final version of which was completed in 1914–15, took their themes, instead, from ancient Norse mythology. These exerted a less wide appeal and it would take several generations before the intrinsic artistic value of some came to be appreciated. Only in 1997 was *Midwinter Sacrifice* finally installed in its rightful place in the National Gallery of Sweden, in Stockholm, for which it had initially been commissioned so many years before.

Zorn, the son of an impoverished rural labouring woman who had gone to Stockholm to seek work and a prosperous German brewer, was well educated by his father, and went on to become an immensely popular society painter, international in scope – he eventually carried out a specially commissioned portrait of the American president Grover Cleveland and painted various member of the British aristocracy. That said, it is his paintings of outdoor scenes which now elicit the greatest appeal. His *Midsummer Dance* of 1897 captures the joyous atmosphere of the Nordic calendar's most festive evening, an iconic image in which the whirling dancers, set against a luminous sky, evoke the *stämning*, or mood and atmosphere, of the occasion, which provides the subject of so many Swedish works of art of this time but none so multifaceted. Very different to this public image is his *Première*, a work in which a mother is depicted naked with her child in the water, which allows the viewer to peep into a private work of maternal affection set

13 *Midwinter Sacrifice* (1914–15), oil an canvas, by Carl Larsson (1853–1919), one of Sweden's most important artists of his generation. The sacrifice was an ancient Swedish religious rite at a time of year when the powers of darkness and famine seemed most to threaten humankind. By the early twentieth century, however, it had become a powerful cultural symbol, embodying a self-conscious national identity, at the very time when war was raging in the Baltic, threatening not only Swedish neutrality but its political and economic existence. Photo: National Museum, Stockholm.

14 *Midsummer Dance* (1897), by Anders Zorn, oil on canvas. The 'White Nights' of the Nordic summer, in which the sun hardly sets below the horizon, have long been a famed subject of Swedish artists, but Zorn has here created an iconic image of young love, elevating light, nature and human relationships to a metaphysical level of poignancy. Yet on a more earthly level, it was at age-old events such as these, with their pagan pre-Christian resonances, that many young men and women found marriage partners. National Museum, Stockholm.

against a backdrop of shimmering water and dazzling light, certainly the most virtuoso depiction of its type in Swedish art history.

The artist Ernst Josephson (1851–1906), the scion of a rich Jewish family which had immigrated to Sweden in the nineteenth century, in his turn focused upon themes of nature and mood. In such works as *Water Sprite* (1884), actually painted while on a visit to Norway, he infuses a pantheistic spirit which would later find expression, not only in the Nordic world, but in Germany and that artistic circle which formed around the Berliner journal *Pan*. On the other hand, the royal artist Prince Eugen (1865–1947)), a brother of King Gustaf V of Sweden, focused in his Symbolist works on a different type of *stämning*, one in which overt mythological figures are eschewed, but in their place, nature itself – woodlands, clouds, even swamps – seems to allude to higher spiritual and philosophical realities. In his painting *The Forest* (1892), a pantheistic allusion is made in which the forest itself seems to possess its own self-conscious identity, as if reflective of some neo-Platonic other-world reality.

MUSICAL LIFE

As in the arts, so music, too, came to assume a more prominent place in the cultural life of Sweden as the second half of the nineteenth century progressed, one in which the mood and atmosphere of the natural world finds its multifaceted and vibrant expression. Already, during the middle years of the nineteenth century, the music of Romanticism found a strong resonance in Sweden, in particular under the musical initiatives of Sweden's greatest composer of the period, Franz Berwald (1796–1868). Berwald, from a family which for four generations had produced musicians, had studied composition under the Frenchman J. B. E. Du Puy, but had then gone on to study first in Berlin, in 1829, and then in Vienna, in 1841. After a brief sojourn in Sweden thereafter, he returned first to Paris and again to Vienna, during the years 1846–9. By this time he had produced six symphonies, the fourth of which has been lost. Unfortunately, however, during most of the 1850s, he was unable to support himself by music and so assumed the management of a glass manufactory in Ångermanland for most of that time. Finally, though, in 1867, he was appointed teacher of musical composition at the Stockholm Conservatory.

If much of Berwald's musical output is influenced by the compositions of Louis Spohr and Carl Maria von Weber, the musical harmonies, as his opera *Estrella di Soria* evinces, are his own. Largely unappreciated in his own life time, his importance for the musical world of Sweden later came to be fully appreciated in the twentieth century and Stockholm's most famous contemporary concert hall, Berwaldshallen, has been named in his honour.

Another major figure of the musical world at this time was Carl Stenhammar (1871–1927), composer, pianist and conductor. Having been especially influenced by Wagner and Bruckner, he then attempted to develop a more typically Nordic musical style, producing two symphonies along with a number of concertos and sonatas in this vein, among which the cantata *A People*, from 1905, is a leading example. Yet there is also an international dimension in many of his works, made clear by the fact that for many listeners, his six string quartets form a link between the music of Brahms and Bartok.

Hugo Alfén (1872–1960) is the latest and final figure in this triumvirate of Swedish musicians of the period. A composer, violinist and conductor who was very much influenced by Mendelssohn, his later works also evince the importance of the music of Richard Strauss for his compositions, not least his best-loved and most famous work, *Swedish Rapsody*, completed in 1903. He also composed five symphonies and, while his collection of folk songs from Dalecarlia exerted a profound influence on some of his musical production, his *Third Symphony, Opus 23 in E Major*, was more profoundly influenced by a sojourn in Italy.

As for operatic performers on the international stage no one achieved greater fame than the so-called 'Swedish Nightingale', Jenny Lind (1820–87). Her role as Agathe, in Carl Maria von Weber's *Der Freischütz* carried her name throughout Europe and across the Atlantic. In 1850, under the auspices of P. T. Barnum, the circus impresario, she carried out an extensive musical tour of the United States, performing with great success in the newly built National Theatre in Washington, DC, newly renovated and enlarged to accommodate her audience. Later in life, after giving many performances in England, she settled near Malvern, in Worcestershire, where she remained Sweden's greatest and most admired ambassador of high culture until the end of her life. The period was to close, however, not on the high notes of classical musical culture, but on the thunder of guns which burst out to cataclysmic effect on the other side of the Baltic, heralding the advent of the First World War.

9

The world wars and Swedish neutrality

The outbreak of the First World War during the summer of 1914 was a major test of Sweden's military neutrality. Many Swedes continued to fear, as their ancestors had done for centuries, that Russia might make a concerted push across the Baltic Sea. Yet, like Denmark and Norway, it maintained its neutral stance vis-à-vis the belligerents. For most of the Swedish population saw little to be gained by entering the war. Russia may have feared a Swedish attack, in 1915, in concert with Germany, but from the Swedish side there was little appetite for such a military adventure. The Independent Conservative prime minister, Hjalmar Hammarskjöld (1862–1953), though sympathetic towards Germany, strove consistently to keep Sweden out of the affray. Even the Social Democrat Hjalmar Branting (1860–1925) supported neutrality, despite the fact that he imputed military responsibility for the war to the Central Powers, Germany and Austria-Hungary. With overwhelming popular opinion against entering the war on both sides of the political spectrum, therefore, Sweden maintained its formal neutrality throughout the war.

It was no easy task. Both Entente and German pressure on Swedish neutrality was considerable, but it took an economic, rather than military, form. By satisfying many of the material demands of both sides, Sweden prevented any military infringement of its stance and this brought in considerable economic benefits in the process. In the spring of 1915, for example, Britain was in especial need of Swedish timber and Germany of Swedish horses, so both sides benefited from the country's neutrality, and the sales proceeded with little hindrance. Sometimes, however, actions by Sweden, under heavy pressure from one of the belligerents, did arouse conspicuous annoyance, even retribution, from the other. For example, Swedish mining of the Kogrund Channel, on the Swedish side of the Sound, in the summer of 1916, under pressure from the Germans, seriously antagonised Britain, closing, as it did, the latter's maritime access to and from the Baltic. On the other hand, the negotiations of the pro-British industrialist Marcus Wallenberg (1864–1943) that same year helped to ameliorate the situation, facilitating both diplomacy and trade between the two countries. That said, Sweden suffered increasingly from an ever tighter British blockade of its German imports and exports, a state of affairs which led to considerable economic hardship throughout the country. Staple commodities became scarce and bread rationing was introduced in September 1916.

By now, the writing was on the wall for Prime Minister Hammarskjöld and his conservative political agenda. Even a fellow conservatively minded aristocrat, Count Wrangel, Sweden's ambassador in Britain at that time, was aware of this fact and lamented that, 'The Hammarskjöld way of conducting policy might perhaps suit a peasant republic like that of the Boers, but is not appropriate to a diplomacy that counts the names of Axel Oxenstierna and Hugo Grotius among its practitioners.'

Then in April 1917, food riots broke out in Sweden. The government of Hjalmar Hammarskjöld collapsed, the prime minister now popularly ridiculed with the nickname 'Hungerskjöld'. Then that of National Party leader Carl Swartz (1858–1926), who had succeeded him, followed suit. Coupled with the eruption of the notorious Luxburg affair, in which the Conservative government, as intercepted by British intelligence, was implicated in the transmitting of secret German diplomatic messages from Argentina to Berlin ordering the sinking of Argentine shipping, the scenario was set for a major overhaul of the Swedish political system and a victory for the left. Professor Nils Edén (1871–1945) of the Liberal Coalition, a professor of history from Uppsala University, was then elected as Sweden's first full parliamentary prime minister.

Meanwhile, by 1917, under the pressure of political events outside Sweden, not least the disruptions and outbreak of revolution in Russia in October, the Swedish left was experiencing acute internal factionalism. Hjalmar Branting, with little sympathy and no patience for Communists or other Socialists of the extreme left, expelled them from the Social Democratic Party. Those who left then formed *Vänsterpartiet* (the Party of the Left) in 1917. This enabled the broader left-wing majority, solidly behind Branting, to consolidate its position vis-à-vis the rest of the political spectrum.

On the diplomatic level, after strenuous negotiations with numerous compromises on both sides, accords were finally reached with the Entente, in February 1918, according to which Sweden was permitted to import large quantities of grain and fodder from them, in return for a major reduction of iron ore exports to Germany. At first there were fears that the hackles of the Central Powers would be raised in response, but the accord reached by Sweden with Germany in April 1918 ensured their acquiescence in the new arrangement.

Yet there was still another issue of considerable importance which had to be resolved: the sovereignty of the Swedish-speaking Åland Islands, in the middle of the Gulf of Bothnia. This had become an even thornier problem than had previously been the case because, in 1915, Russia had re-fortified the islands, the 1856 prohibition in settlement of the Crimean War notwithstanding. Therefore, on 13 February 1918, in reaction to inflammatory reports of alleged Russian atrocities on the islands, Sweden sent troops to occupy them, the first time such forces had been ordered abroad since 1808. Clearly, the Swedish minister of the navy, Baron Erik Palmstierna (1877–1959), considered annexation an option. However, the following week, German troops also arrived, placing Sweden in an awkward position, a situation aggravated by the hostility of newly independent Finland which now had legal sovereignty over the islands.

At first, a condominium approach was taken, the occupation of the islands being divided between Sweden and Germany. But on 25 April, Sweden began evacuating its forces, deeming its interest on the islands better supported by a non-confrontational approach. Germany, after all, had agreed to Sweden's right to negotiate over the islands' de-fortification and sovereignty, while the Entente powers had not. The likelihood of military confrontation dramatically receded.

Yet Sweden was by no means out of troubled waters, as the war drew to its close. Other threats loomed which no amount of negotiations could eliminate: the arrival of Spanish influenza in June 1918, which devastated the country in a way the war itself had not accomplished. Its spread was facilitated by the returning armies of neighbouring countries and the vast migrations of people which affected neutral countries in almost equal measure to belligerent ones. Several hundred thousand Swedes fell victim to the disease, some 85 per cent of them between the ages of seventeen and forty. A wide variety of public buildings were turned into hospitals to accommodate them and a wide range of public assistance was provided. Nonetheless, well over 20,000 people died, most of them young adults. Though no real famine broke out, food shortages were also a problem and in July 1918, the rationing of potatoes, the country's staple crop, was reluctantly introduced.

SWEDEN IN THE AFTERMATH OF THE FIRST WORLD WAR

Despite the loss of life caused by what was now seen to be the great world influenza pandemic, Sweden's political and economic position in the aftermath of the First World War was strengthened, in particular vis-à-vis its neighbours Russia and Germany. With the end of the war, even Germany was happy to see the Åland Islands demilitarised, since shipments of iron ore to Germany in the case of future hostilities would be less likely thereby to become impeded. A referendum was finally also held in the Åland Islands, according to which more than 95 per cent of the population voted for reintegration with Sweden. This result, nonetheless, was rejected by the newly formed League of Nations, the new international organisation founded at the Paris Peace Conference in 1919 to secure future peace among the nations of the world, under considerable pressure from Britain, which feared a resurgence of German influence, and the islands remained under Finnish sovereignty, but with autonomy in internal matters and the use of Swedish as the only official language.

During the early post-war years, Arvid Lindman (1862–1936), prime minister of Sweden from 1906 to 1911, again came to the fore as a leader of the political right, but the left was now in political ascendancy. In 1920, Hjamlar Branting began his first term as Sweden's first Social Democratic prime minister. That same year, the country joined the League of Nations and, in 1923, occupied a temporary seat on the organisation's council. However, this position was renounced in 1926, to enable Germany, now partially rehabilitated, to become a permanent member. Its membership of the League notwithstanding, Sweden continued upon its path of neutrality, reducing the size of its armed forces in 1925.

Although many intellectual Swedes still took an interest in elements of common Nordic co-operation, this remained limited in scope but some initiatives were undertaken. In 1918, *Föreningen Norden* (the Nordic Union) was founded to foster co-operation and this soon came to encompass the economic as well as the political. However, its political dimensions were weak in the extreme, especially as the countries of the Nordic region, in particular Norway, feared Swedish domination of the others. That said, all did sign up and even Finland, though long characterised by an almost exclusive Fennomania, became a member.

During the 1920s and early 1930s, no single party, whether of the right or left, was able to dominate Parliament and governments changed on average every two years. In one instance, Branting was forced out of office in less than one year and, in 1920–1, Louis De Geer the Younger (1854–1935), an Independent Liberal and son of Sweden's first prime minister, assumed the premiership in what proved to be a largely uneventful period in office.

On the left, Per Albin Hansson (1885–1946), the son of a stone-mason, became one of Sweden's most prominent young politicians during these years. A Social Democrat, in favour of alcoholic prohibition, he had become the protégé of Branting, who helped him to get a job as a journalist in Stockholm with the newspaper *Social-Demokraten*. He was eventually elected to Parliament in 1918, becoming defence minister during the 1920s.

In 1921, Oscar von Sydow (1873–1936), like De Geer of the Independent Party, became prime minister. During his short term of office, one significant legal reform was introduced: the abolition of the death penalty. However, in general, he received little support in government and was succeeded later that year by Hjalmar Branting.

His second term of office would last until 1923 and saw a further consolidation of Social Democratic power.

After the First World War, economically enmeshed as it was with the rest of troubled Europe, its neutrality and trade during the war not withstanding, Sweden's economy was in a grievous state. In the immediate aftermath, it suffered severe unemployment, with up to a quarter of the working population without a livelihood. Matters then began to improve, as industry once again began to develop, and by 1925 unemployment had fallen to only 10 per cent. Indeed, between 1919 and 1939, the annual growth rate of the Swedish economy increased by 3.3 per cent. That said, in terms of trade the economy still languished. From an export level of 20.8 per cent of GNP in 1913, it had fallen to only 16 per cent in 1925. Imports, too, remained lower: from 21.6 per cent in 1913, they had dropped to 17 per cent by 1925.

As for Germany, its political and economic collapse notwithstanding, it remained one of Sweden's major trading partners. Indeed, in the following years, as German industry revived, German imports of iron ore increased dramatically, especially in the late 1920s, after Sweden's own production had, in 1927, been fixed at 10.5 million tons per annum *in toto*, the overwhelming majority from its northern iron ore fields.

The upheavals in Russia, in particular, the civil war which raged in the aftermath of revolution until 1922, also brought considerable financial benefits for Sweden. The country had become revolutionary Russia's most important trading partner and acted as a conduit for the sale of Russian gold, of which the Swedish mint processed large quantities, despite the British and American blockade during the years 1920–1.

With the advent of the Great Depression, however, after the collapse of the Wall Street Stock Exchange on 29 October 1929, Sweden's economy virtually collapsed. The gold standard on which its currency was based was now rapidly abandoned. Economic losses in Sweden were vast and both rich and poor suffered. As in New York, major figures from the world of finance committed suicide in reaction to their losses, among them the famous entrepreneur and industrialist Ivar Kreuger (1880–1932). Popularly known as the 'Match King', his *Svenska Tändsticks* AB (Swedish Matches Ltd) was affiliated to the International Corporation in the United States, which had come to produce some two thirds of the world's matches. His empire had also come to encompass much of the forestry production of northern Sweden and he was heavily involved in the production of cellulose. His financial rise and dramatic fall eventually became the subject of the Russian-born American playwright Ayn Rand's Broadway hit of 1935, *Night of January 16th*, in which he inspired the character Bjorn Faulkner.

As unemployment surged in Sweden, discontent among factory workers and miners burgeoned. Serious strikes broke out, at the Stripa Mine, in Västmanland, and at Ådalen, in which five of the strikers were shot dead. Memories of these events and the hardships of the period would in consequence lead many Social Democrats over the following years to strengthen their main agenda: the creation of the so-called *folkhem* (literally, people's home) or Swedish welfare state. Among the most ardent of these supporters was Gustav Möller (1884–1970). It was he whose polemical skills, while minister for social affairs, helped to mould a positive public opinion for its implementation. Keynesian economic solutions were also adopted to overcome the economic depression, brought in by the Social Democrats who, from 1932, joined forces with the Agrarian parties, a government which would dominate Sweden for almost two generations.

Their successes led the American economist Marquise Child to publish his famous book *The Middle Way* in 1936, in which the Scandinavian economies were seen as offering viable alternatives to both Communism in the Soviet Union and capitalism in the United States. As such, it served to nurture the roots of the budding Swedish welfare state, which reached its full maturity only after the Second World War and in the decades which followed.

Despite contemporary expectations to the contrary, severe economic decline by no means encouraged criminality in Sweden. On the contrary, during the interwar years, crime, as such, was held at a relatively low level. In consequence, few new gaols or prisons were built, the prison stock of that century still serving its purpose well.

The efforts of that century in fostering a civic society in Sweden, in all segments of the population, were still bringing in dividends.

Despite the best intentions of the Social Democrats and the initiatives which they undertook to boost the economy, unemployment continued to burgeon in Sweden in the wake of the world-wide Great Depression, as almost 30 per cent of the population were thrown out of work by the end of 1932. In consequence, the severely weakened Swedish economy limped on more and more feebly and, by 1938, despite some minor gains in limited sectors, its ratio of exports to imports remained at a very low ebb. Indeed, only 15.7 per cent of GNP was now exported, as compared with 17.7 per cent imported, an unhealthy balance. While timber as a commodity of foreign trade had declined only slightly from pre-war levels down to 22 per cent in 1924-5, it had fallen more sharply down to 13.2 per cent during the years 1934-8. That said, some important industries did show signs of progress, in particular those of iron and steel. For, from a low of 5.3 per cent of foreign trade in 1924-5, they rose to 7.2 in the years 1934-5. The production of iron ore now came to assume a new importance, rising from 7.9 to 9.5 per cent of overseas trade between 1924 and 1935.

Sweden's engineering industry was also proving a boon for the otherwise debilitated economy, as its products rapidly acquired an international renown for quality, which made them highly competitive on the world market, even in these extremely difficult times. As a result, such goods formed an increasingly large share of the foreign export trade, as much as 21.3 per cent by the period 1934-8.

By 1938, Britain had become Sweden's most important export partner, taking 24.5 per cent of the total. Timber was just one of a number of important export commodities, a prerequisite for Britain's burgeoning building trade. Germany came second, with 18.2 per cent of the export market. With respect to imports, however, the roles were reversed: German imports totalled 24.0 per cent, but British only 18.3 per cent. During the late 1930s, Sweden's fledgling aircraft industry also achieved considerable economic prominence. SAAB (Svenska Aeroplan AB) was founded in 1937, at Trollhättan, near Gothenburg, and rapidly became an international byword for the country's growing reputation for high technological expertise, increasing in importance as war in Europe loomed ever closer.

By now, iron ore imports from the north of Sweden had assumed a significance for Germany that can hardly be overestimated. For by the later 1930s, no less than 60 per cent of its total iron ore imports were coming from Sweden. Indeed, it purchased some three quarters of all the total Swedish export of that material, vastly more than Britain, which only imported 12 per cent at this stage. This proved insufficient for British needs and, therefore, in 1937 it too attempted to purchase greater quantities of ore, which could be made possible, not so much at the expense of the Germans, but by encouraging the Swedish government to increase its overall production. This Sweden did, but it was not Britain which benefited most, since a recession in the steel industry in the latter meant that demand for iron ore was far less than had initially been anticipated. This surplus Germany greedily gobbled up.

New technological innovations, with major implications for communications, had by now come to the fore, with great import for the Swedish economy and social development. Public radio broadcasting commenced in 1922 and soon reached into the homes of virtually all Swedes. It was not only its entertainment value which was of significance, but the powers it exerted for opinion formation and public awareness of social problems and issues. When, in 1938, the author and journalist Lubbe Nordström (1882–1942) held a series of radio talks entitled *Lort-Sverige* (Crappy Sweden), it proved very important in bringing to a wide public an awareness of the acute housing shortage the major cities were suffering. This, too, further served to stimulate initiatives in the development of Sweden's nascent welfare state.

The motorcar was also becoming extremely important in Sweden, as its use spread increasingly through the general population. The first Volvo rolled off the assembly line in Gothenburg in 1927, under the direction of two men of vision, the industrialist Assar Gabrielsson (1891–1962) and the engineer Gustav Larsson (1887–1968). Like SAAB, Volvo, too, eventually entered the aeroplane market, though it was never as successful as its rival. Nonetheless, both companies proved indispensable in the production of aeroplanes in significant quantity to secure the country's aerial defences during the Second World War.

HEALTH, HYGIENE AND SOCIAL WELFARE

Despite the visitation of Spanish influenza in the wake of the First World War, life expectancy, in general, was on the increase throughout Sweden, where improved diet and hygiene helped to limit the spread of the old infectious diseases. This led to an increasingly older population, so new measures had to be taken in order to accommodate the growing numbers of elderly people who were physically incapable of looking after themselves or were suffering from senility. Age-old institutions like the Queen's House, in Stockholm, catering for the needs of impoverished ladies, found the demand for their services ever greater and, in 1924, the latter subdivided its rooms into smaller ones, along a central corridor, to accommodate more people in greater privacy. A large number of new establishments were also founded, catering for old people from all segments of the population.

Growing social dislocation and an ever more anonymous urban milieu, among the other physical and social causes of mental illness, also led to a growth in the numbers of people needing treatment for such problems. Along with traditional treatments in mental hospitals, the new, now notorious technique of lobotomy came into fashion towards the end of the 1930s. First performed by the Portuguese physician and neurologist Antonio Egas Moniz in 1936 – a treatment for which he won the Nobel Prize for Medicine in 1949 – its use became very popular in Sweden in the following decades as a means of dealing with mental disturbances. Up to 50,000 people came to be surgically operated on in this way, a technique which continued to be used in Sweden, with considerable regularity, until well into the 1970s. By then other forms of psychiatric treatments, some of which involved the administration of the pharmaceutical drug thorazine, useful for a wide range of pathological conditions, physical as well as mental, had supplanted the invasive surgical treatment.

Alcoholism also continued to be a problem in Sweden, as in other northern European countries, and numerous private clinics opened their doors to treat those suffering from it. However, its influence remained an all too frequent component in the commission of many violent crimes and, despite state control of the sale of alcoholic beverages, alcoholism continued to be a major social health problem.

Malaria, on the other hand, was finally eradicated from Sweden by the mid-1930s.

Child care also improved in the interwar years, the Municipal Child Care Boards having first been set up in 1902, but thoroughly reorganised in 1917. By the following year, it had become the custom for children without means of maintenance to be accommodated in newly established institutions created for that purpose. These no longer formed parts of larger institutions for adults, but were set up on their own, exclusively for the young, in response to growing public fears that the previous association of children with adults with whom they were not related had been the occasion for 'moral corruption' of them.

A variety of legal reforms were also enacted at this time. The death penalty was abolished in 1921, as we have seen, and that same year, women were granted the vote, as well as judicial rights of equality within marriage. Most significantly, for the rights of women, Kerstin Hesselgren (1872–1962) took her seat as the first female to be elected to the Swedish Parliament, in 1922.

Reforms, in these interwar years, were also taking place within the Swedish Church, as ecumenicism grew apace, culminating, in 1925, in a great congregation of churchmen in Stockholm, under the leadership of Archbishop Nathan Söderblom, which stressed the common ground held by all the mainstream Christian denominations. Only Roman Catholics, from the major Christian denominations, were not in attendance, their representatives having refused for theological reasons.

Among the Free Churches, the Pentecostal Church, in particular, continued to grow, drawing its burgeoning membership from disaffected Lutherans as well as Baptists. That latter loss notwithstanding, membership of Baptist churches remained strong, encompassing some 68,000 adherents in 1938. The greatest inroads, however, were those made by the *Svenska Missionsförbund* (Swedish Missionary Society). Not only did it continue to grow from strength to strength in Sweden, but its prominence overseas continued, with its focus on missionary activities, especially in Africa and Asia.

THE ARTS

If the Swedish Church and the other major Christian denominations of the country were becoming more international in their vision, the arts, too, were following suit. A number of painters, in particular, took an active part in wider artistic movements, international in scope. For example, Adrian Gösta Nilsson (known as GAN, 1884–1965) was deeply influenced by both Futurism and Cubism during his many sojourns to Berlin. Indeed, one of his most famous works, *City at the Seaside* (1919), combines elements of both, in its depiction of Halmstad, on the south-western coast of Sweden. Along with its vistas of the city itself, numerous vignettes are contained within its fractured surface, including an attempted burglary and the cosy sitting room of his friend Egon Östlund. The train that steams through the centre of the picture, in Futurist fashion, emphasises movement, seeming to accelerate as it approaches the viewer.

Another artist of considerable note was Sigrid Hjertén Grünewald (1885–1948), who was also very much influenced by Cubism, inspired in part by the works of her husband, Isaac, an artist of German-Jewish extraction who had spent many years in Paris. Her *View over the Sluice*, painted in 1919, evinces this fact and demonstrates the use of a one-point fragmented perspective to create the effect of a kaleidoscope in its depiction of Stockholm life, one in which the viewer is drawn into the work by a statuesque figure standing on a balcony, which seems borrowed from Picasso. The aristocratic Swedish painter Nils von Dardel (1888–1943) should also be mentioned, not least because of the important influence the international world of French, Russian and Swedish ballet had on his works. A grandson of the nineteenth-century history painter Fritz von Dardel, his *Visit at the Home of an Eccentric Lady* from 1921 depicts a bizarre array of events, with a perspective which twists three-dimensional reality, to create a modern, if naive, Bosch-like vision. The influence of the French artist Henri Rousseau is also present, for a lady dances with a monkey perched on her head. At the same time, motifs from oriental animal paintings seem to be present, hardly surprising, since von Dardel travelled extensively in Mexico and Japan, in the company of the impresario Rolf de Maré (1888–1964), the rich and brilliant founder of the Swedish Royal Ballet.

Finally, the sculptor Carl Eldh (1873–1954) is of note, not least for his works on Strindberg, in which his muscular ideal as expressive of the human form is used to express the intellectual power of Sweden's greatest playwright, in particular in his monumental sculpture *Strindberg* from 1923. To do this, he drew upon his extensive sojourn in Paris, where he had studied at, among other schools, the Académie Colarossi, receiving an honourable mention at the World Exhibition of 1900. Perhaps it is his much later work, *Runners*, from 1937, a bronze piece erected at the Stockholm Stadium, which is most expressive of the influence Rodin, too, had on his *œuvre*.

In music, the Swedish composer Hilding Rosenberg (1892–1985) enjoyed fame in the 1920s and 1930s. His *Piano Concerto No. 1* of 1930 was a particular success among Stockholm audiences, despite its modernity. His rejection of the romanticism of the previous musical generation inspired others, in particular the Monday Group, whose leading proponent was the composer and conductor Karl-Birger Blomdahl (1916–68).

In literature, the largely self-educated Eyvind Johnson (1900–76) was now coming to the fore with such novels as *Här har du ditt liv!* (Here is Your Life!), which appeared in 1935. Inspired by such intimately revelatory authors as Joyce, Gide and Proust, in much of his writing he drew upon his own experiences from his early life as a logger in the far north of Sweden, by the Arctic Circle. Harry Martinson (1904–78) was also of great note at this time, not least for his novel *Kap Farväl* (Cape Farewell, 1933), an autobiographical book based on his travels in which his imagery and descriptions of wind take on an expressive quality that alludes to human emotions. It took many years for their work to be fully appreciated and, in 1974, both Johnson and Martinson shared the Nobel Prize for Literature.

Swedish theatre was increasingly appreciated by an ever wider public audience, but of especial importance was the birth and development of the film industry. The silent movie had arrived in Sweden as far back as 1896, with native film production commencing in 1907. Films with sound followed in 1929 and towards the end of the following decade the actress Zara Leander (real name, Zara Stina Hedberg, 1907–81) became one of Sweden's most famous international stars, renowned for her husky and powerful voice. From a career in theatre in Stockholm – her first husband was the son of the director of the Royal Dramatic Theatre there – she emigrated to Berlin, where she rapidly became the darling of the Nazi regime.

15 The actress and film star Zara Leander (1907–81) became one of Sweden's most famous international divas during her years in Berlin leading up to and during the Second World War. Renowned for her husky and powerful voice, her collaboration with the Nazi propaganda machine damaged her reputation in the post-war years. Photo: British Film Institute.

Her wartime film *The Great Love* (1942), including the hit song 'I Know One Day a Miracle Will Happen', won her great acclaim throughout the Reich. However, seeing the defeat of Germany approaching, she returned to Sweden shortly thereafter. After the war, her career in her native country was in tatters, severely undermined by the propaganda contribution which her films had provided to the Nazi war effort. That said, in Germany and Austria she remained very popular and continued to perform on tours there for the rest of her life.

Even more successful internationally was the actress Greta Garbo (real name, Greta Lovisa Gustafsson, 1905–90). Her role in the

Swedish silent film *Gösta Berlings Saga* (Story of Gösta Berling, 1924), based on the novel by Harry Martinson, won her critical acclaim, but it was her move to Hollywood, where she began work at Metro-Goldwyn-Mayer, which provided her with the opportunities to become one of the world's most famous divas. Her role as the monarch in *Queen Christina* (1933), a highly fictionalised film about Sweden's seventeenth-century monarch, has become iconic, her private reclusiveness and facial inscrutability contributing to a mysteriousness which remains untarnished to this day, only added to by her decades of retirement in New York. She became naturalised as an American in 1951 and was awarded an honorary Oscar in 1954, for 'unforgettable performances'.

The final member of this great Swedish film triumvirate was Ingrid Bergman (1915–82), who also found her fame in Hollywood. Her most famous film was, without doubt, *Casablanca* (1942), in which she performed opposite Humphrey Bogart, in what was the most famous and admired film of that decade. By contrast to Leander and Garbo, however, she continued to act in internationally acclaimed films for decades, her later collaboration, in a variety of roles, with the film director Roberto Rossellini (who became her second husband), as well as Ingmar Bergman, among others, earning her three Academy awards.

SWEDEN MOVES TO THE POLITICAL RIGHT

If the arts in Sweden were becoming increasingly international in their sources of inspiration, on the political plane the country was entering a period of retrenchment and greater insularity. As in most other European countries, the parties of the political right increased their support during the 1930s. In 1936, the National Socialist movement in Sweden, despite its splintered state, achieved its greatest popularity, with some 20,000 voters supporting it in parliamentary elections. The *Nationalsocialistiska arbetareparti* (National Socialist Workers Party), which stood in close rapport with its German counterpart, under the leadership of Sven Olof Lindholm (1903–98) received 17,383 of the votes, the Swedish National Socialist Party the remainder. Lindholm's organisation Nordic Youth was, at this time, a particular focal point for spreading his propaganda among the rising generation of potential supporters. However, with only 0.7 per cent of the total vote, none of the Swedish Nazi candidates actually took seats in Parliament.

The extreme left was also in a poor and disorganised state. The Swedish Communist Party was both badly splintered and marginalised, unable through these weaknesses to influence the majority Social Democrats in any significant way. Thus, Sweden continued upon its middle road, carefully laying plans to bolster its military strength now that the League of Nations had shown itself to be powerless in the wake of Italy's invasion of Ethiopia, and the international situation worsened. When, in 1936, the Social Democrats and *Bondeförbundet* (Farmers' Union Party) came together to form a coalition government, the country's governing stability was secured until 1939. Then, in consequence of the outbreak of the Second World War, a coalition government including all democratic parties was formed.

With the prospects of war looming ever more threateningly on the horizon, initiatives were undertaken to create a Nordic defence pact in the spring of 1937. Plans were also made by the Swedish General Staff to provide military support for Finland in the event of the latter becoming involved in a war with the Soviet Union. When, though, Denmark's prime minister, Thomas Stauning, rejected the idea of a pact, Sweden fostered, instead, closer contacts with Finland. As a result, in 1939, Sweden, under its foreign minister, Rickard Sandler (1884–1964), endeavoured to secure for Finland the right to re-militarise the Åland Islands. However, the hostility of the Soviet Union prohibited its implementation. Swedish support thereafter became more discreet and largely economic in scope.

When the Second World War subsequently broke out on 1 September 1939, Sweden declared its neutrality. A meeting of the Nordic heads of state, of Sweden, Finland, Norway and Denmark, was convoked in Stockholm in October but the practical results, with respect to any possible concerted action, political or otherwise, were minimal. That said, Sweden put its defences in a state of military preparedness and General Olof Thörnell (1877–1977) was placed in overall command, supplanting the king as commander-in-chief of all Swedish military forces, a post he continued to hold until 1944. Yet Sweden's stance of neutrality was maintained: Russia's attack on

Finland on 30 November, while stimulating much popular sympathy, did nothing to change this situation, even if many Swedes, in a private capacity, enrolled as volunteers to fight for Finland.

With respect to Germany, Sweden endeavoured to maintain a strict political and military neutrality, but one which brought considerable economic benefits to the country. In April 1939, Sweden formally confirmed to the German government that the supplies of iron ore it so desperately needed would continue to be supplied. More concrete measures, though, including plans to create stockpiles of the material in the south of Sweden, from the ports of which export to Germany would be less risky in time of war, were not implemented.

THE SECOND WORLD WAR

When the Soviet Union invaded Finland on 30 November 1939, most Swedes sympathised with the long-lost former province. However, with the departure of the Social Democratic foreign minister Sandler, an uncompromising partisan who advocated aid for Finland, a major opposition to the maintenance of strict Swedish neutrality was removed. Career diplomat Christian Günter (1886–1966) was then appointed foreign minister. Hansson, now in his third term as Social Democratic prime minister, had won some 53.8 per cent of the vote. Forming a government of unity with a wide spectrum of political parties of both the right and the left, he successfully continued the maintenance of Sweden's official neutrality throughout the war. That said, covertly he and his government now came to provide Finland with both weapons and much needed credit. Some 12,000 Swedes also volunteered to help the Finnish struggle generally, many engaged in non-combative capacities in Finnish Lapland.

The industrialists Marcus Wallenberg (1899–1982) and his brother Jacob (1892–1980), sons of the elder Marcus Wallenberg, so active in negotiations during the First World War, also now assumed key roles, securing substantial economic benefits for Sweden during the course of the Second World War. Once again, as with their father, these entailed complex negotiations beneficial to both Britain and Sweden, which nonetheless left the country's official neutrality with respect to the Axis Powers largely undamaged. However, some areas of friction remained, for iron ore continued to be exported to Germany, fuelling its war effort. British plans were, therefore, laid to disrupt this and, in early 1940, the British MI6 agent Alfred Rickman led a commando group to sabotage its export from Oxelösund, on the Swedish Baltic coast. However, the attempt failed and the iron ore exports continued.

By now, a Russian presence in Sweden was also making itself felt, not least in the realms of diplomacy. The charming and brilliant Alexandra Kollontai, the Soviet Union's minister in Stockholm from 1930, and then ambassador from 1943, was an especially great asset to the new rulers of Russia, for she was skilful not only in keeping relations relatively smooth between the two countries but in co-ordinating negotiations between Finland and the Soviet Union, which later resulted in the conclusion of hostilities in the so-called Continuation War between the two countries, in 1944.

With respect to Norway, Sweden's response was perceived as less than fraternal by that country, to say the least, and led to resentments which have lasted to our own day. For, after the German occupation of Norway in March 1940, German military forces were permitted to use Swedish railways to cross the country. The scale of this transport became apparent in June 1941, when an entire German division of more than 18,000 men did so, travelling from Norway to Finland. This greatly facilitated the Nazi war effort and was only stopped in 1943, when German military might was on the wane. Many Swedes, particularly those on the political left, were unhappy with this state of affairs from the beginning of the arrangement and some of these found a voice through Torgny Segerstedt, Senior, editor-in-chief of the newspaper *Göteborgs Handels- och Sjöfartstidning*, and through Ture Nerman and his broadsheet *Trots Allt* (Despite Everything), which was full of sharp criticisms of the Swedish government on this issue.

Others, on the political right, were more worried about the threat from the Soviet Union, fearing the spread of Communism to Sweden, were the war with Finland to be lost. A strict government censorship, however, frequently lessened the impact of their publications, and issues which might have proved offensive to the belligerent powers were frequently confiscated, even those which cast a light on the torture of Norwegian resistance fighters by the Nazis. As a result, Sweden continued to meander down its path of official neutrality, edgily watching the great warring powers to the east and south, while allowing *in toto* more than two million German troops to crisscross its territory during the course of the war.

For all the flaws of its policies, however, one fact was appreciated by all: Sweden successfully avoided the fate of Denmark and Norway, occupied by German troops in April 1940. That said, the fears of the Allied Powers that Sweden would be brought within the Axis orbit, by one means or another, almost led to an invasion by Britain and France that same year. On 5 February 1940, the Allied Supreme War Council authorised, as part of Operation Stratford, the occupation of central Sweden by 100,000 soldiers, supported by 11,000 vehicles. In the absence of sufficient manpower and resources, however, such a grandiose scheme of occupation and defence against Nazi Germany was never realised. The maintenance of Swedish neutrality, in any case, had made it unnecessary and Swedish territorial integrity remained uncontested by both the Allies and the Axis.

THE ECONOMY IN WARTIME

The turning of the North Sea into a battleground during the Second World War greatly inhibited Swedish trade to the west, despite British willingness to keep certain maritime channels open for Sweden. It, therefore, willy-nilly, became even more dependent on trade with Germany across the Baltic Sea than had previously been the case. Iron ore was a primary resource desperately sought by Germany, as we have seen, and no fewer than 38 million tonnes of it were exported between 1940 and 1944. Coal and coke, on the other hand, were crucial commodities needed for the maintenance of Swedish energy supplies for industrial and domestic use. Naturally, in the difficult circumstances, imports declined and the government, in 1942, imposed increasingly strict regulations on the economy, which came to include caps on wages and prices, as well as rationing. That said, with the competition of foreign imported foodstuffs sharply reduced, agriculture in Sweden received a boost and prices rose significantly. The military, also, swelled beyond recognition. Having been funded to the tune of 148 million crowns in 1936, expenditure soared to 1,846 million in 1941–2.

Wartime difficulties in industry sometimes led to such stresses that the relationship between workers and the industrial management broke down completely. When industrial unrest in some sectors led workers to declare a strike on 5 February 1945, it was swiftly quelled but not before it had become the most serious industrial unrest in Sweden since the Great Strike of 1909.

A JEWISH HAVEN

Swedish neutrality, at least its aloofness from the devastating effects of war which engulfed its neighbours, had one further positive consequence and this proved an incredible boon to refugees who had reached the country from abroad: it provided a haven for thousands of people for whom persecution and death waited in the wings. Among the most famous cultural figures who fled to the country was the German socialist playwright Berthold Brecht, long settled in Denmark since 1933, but who arrived in Stockholm with his family in April 1939. He departed the following year, by way of Finland and the Soviet Union, from which he made his way across the Pacific Ocean to the United States. Of the greatest significance, however, was the asylum Sweden provided for European Jews, fleeing the Nazi holocaust. German pressures on the country notwithstanding, Sweden continued to provide a refuge for thousands of Jews from occupied Europe throughout the war, not least most of Denmark's Jews who had fled across the Sound in October 1943.

Sweden's profile elsewhere in Europe in saving many Jews from the gas chambers was also high: in 1944, Raoul Wallenberg (1912–47?), assisted by Carl Ivan Danielsson, Per Anger and Valdemar Langlet, helped many escape from Nazi-occupied Hungary by issuing them with Swedish passports. In this he was supported by King Gustaf V, who went as far as to write a personal letter to the Hungarian dictator Admiral Horthy enjoining him to stop the persecution. Wallenberg himself eventually fell into Soviet hands and is thought to have been sent to a labour camp, but the circumstances of his disappearance and death have yet to be fully clarified.

Folke Bernadottte (1895–1948), a cousin of the Swedish crown prince, the future King Gustaf VI Adolph, and vice-chairman of the Swedish Red Cross, was long said, also, to have assisted in a variety of humanitarian actions concerning the salvation of Jews in central Europe. However, the most recent conclusions are not edifying. It was long maintained that not only ten thousand members of the Norwegian, Danish and French Resistance movements, but a further eleven thousand Jews who had fallen into Nazi hands, were repatriated through his efforts, utilising the so-called 'White Buses' transport to Sweden, after successful negotiations with Heinrich Himmler. In reality, however, the scenario appears to have been rather different, if the recently published letters of Sir Hugh Trevor-Roper are to be believed. Trevor-Roper wrote to his friend the art connoisseur Bernard Berenson in 1952:

The negotiations which ensured the rescue of the 19,500 prisoners were almost exclusively the work of Felix Kersten, Himmler's doctor, who had concerted the plan with the Swedish Foreign Minister, Gunther, long before Bernadotte appeared ... When it came to implementing these plans, Bernadotte explicitly *refused* to save any Jews, telling Himmler that he shared his racial views.[1]

In the event, according to this account, Bernadotte was overruled and the plans for rescue were carried out. However, in the aftermath he claimed the credit, bolstering the prestige of both Sweden – tarnished by its acceptance of the Nazi troop transports to Norway – and himself.

As the Second World War drew to a close in the spring of 1945, Sweden could count itself most fortunate to have escaped the losses counted in tens of thousands by such other neutral countries as the Netherlands and Belgium which had also endeavoured, though with no success, to remain neutral. True, many Swedish seamen lost their lives on vessels of various nationalities during the course of hostilities, but Swedish ships themselves had avoided attack, albeit with two significant exceptions. In one, some thirty-three sailors died

---

[1] Hugh Trevor-Roper to Bernard Berenson, *Letters from Oxford* (attached to a letter written at Christchurch, Oxford, on 30 August 1952), in 'The Bernadotte Myth', edited by Richard Davenport-Hines, London: Weidenfeld and Nicholson, 2006, pp. 96–8.

when the Swedish submarine *Ulven* struck a mine in April 1943. In another, the ferry boat *Hansa* was sunk by the Germans – in what is believed to have been a mistake – sailing between Gotland and mainland Sweden on 24 November 1944, costing the lives of eighty-four passengers and crew.

The country had also escaped the carpet-bombing that had afflicted so much of the rest of Europe, although one load of bombs was dropped by mistake on Stockholm by a Soviet airman. In any case, on that occasion no one was hurt and the damage was minimal. Thus, Sweden had escaped virtually all the horrors of the Second World War, through its political and military neutrality, in stark contrast to all its other Nordic neighbours. It had also reaped considerable economic gain from both sides in the conflagration, resources which would prove of great usefulness in the development and funding of its still-unfolding welfare state. Most importantly, too, it continued to welcome many refugee children from Finland and elsewhere in central and eastern Europe, who arrived there at the end of the war, and it provided them with generous support, in a world and at a time when such comforts were in short supply.

10

Triumph of the Swedish welfare state

At the conclusion of the Second World War, from which Sweden had emerged largely unscathed, the country enjoyed greater social cohesion than ever before. With its social welfare infrastructure now firmly established, its benefits now came to be widely extended throughout its relatively homogeneous society, in which the overwhelming majority of citizens shared common ethnic, cultural and religious values, much as they had done for centuries. Immigration was limited largely to refugees who had escaped religious or political persecution, whether from Nazi Germany and the Soviet Union, or after the war from the Soviet-occupied states of eastern Europe, in particular from Poland, Estonia and Hungary. Later, they came to help carry out much of the work needed for the physical extension of the welfare state into which Sweden was being moulded, but in the immediate post-war years, their settlement – or removal – was a major problem. Deciding who could or could not remain permanently in Sweden was an especially thorny issue, often with life and death implications for the refugees.

More than 30,000 refugees from the Baltic states, now occupied by the Soviet Union, were allowed to remain. On the other hand, 2,700 German soldiers, with another 145 Latvians, Lithuanians and Estonians who had fought alongside the Germans but later taken flight to Sweden, were expatriated eastwards, either to prison camps or certain death. In these cases, Swedish fears of inflaming Russia,

Map 3 Sweden today. Sweden's borders have remained unchanged since 1809, when Finland, during the Napoleonic period, was transferred to the Russian tsar. The stability of Sweden's frontiers is a byproduct of the fact that the country has successfully maintained political and military neutrality from that time until the present day.

were they to permit the latter's former enemy combatants a lasting refuge, had proved too great to overcome. Many of these refugees to Sweden, therefore, ended their lives in the Soviet labour camps to which they were ultimately sent.

The post-war years formed a highly unsettled period on the international plane, as the former Allies – the United States, Britain and France, on the one hand, the Soviet Union, on the other – stood in increasingly acrimonious confrontation. While the death of Gustaf Adolph, Duke of Västerbotten, grandson of the king and father to the future Gustaf VI Adolph, in an aeroplane crash in Denmark in 1947 could hardly be blamed on politics, that in 1948 of Count Folke Bernadotte, now ironically – bearing in mind his alleged anti-Semitic feelings – United Nations representative in Jerusalem for the purposes of mediation in the Jewish–Palestinian conflict, was: he was assassinated by Jewish terrorists who resented what they perceived to be his deleterious interference, as they attempted to secure the foundations of the new state of Israel.

POLITICAL REFORMS

With the end of a government of unity under the premiership of Per Albin Hansson during the Second World War and his sudden death shortly thereafter, Tage Erlander (1901–85), former minister of education, was elected prime minister in 1946. He was to occupy this office for three terms, until 1969, becoming not only the country's longest-serving prime minister, but the longest-serving prime minister in any western European country of that period, and, as such, a symbol of the political and social stability of Sweden. Advocating the establishment of 'the strong society', that is, one in which a vast infrastructure of social services would be provided, he set both his own personal imprint, as well as that of the Social Democratic Party he so steadfastly represented, upon Sweden in a lasting and powerful way, making the country into what has since become the archetypal model of the welfare state. At the same time, he and his government rejected any totalitarian or aggressive imposition of their, largely, socialist goals, as was taking place in a number of Sweden's neighbours, now occupied by Soviet troops: censorship was abolished in 1949 and confiscation of property and wealth remained anathema.

In view of the growing confrontation between the western Allies and the Soviet bloc, imposing its 'Iron Curtain', as Churchill put it, on virtually the whole of eastern Europe, Sweden once again, in February 1948, stressed its official military and political neutrality in the new post-war Europe. This policy was championed by the Swedish foreign minister, Östen Undén (1886–1974), appointed for the second time in 1945 to this position which he had held previously a generation before, in the years 1924–6. A left-wing Social Democrat, he remained in office until 1962, but earned much criticism from those on the right of the political spectrum for his somewhat sympathetic stance towards the Soviet Union. That said, it was under his aegis that many unofficial rapprochements were made towards the United States and NATO, to secure the defence of Sweden in the event of a sudden Soviet attack.

This new stance in no way prevented the government from advocating the creation of a new Nordic defence alliance, committed to neither of the superpower blocs. As so often in the past with such pan-Scandinavian visions, however, no such alliance materialised: both Denmark and Norway joined NATO, while Finland maintained a political non-alignment in friendly co-operation with the Soviet Union, a process which came to be known as *Finlandisation*. It also signed a pact of mutual assistance and friendship with its erstwhile enemy. Therefore, a more modest and non-military Nordic Council came to be established in 1952, with the much more limited goals of encouraging economic, social and political co-operation among the Nordic countries. Finland joined it nine years later.

In 1951, the two principal political parties of the left, the Social Democrats and the *Bondeförbundet* (Farmers' Union), once again came together to form a government, as they had done in pre-war years. They continued to carry out a basically Social Democratic programme. In opposition, Jarl Hjalmarson (1904–93), leader of the *Högerpartiet* (Party of the Right), and Bertil Ohlin (1899–1979), the head of the *Folkpartiet* (People's Party), attempted to curb the state's intrusions into the private sector, but with ever diminishing success. Many of the political right and those who supported a more open market economy now lamented the fact that Sweden was increasingly becoming the model 'nanny state', in which the weaker members of society found an abundance of material support, but one in

which creative initiative, individuality, entrepreneurship and hard
work were now, to a considerable degree, stifled.

As the military might of the Soviet Union strengthened in the post-
war years, especially after its development of a nuclear bomb, fear of
this eastern imperium burgeoned, not least after the disclosure of
the alleged espionage activities of Fritiof Enbom (1918–74) and six
of his colleagues in the years from 1943 to 1951. When, in 1952,
the Russians shot down two unarmed Swedish reconnaissance
planes over international waters tensions heightened still further, but
Swedish neutrality remained uncontested.

Indeed, on a wide international plane, Sweden achieved an extraordinarily well-respected status by virtue of its neutrality, not only
in European affairs but elsewhere. This achievement was gained,
not through power politics, but through the humanitarian activities
of a number of Swedes, in particular that of Dag Hammarskjöld
(1905–61). Appointed Secretary General of the United Nations in
1953, a time of especial crisis because of the outbreak and unsatis-
factory conclusion of the Korean War, he continued to hold the post
until his death.

Already in 1946, Sweden had joined the United Nations, taking a
highly visible stance as mediator between the two political blocs.
When subsequently Hammarskjöld assumed his office, he was able
to draw upon Sweden's even-handed reputation to play a key role in
the negotiations in which he was involved. Among the most difficult
were those which sought to settle the political and military conflicts
aroused by the collapse of the Belgian Congo, a period when other
European colonial powers were relinquishing many of their colonies,
either voluntarily or through force. Hammarskjöld's sudden death in
an air crash in Africa – possibly provoked by South African secret
agents with their own political agenda – served to create a myth of
veritable martyrdom. His book *Vägmärken* (Markings), posthumously published in 1963 and infused with mystical Christian
values derived from the German medieval mystic Meister Eckhart
and other spiritual figures of earlier ages, helped to sanctify him
further in the public mind. He was awarded the Nobel Prize for
Peace in 1961, shortly before he died.

During the 1960s, both the Social Democrats and the more
radical parties of the political left gained considerably in popularity

and strength, as the multiplying benefits of the welfare system spread throughout society, most of whose members remembered the difficult days of the Great Depression. Then, the invasion of Czechoslovakia by troops of the Soviet Union erupted upon the scene, dampening much of the more radical left-wing enthusiasm. Nonetheless, in 1969, the left-wing politican Olof Palme (1927–1986), who had revolted against his upper-class background to pursue a radical, socialist-inspired political programme, became leader of the Social Democrats and therefore prime minister, and Sweden lurched further to the left. Over the following months, in consequence, the country became an ever more vociferous opponent of the American stance in the Vietnam War, thereby incurring the opprobrium of Washington, while turning a blind eye to the horrors of Communist repressions in the Soviet satellite states to the east and south. That said, Swedish co-operation with the Soviet Union and North Vietnam was less real than apparent, as an embarrassing report by Swedish journalists at the time indicated, revealing to the general public the great scope of Swedish anti-Soviet espionage. Nonetheless, a further shift to the left was facilitated in 1970, when the Swedish Parliament was made uni-cameral, with 350 members, a figure lowered to 349, for technical electoral reasons, two years later. Therefore, with the right marginalised, the Centre Party (a reincarnation of the old Agrarian Party) had become the leading opposition party by 1973.

Sweden, though, for all its political neutrality, was by no means immune to the rise of terrorism which by now had begun to plague so many other European countries under attacks from their radical fringes. Indeed, its presence in Sweden became all too obvious when, on 24 April 1975, members of the German-based Baader–Meinhof Group seized the embassy of the Federal Republic of Germany in Stockholm, in the aftermath of which three people were killed. The reality of the continued threat of the Soviet Union was also brought home to Swedes by the discovery, in 1981, of a Soviet submarine U 137, which had accidentally run aground in the archipelago of Karlskrona, a closed naval zone.

By the mid-1970s, the drawbacks, as well as the benefits, of Sweden's monolithic social democracy began to draw the attention of Swedish voters, increasingly desirous of ending what was threatening to become permanent one-party rule. In consequence, in 1976, Thorbjörn Fälldin (born 1926) of the Centre Party was elected as prime minister, ending more than forty years of Social Democratic rule. Except for a brief interlude under Ola Ullsten (born 1931) of the People's Party in 1978–9, Fälldin and his party remained in power until 1982. However, these parties of the right now came to maintain their period of power not through their own strength alone, but in coalition with one another. In 1982, this arrangement broke down, in consequence of which the Social Democrats, under Palme, were once again returned to office. He was now able, therefore, to pursue his radical agenda with even greater determination than before, taking stronger international initiatives which served to bolster his image as what many, both at home and abroad, called that of 'the world's policeman'. While the dismantling of the apartheid regime in South Africa became his primary focus on an international plane, the horrors faced by political dissenters in Erich Honecker's iron-ruled German Democratic Republic just across the Baltic hardly seemed to rise above his radar screen.

Political opposition to him from Sweden's political right was considerable but it was in no way implicated when, on 28 February 1986, Palme was assassinated while on a visit to the cinema with his wife. The crime has never been resolved. Whether he was murdered by the disgruntled and mentally disturbed young man who was at first accused of the *attentat*, or whether it had wider political dimensions, with tentacles spreading out amongst the great powers, remains unclear. He was then succeeded by Ingvar Carlsson (born 1934), a Social Democrat it is true, but one who was far less radical and controversial than Palme.

As the political stage, both international and domestic, shifted to the right, Carlsson was voted out in 1991 and, from 1991 to 1994, conservatives once again gained control of Parliament, with Carl Bildt (born 1949) from the *Moderata samlingsparti* (Moderate Party) elected as prime minister. The world was, by this stage, different from what it had been at the time of the previous election campaign: the collapse of the Soviet Union and the eastern bloc had served dramatically to encourage Sweden's continued political and economic shift to the right. Thus, as in other western European countries, the privatisation of formerly nationalised industries and services became the economic hall-mark of the day. Institutions like the post, rail and telephone were now, to varying degrees, rapidly privatised. This increasing market economy orientation was of particular importance for the Swedish economy, because one company, Ericsson, originally established in the nineteenth century, had now become the country's leading telecommunications player, cornering, by the early 1990s, more than a third of the entire cellular telephone system market world-wide.

The establishment and development of the European Union was another especially significant event, with major import for Sweden's political and economic identity. Sweden had for decades held aloof from the European Common Market, but with the European Union, in the post-Soviet period, it was a different matter. Despite the strident opposition of both the left and the Environment Parties, after a referendum on 13 November 1994, 52.3 per cent of voters supported the idea of Swedish adherence to the new pan-European organisation. The initiative was then taken and, on 1 January 1995, Sweden joined the European Union.

The country's political shift to the right was further underscored in the 1998 election, when the Social Democrats faced their lowest popularity since 1921, only 36.4 per cent of the vote. Nonetheless, together with the other left-wing parties, they continued to dominate Parliament. Therefore, in 1994, Carlsson was once again elected Swedish prime minister, a post he kept until 1996. He was then succeeded by fellow Social Democrat Göran Persson (born 1949). He remained in office until 2006. The economic and political values of the last few years, however, were a far cry from those of the heady radical days of Olof Palme. Moreover, today, the newly formed conservative *Allians för Sverige* (Alliance of Sweden), formed in the mid-1990s, has come to dominate government, through its four constituent parties, the Moderate, Centre (*Centerpartiet*), Liberal People's (*Folkpartiet liberalerna*) and Christian Democrats (*Kristdemokraterna*). Under the leadership of the Moderate Party politician Fredrik Reinfeldt (born 1965), a young prime minister with little of the social baggage of the earlier generation, they have served to consolidate Sweden's rightward political swing.

THE SAAMI IN SWEDEN AND THEIR
GROWING POLITICAL POWER

As in the other Nordic countries in the last decades of the twentieth century, ethnic minorities in Sweden were given new rights, both political and social. This was especially true of the indigenous northern people, the Saami (the term by which the people formerly known as Lapps prefer to be called). In 1993, the Saami were granted their own parliament, even if, by now, they were hardly a homogenous people. With Saami people across the Nordic world and the Kola Peninsula speaking some nine different dialects – some would say languages – this is not surprising, but there were also economic reasons. Even in Sweden itself, only 10–15 per cent of the 18–20,000 people who considered themselves Saami were now active in reindeer herding. In any case, this activity was no longer carried on in the ancient traditional way of past centuries, but now was facilitated by high technology, including aeroplanes and snowmobiles. With the majority now engaged in other forms of employment, the Saami often had other economic, social and political priorities. For many, therefore, a reassessment of what it actually meant to be Saami was needed. That said, certain aspects of Saami life were no longer negotiable, as they had been in the past, in particular the use of their language. In consequence, Saami has become one of the five official minority languages of Sweden today, along with Romani (Gypsy), Finnish, Meänkieli (a Finnish dialect spoken in the far northern region of Tornedal) and Yiddish.

THE POST-WAR ECONOMY

The post-war years in Sweden were ones of massive economic development, much of the fruits of which were required to pay for the burgeoning welfare state. In 1946, the Scandinavian Airlines System (SAS) was established by an inter-Nordic consortium, setting up regular flights to the Americas. That same year, an important credit and trade agreement was signed with the Soviet Union, which also proved mutually beneficial to both countries, as trade between them increased significantly. Sweden also reaped rewards from joining the Marshall Plan programme, in 1947, which provided money for

European redevelopment in the wake of the Second World War. It became a member, too, of the OEEC, an organisation which furthered economic co-operation among the free-market western European countries. That said, the Social Democratic government's imposition of a much higher tax burden on Swedes in 1947, under the leadership of the new finance minister, Ernst Wigforss (1881–1977), slowed down the economy and impeded its competitiveness. An equally problematic issue was more practical in scope, but equally difficult to resolve: a shortage of urban housing for an increasingly urban population was a serious problem during the first few decades of the post-war years but one which the state and its citizens were determined to resolve.

When regular television broadcasting commenced in 1950, on the occasion of the anniversary of the establishment of the Nobel Prize, first awarded in 1901, Sweden was clearly on the cusp of a new era. Yet during the 1950s, inflation became a significant problem in Sweden, despite the fact that growth in the import-export sector had occurred, even if the level reached was only that enjoyed by the country in 1900, including exports of 17.5 per cent of GNP in 1955, and imports of 20.3 per cent. Britain was by now the country's most important export partner in trade, accounting for 19.7 per cent of its exports, with the Federal Republic of Germany second, at 13.3 per cent of the total. The latter provided the lion's share of imports, though, some 21.9 per cent, while the British share now was only 13.7 per cent. As for the United States, it provided another 13.7 per cent. While imports at first predominated, the scales tipped in favour of exports over imports during the following decade, reaching 19.2 and 19.9, respectively, by 1969.

The timber industry and its ancillary products had clearly fallen to secondary significance. In the post-war years, the importance of timber in Swedish foreign trade had diminished dramatically, compared with other export commodities. From 10 per cent in 1947–50, it had declined to 7.7 per cent by 1967–70. Paper and pulp also assumed a less prominent role in foreign trade, down from 33.3 per cent to 15.8. Iron and steel, on the other hand, continued their unarrested rise, from 5.4 per cent in 1947–50, to 8.9 in the latter period. That said, engineering products now came to play the most prominent role, their share rising from 27 per cent to 42.7 per cent, during this time span.

From the 1950s to the 1960s, Sweden's shipbuilding industry continued to thrive, with more than 30,000 people employed in this sector. Kockum Wharf, in Malmö, was just one of a number of such successful construction sites. However, increasing competition from abroad, especially from east Asia, undermined this trend and the industry contracted over the following decades. By 1990, only 6,000 people were still employed in shipbuilding. As for the venerable Swedish-America Line, which had, in recent years, come to focus upon the demand by tourists for cruises, it, too, fell victim and finally ceased its passenger operations altogether in 1975.

Banking, on the other hand, continued to be a highly lucrative branch of the economy. Marcus and Jacob Wallenberg remained the two leading men of Swedish industry during this period, and their power base was consolidated by their control of *Enskilda Banken*, which merged with *Skandinaviska Banken* in 1971.

The creation of energy for public, industrial and domestic consumption had by now developed into a major industry in its own right. During the mid-1970s, the issue of nuclear energy became a source of considerable contention, since many people were fearful of its safety and health implications. Growing numbers of political activists began vociferously to object to its further implementation. Some, indeed, demanded that its use cease altogether.

Meanwhile, the car had come to be an indispensable form of transport for much of the population of Sweden. Unlike other countries in the Nordic region, however, it had implemented left-hand traffic, which now, with increased communications with its neighbours, had created considerable problems. Therefore, in September 1973, the country took the step and changed over to right-hand traffic. Other difficulties caused by the automobile, however, have proved themselves less easy to resolve: air pollution and the destruction of areas, both urban and rural, through which new roads have had to be built to accommodate the increased volume of cars and to provide more efficient access.

RISING COSTS OF THE WELFARE STATE

High taxation, too, had now became a bugbear for many, not only from the political right but among centre and even left-wing voters too, as many affluent people saw the bulk of their income gobbled up by the taxman to pay for the country's increasingly top-heavy social infrastructure. When Sweden's most famous author of children's books Astrid Lundgren (1907–2002) – *Pippi Longstocking* is amongst her most popular stories – publicised the fact that, in 1976, she had been obliged to pay more than 100 per cent of her income in tax – a situation quipped the 'Pomperipossa effect', after a name in a story which she published that year – even many life-long Social Democrats came to the conclusion that the wild spiral of taxation upwards had overstepped its mark.

Yet on the international stage, away from Sweden, where its disadvantages were becoming all too apparent, the reputation of Swedish Social Democracy as a model for providing the benefits of the welfare state was growing. In this trend, the economist Gunnar Myrdal (1898–1987), winner of the Nobel Prize for Economics in 1974, played a prominent role. During the years prior to his award he was a Visiting Research Fellow at the Center for the Study of Democratic Institutions at Santa Barbara, California, and from 1974 to 1975 he was Distinguished Visiting Professor at New York City University, too. Many of his writings focus on the issue of world poverty and the means to eradicate it, namely, Swedish Social Democratic values and methods.

Back in Sweden, however, the economy itself was confronting its own difficulties, many of them the product of this self-same Social Democracy, and many of its rich businesspeople, industrialists and landowners were gradually going into tax exile, often to Britain, taking much of their wealth and expertise with them. The economy was suffering and in 1977, the Swedish crown was devalued by 10 per cent. This served the beneficial purpose of encouraging Swedish industrial exports, which had begun to lose their economic competitiveness because of heavy taxation and the massive bureaucratic infrastructure which administered the welfare state.

Nonetheless, some branches of industry did rather well. During the 1980s, the Swedish motor-car industry was now able to compete more successfully with those of the United States and Japan. In consequence, by the 1980s Volvo, under its director Pehr G. Gyllenhammar (born 1935), had become one of the world's most sought-after automotive brands. The company launched the first front-wheel drive executive car with a transverse, five-cylinder engine in 1991 and a merger with Renault was mooted shortly thereafter. This never materialised and the company remained one of the few independent companies of its type, not only in Sweden but throughout the world.

SAABs, meanwhile, had become one of the most popular cars internationally for those who had achieved middle-age prosperity, after the *Svenska Aeroplan Aktiebolaget* started producing cars, as well as aeroplanes, for domestic needs in December 1949. The majority shareholding was sold to General Motors in 1989 and, in truly global fashion, the American-based company has since become part-owner of the Japanese-based Fuji Heavy Industries, so the Japanese, too, now play a role in the production of SAAB motor cars, in particular, the Saab 9-2X model.

Yet despite these undoubted success stories, the Swedish economy remained troubled. In 1982, the Swedish crown was again devalued, this time by 16 per cent of its value. That was a dramatic reduction, but far more disturbing to broad sections of the Swedish population was the Social Democratic attempt to propagate the so-called 'employee funds', collective financial bodies which were attempting to buy up large swathes of industry, ostensibly to further the financial interests of working people and as a means of achieving greater egalitarianism. This had been a controversial matter even within the party and one of its leading members, the minister of finance, Kjell-Olof Feldt (born 1931), had been set against it from the beginning. Horrified by what seemed to be a covert attempt to nationalise the private sector, many Swedes protested vociferously, marching in a demonstration of more than 75,000 in front of Stockholm's City Hall in 1983. Protests continued throughout the 1980s and, in a victory for 'people power', after the return of the right to political power, the 'employee funds' were finally dissolved, as even large segments of the left had turned against them.

By the 1980s, with its governmental intrusion into all aspects of public and private economic life, the public sector had become Sweden's primary employer, with its top-heavy involvement in all facets of regulation and control. Among its many competing priorities was the issue of sustainable energy. Nuclear energy had by now become more acceptable, as an unwelcome but necessary solution for the country's growing energy problems, and in 1980 permission was granted for the building of twelve new reactors. The reactor at Barsebäck, on the south-western coast of Scania, by the shore opposite Copenhagen, remained nonetheless a source of contention for many living in its vicinity on both sides of the Sound. For the quandary remained: where was the energy required for Sweden's future industrial and domestic use to be found, if the cheapest and most accessible resource was undesirable for ideological or ecological reasons?

Sweden's welfare state was now a long-standing and consolidated reality, but one which took its own toll on society, in a plethora of ways. For one thing, the political centralisation of the country increased dramatically, as some 2,500 communes were consolidated into only 284. Local regions and communities increasingly felt themselves isolated and ignored, as powers from on high determined the policies, political, economic, social and cultural, to be implemented.

During the early 1990s, the Swedish economy suffered considerable setbacks, not all of which could be blamed on Social Democracy, but were part of wider world market trends and increased competition. The stock exchange declined dramatically, losing some 40 per cent of its value, while the housing market virtually collapsed. However, even then, some companies thrived and they helped to boost the economy.

The packaging company Tetra Pak was certainly one of the great success stories of the 1980s. Founded in 1951 by Ruben Rausing (1895–1983) and Erik Wallenberg (1915–99) and employing a system of plastic-coated paperboard to make four-sided cartons, it went on to become the largest packaging company in the world, making Rausing's sons Gad (1922–2000) and Hans (born 1926) two of the richest men on the planet: that section of the company which produced cartons for asparagus juice in China alone was worth vast sums.

During the mid-1990s, Swedish exports increased by more than 10 per cent each year, while inflation plummeted to its lowest levels in almost forty years. Then, the next Swedish global industrial success story burst upon the scene. It was the phenominal growth of IKEA (an acronym of the owner's name joined to that of his family farm, Elmtaryd), the furniture manufacturers. Originally founded in 1943, it has become in recent years Sweden's most successful industrial and retail venture, making its owner, Ingvar Kamprad (born 1926), one of the richest men in the world and the richest in Sweden itself in the process. The Rausings and Kamprad made the system work for them, but for most people, consistently high Swedish taxes remained a serious issue, preventing the accumulation of capital. Indeed, by 1997, Sweden's tax burden on its citizens was the highest in the European Union, that is, some 55 per cent of BNP that year. In consequence, the country's economic competitiveness in market terms internationally continued to be troubled.

SOCIAL REFORMS

One of the most important issues to be dealt with in Sweden after the Second World War was the housing shortage. Therefore, in 1950, Sweden's Beneficial Building Society or SABO was founded as a nation-wide organisation to help in the provision of new, much needed, residential accommodation. This was aggravated not only by the arrival in cities of many Swedes from the countryside, but by growing immigration from Finland and Communist-occupied Poland, as well as from the formerly independent Baltic countries, now forcibly absorbed into the Soviet Union. Housing shortages were acute not only in Stockholm and the Swedish heartland but even in more remote parts of the country, where the population, though increasing, was relatively sparse, as in Norrland. There in Luleå, for example, the population had multiplied sevenfold between 1800 and 1950, while in the province taken as a whole, it had grown from 66,000 to half a million over that period.

As a result of these new initiatives, more than 100,000 rental flats were built in Sweden by 1970 and just five years later this figure topped a million. Most of them were unattractive rows of multiple blocks of flats, though a sizeable minority were small private houses – in contrast to the housing situation in most other European countries, including the Nordic ones, where relatively few single-family dwellings were constructed at this time. The people were, therefore, accommodated, but, already by the late 1960s, the failings of the new soulless satellite cities were already becoming all too apparent. Indeed, as the twentieth century progressed, many later became what some critics branded veritable ghettoes for Sweden's own marginalised underclass, many of whom, in the final quarter of the twentieth century, came increasingly from refugee Third World backgrounds. These included first Kurds, Iranians and Turks, then Albanians, Serbs, Croats and Somalis. A small minority of Swedes were alarmed by their arrival and a new phenomenon, that of violence perpetrated by small groups of Swedish neo-Nazis, came into being. A few people even lost their lives in consequence of these various incidents in different parts of the country, crimes previously virtually unheard of in Sweden up to that time.

However, if new problems were arising from changing social circumstances, others were being settled through improved infrastructure, which facilitated the availability of a wide range of public amenities. This was particularly the case in the realm of higher education, through which an ever greater proportion of the population now passed. To serve these new needs, Gothenburg University was established in 1954 and Stockholm's University opened six years later, when the former College of Higher Education was given a more elevated university status. This, in turn, was followed in 1965 by the establishment of Umeå University, in Norrland, and since that time a whole new range of institutions and academies of learning have opened their doors throughout the country.

Public transport, in particular air travel, was also in rapid development. Arlanda Airport, north of Stockholm, opened to the public in 1959 and has since become one of northern Europe's most important airports, facilitating the arrival in Sweden of millions of overseas visitors. Many other Swedish cities also obtained their own airports, providing rapid accessibility to virtually all parts of the country in a matter of a few hours.

Greater and better access to medical treatment now also became available. In 1955, public medical insurance was introduced and a high quality health care became available to all. Later, between 1957 and 1960, public opinion became deeply engrossed in the issue of service pensions, which arose in the wake of burgeoning inflation and the cost of higher post-war living standards. With opinions in the governing coalition diverging, a referendum on the issue was held, which chose the Social Democratic option, enabling the establishment of obligatory salary-related service pensions, financed by

employers, but with monies held in funds administered by representatives of government, employers and employees. In the wake of this
confrontation, the Social Democrats and the People's Party went
their separate ways, the latter in a severely weakened position.
When subsequently the issue went to Parliament, it was the People's
Party whose support led the establishment of these pensions along
the lines envisioned by the Social Democrats, who won out, a law
being promulgated to the effect in 1959. At first, the national pension
age was set at sixty-seven, but, in 1974, it was reduced to sixty-five.

Other more confrontational aspects of modernity also arrived in
Sweden at this time, much as they did in the rest of Europe and the
United States. The student occupation of the Student Union at
Stockholm's University in 1968 was just one of the many throughout
the western world which followed, in copycat fashion, that of Paris.
Feminism also increasingly came to permeate Swedish educational
life and society. The occupation of the *Kvinnohuset* (House of
Women) in Umeå, Norrland, was perhaps the most famous event in
respect to it, but nonetheless just one of a number of such sit-ins which
sought to focus upon gender issues in Sweden in the late 1980s.

A dramatic liberalisation of sexual attitudes occurred in Sweden in
the post-war years, in particular concerning homosexuality, after its
legalisation in 1944, some eleven years following legalisation in
neighbouring Denmark. From 1996, partnerships between members
of the same sex could be registered, with a wide range of economic
benefits. New measures were also introduced for the greater protection of women in other respects. In 1999, a law was enacted in which
the procurement of sex for money was criminalised in Sweden,
though not the selling of sex itself. New laws were introduced, too,
with respect to the workplace, prohibiting discrimination on the
ground of race and sexual inclination. It is against this background
that the consecration of the first female bishop of the Church of
Sweden, Christina Odenberg, took place in Lund in 1997, consolidating that process of gender liberalisation in the Church which had
begun when female priests were first ordained in 1954. In 2000, the
Swedish government finally disestablished the Church of Sweden,
thereby formally separating Church and state, an action of which
Archbishop Karl Gustav Hammar (born 1943) approved, despite the
fact that 87 per cent of the country's population were still officially

members. In 2006, Anders Wejryd (born 1948) succeeded Hammar as Sweden's sixty-ninth archbishop and the Church's journey down the path of liberalisation continued.

Despite growing secularisation and the movement to disestablish the Swedish Church, Christianity had, over the preceding decades, flourished. On 23 July 1973, the Lutheran Sisters of Brigitta Convent opened its doors again at Vadstena after a lapse of several hundred years, in celebration of the six-hundredth anniversary of St Brigitta's birth. Other churches also did well. Indeed, during the second half of the 1980s, the Catholic Church had become the fastest-growing religion not only in Sweden, but in the other Nordic countries as well. The first papal visit to Sweden took place in 1989, on which occasion Pope John Paul II visited Uppsala Cathedral, praying in the company of the Lutheran archbishops of Uppsala and Turku and of King Carl XVI Gustaf (born 1946) and Queen Silvia (born 1943). As for the Swedish Missionary Society, it too continued to thrive, but changed its name in 2003, in view of its growing autonomy, to the Swedish Missionary Church.

HEALTH, HYGIENE AND CHERNOBYL

By the 1950s, Sweden was definitely a far healthier place to live than it had ever been. The country's last native leper who had contracted the disease in Sweden had died in 1951. However, there were little grounds for complacency in terms of measures to prevent the spread of disease. Indeed, a failure to implement such proper measures led, in 1963, to the last smallpox epidemic to afflict the country. It affected Stockholm specifically, apparently imported by air from south-east Asia by a Swedish seaman returning home. Twenty-five people fell victim to the disease, of whom four died. Massive vaccination was then implemented and the disease rapidly disappeared, never to reoccur.

The political shift away from the left has also brought other medical changes. Towards the end of the twentieth century, privatisation once again began to make inroads into the Swedish health system, much as has been the case elsewhere in northern Europe. In 1999, Sankt Göran's Hospital, in Stockholm, became the first of Sweden's hospitals where emergency treatment was privatised and others have since followed.

The care of the mentally ill has also changed radically during this period, as many such individuals were released into 'care in the community'. Lobotomy as a surgical treatment for those with mental illnesses also fell out of favour with psychiatrists who increasingly preferred administration of medicines and analytical therapies to treat their patients. The sterilisation of those deemed unfit to bear children also diminished dramatically during this period until it ceased altogether in 1976. By then, though, since 1936 no fewer than 63,000 women had been sterilised.

Alcoholism continues to be a significant health problem and suicide levels reached record highs during this period. Increased wealth, a growth of the provisions of social services and the easy availability of psychotherapy have failed to stem its inroads.

Many accidental deaths in Sweden continued to be caused by the failure to implement appropriate safety measures, in particular with respect to 'do-it-yourself' household activities. However, these were brought to public attention and the incidence declined. That said, the growth of mass tourism brought its own risks to life and limb. The sinking of the German-built ferry boat the *Estonia* off the coast of Finland on 28 September 1994 took the lives of 852 passengers, 501 of them Swedes, its improperly designed bow door one of the contributing causes. More recently, the *tsunami* which afflicted the eastern Indian Ocean littoral in late December 2004, killing hundreds of Swedish tourists, among the hundreds of thousands of dead, brought home the fact that natural cataclysms were by no means just the rare eventualities of past millennia. This has served to focus the Swedish mind on related ecological issues, not least that of global warming.

Other problems of great gravity from beyond its borders also confronted a Swedish populace which had thought that by bringing its own house into order new health threats could be prevented. On 26 April 1986, the Chernobyl nuclear energy station in northern Ukraine, then a part of the Soviet Union, exploded with dire consequences. The local environs were devastated, hundreds of nearby residents killed and the land polluted, but Sweden, too, in the direct path of much of its fallout, was also affected. In particular, the Saami people, many of whom were still involved in reindeer herding, found not only their long-term health but their livelihood undermined, as the Swedish government imposed bans on the sale and export of reindeer meat, their primary export. This situation was aggravated by the fact that in Norway the authorities permitted the sale and export of such meat with vastly higher concentrations of radioactivity than in Sweden. Even then, over time, when in Sweden the export of meat with higher concentrations than before was permitted, the action only served to undermine public confidence, rather than to boost it. Only the introduction of artificial fodder for the reindeer, which enabled them to avoid food contamination from local pasture altogether, helped to relieve matters. Nonetheless, large numbers of the reindeer which had been affected were killed and their meat destroyed, a lost generation of food produce. As a result and despite some financial compensation, this most traditional of Saami livelihoods was undermined. In consequence, fewer and fewer Saami are now engaged in such animal husbandry, having become diversified into the other, more sedentary, activities usual in Sweden.

LITERATURE

During the second half of the twentieth century, Swedish literature thrived, sometimes gaining an international reading public in translation. Harry Martinson and Eyvind Johnson, whose careers had already blossomed in the interwar years, now achieved their full maturity, jointly winning the Nobel Prize for Literature in 1974. Martinson's *Vägen till Klockrike* (The Road), which was published in 1948, considered the plight of tramps and other social outcasts in a sympathetic fashion. Johnson's *Hans nådes tid* (The Days of his Grace) first appeared in 1960, but was later translated into a plethora of languages. A historical novel set in the court of Charlemagne, its focus is sombrely political and social, with reflections more of twentieth-century totalitarianism than of life in the Middle Ages.

One of the most important literary figures of the period was Sven Delblanc (1931–92), born in Canada to a Swedish immigrant family, who later resettled in Sweden. His first novel, *Eremitkräftan* (The Hermit Crab), published in 1962, used the medium of allegory to examine a wide range of political and spiritual issues. Later works included *Stadsporten* (The Town Gate), which appeared in 1976, focusing upon life in the countryside in Sweden of the 1930s.

Perhaps the greatest literary accolades, however, have gone to Torgny Lindgren (born in 1938), one of the most profound novelists of the later twentieth century. A convert to Roman Catholicism in 1980, much of his work thereafter has a rich spiritual dimension, not least *Ormens väg på hälleberget* (Serpent's Way on Halle Hill), published in 1982, which focuses, in an almost biblical style, upon a remote community living in the north of Sweden, drawing inspiration from Vastrabothnia, where he himself was born. It was made into a film in 1986, with the Swedish-Finn Stina Ekblad (born 1954), now one of Sweden's leading contemporary actresses, as Tea. In recognition of Lindgren's extraordinary literary skills, he was made a member of the Swedish Academy in 1991 and of the Nobel Prize Committee as well.

Yet another important literary figure was Sara Lidman (1923–2004), whose *Hjortronlandet* (Cloudberry Land), published in 1955, considered her childhood experiences of rural life in the north of Sweden. Other works focused upon the war in Vietnam and the role of the United States, of which, being active in the Communist movement, she vehemently disapproved, as well as on apartheid in South Africa, which she also strongly opposed. Later novels, on the other hand, including *Järnkronan* (The Iron Crown), which appeared in 1985, had a strong spiritual, rather than temporal, dimension.

In the detective stories written by the husband and wife authors Maj Sjöwall (born 1935) and Per Wahlöö (1926–75), the literary character Martin Beck achieved wide popularity in Sweden. They include some ten novels, beginning with *Roseanna* in 1964, and concluding with *Terroristerna* (The Terrorists), published in 1975. Since then this genre has achieved a wide following both at home and abroad. Among authors now active in this literary branch, which frequently blends over into so-called Scandinavian Noir writing, are Karin Alvtegen (born 1966), a great-niece of Astrid Lindgren, noted for her novel *Saknad* (Missing), which won the best crime novel award of 2000 in Sweden, and Liza Marklund (born 1962), author of *Prime Time* (2002). The latter's work is stylistically informed by her writings for tabloid newspapers, in which she has often focused on the problems of Norrland, not least with respect to depopulation.

ART

During the post-war years and beyond, the arts in Sweden were deeply influenced by international stylistic trends, including, in particular, those emanating from the United States. For example, the painter Öyvind Fahlström (1928–76), born of a Norwegian father and Swedish mother, but a native of Brazil who settled in Sweden, achieved considerable acclaim through his pop art, which drew its principal inspiration from the USA, although French Situationism also influenced his *œuvre*. Much of his work has political and social overtones, especially his 'happenings', which include *Aida* (1962) and *Mellanöl* (Middle Strength Beer, 1964), both in the Moderna Museet of Stockholm.

Another artist of significance was Phillip Schantz (1928–98), whose works, for all their rich detailing, have a minimalist quality and evince a subtle use of limited tonalities. He is especially noted for the gentle lyricism of his still-life works, many of which are to be found in the Nationalmuseum and Moderna Museet, in Stockholm.

A younger artist, Peter Tillberg (born 1946), has worked in a variety of mediums. His illustrations *Sagas*, intended to accompanying the writings of a Swedish edition of the short stories of Isaac Bashevis Singer, appeared in 1995. Also of note is his painting *Blir du lönsam, lille vän?* (Are You Worth It, My Little Friend?, 1971–2), which depicts the interior of a classroom full of small children at their desks, drawing attention to the realities of the classroom and the often unfulfilled needs of pupils, whose individuality is not always respected by their teachers.

FILM

While the visual arts produced a number of highly talented artists in Sweden, it has been in the world of film that the country has really achieved an international recognition. This is to a large degree because of the world-wide appeal of the films of Ingmar Bergman (1918–2007), undoubtedly not only Sweden's greatest film director but one of the greatest in the history of film production altogether. His collaboration with the innovative cinematographer Sven Nykvist (1922–2006), twice winner of an Oscar, proved a genial

16 One of the greatest film (and theatre) directors in the world, Ingmar
Bergman (1918–2007) explored the most intimate psychological states of his
characters against a lyrical backdrop, rich in metaphysical overtones, which
won him international acclaim for such films as *Wild Strawberries* (1959),
Persona (1966) and *Fanny and Alexander* (1982). © Scanpix/epa/Corbis.

combination. Such films as *Wild Strawberries* (1959), *Persona*
(1966) and *Fanny and Alexander* (1982) insured his place as the
most insightful director of scenarios in which the most intimate
psychological states of the characters are juxtaposed against a
lyricism that seeks to explore metaphysical issues, at the same
time as it does personal ones. His casting of some of the Nordic

world's finest actors and actresses is also of great significance, including as they do such figures as Max von Sydow (born 1929), Bibi Andersson (born 1935), Erland Josephson (born 1923, a relation of the nineteenth-century painter Ernst Josephson) and more recently the Norwegian Liv Ullmann. Other already famous actors, including Jarl Kulle (1927–97), also came to act in his films.

Famously hostile to what he perceived to be the culturally deadening effects of Swedish Social Democracy, Bergman incurred the wrath of many dyed-in-the-wool Socialists who, while appreciating his cinematic genius, nonetheless wished to see him knocked off his pedestal, from which he scornfully but with sadness watched the debasement of much of Sweden's modern artistic culture. This reached its culmination in 1976 when Bergman was arrested at the Dramatic Theatre in Stockholm – he was also an immensely talented director of plays – accused of tax evasion. In its wake, he went into exile from Sweden, although he eventually returned a few years later.

Since then, new film directors like Lasse Hallström (born 1946) have come to the fore, with films such as *Mit Liv som Hund* (My Life as a Dog), in 1985, based on a novel by the Swedish author Reidar Jönsson. Hallström's career since then, largely Hollywood based, has been more populist. This is hardly surprising since in his early days he made music videos for the pop group Abba. Later works include such blockbusters as *What's Eating Gilbert Grape?* in 1992, and *Casanova*, in 2005. *The Shipping News*, in 2001, based on the novel by the American author E. Anne Proulx, attempted to bridge the gap once again between art and a popular box office appeal, but failed dismally in this regard, despite the worthiness of its subject matter.

MUSIC

Popular music in Sweden in the post-war period was highly influenced by trends from across the Atlantic, but in its classical expression, Russian influences came to bear. This was to a large degree because of the world-famous tenor Nikolai Gedda (born 1925, real name Nikolai Ustinov), born in Stockholm to a Swedish mother but a Russian father who was related to the actor Peter Ustinov. Among the most widely recorded opera singers in history, he was particularly famous for his role as Lensky in Tchaikovsky's opera *Eugene Onegin*. Equally of note is the Swedish tenor of Finnish extraction Jussi Björling (1911–60), who also achieved enormous renown, dominating the international Italian opera scene in such roles as Arnoldo in Rossini's *William Tell* and Almaviva in *The Barber of Seville*. Especially renowned was the tenor part he sang under Toscanini in Beethoven's *Missa Solemnis*, performed in New York in 1939, a recording of which is of considerable interest for opera buffs.

The soprano Birgit Nilsson (1918–2005) also achieved immense fame on the international stage, not least for her performances in both German and Italian opera, especially for her rendition of Isolde in Wagner's *Tristan und Isolde*, and later as Turandot in Puccini's eponymous opera.

The greatest musical success of the 1950s was the new Swedish opera *Aniara*, the music of which was composed by Karl-Birger Blomdahl (1916–68) and the libretto by Erik Lindegren, based on the eponymous poem by Harry Martinson. In its premiere on 31 May 1959, Erik Sædén, as Mimaroben, and Loulou Portefaix, as Isagel, took the leading roles.

On a popular level, the singing group Abba, including Benny Andersson, Agnetha Fältskog, Anni-Frid Lyngstad and Björn Ulvaeus, enchanted the world with its songs especially during the years 1972–82, selling more than 350 million records. They were undoubtedly the Nordic world's most popular musical group, adored for such songs as *Dancing Queen* (1976) and *Take a Chance on Me* (1978), both of which remain popular to this day and are the subject of repeated revivals.

SPORT

In sports, as in the arts, the role of Sweden on the international stage was considerable. In the third quarter of the twentieth century, Swedes achieved international renown for their participation in a variety of sports, but none more so than tennis. In this, Björn Borg (born 1956) played the leading role as the world's number one tennis player. Indeed, he has been deemed by many, especially other tennis players, to have been one of the greatest ever to play the game. During his nine years of playing at the highest level, he won no less than 41 per cent of the Grand Slam singles tournaments in which he participated, and additionally 89.8 per cent of his Grand Slam singles matches. Amongst Sweden's numerous Davis Cup winners was the highly famed Mats Wilander (born 1964), who also became world number one. His successes included seven Grand Slam singles title, along with one Grand Slam doubles. While 1988 was his most successful year individually, he helped Sweden to win the Davis Cup in seven consecutive years in that decade. Sweden had, thus, succeeded in achieving an Apollonian eminence on the world stage, not only for its political fairness, model social welfare and technological expertise, but for its cultural and sporting merits as well, no mean feat for a small country on the northern European periphery.

Conclusion

The beginning of the new millennium witnessed Sweden's continued but gradual shift to the right and a departure from the political aloofness which had characterised its relation to the rest of Europe for decades. In September 2006, the Moderate Party led by Fredrik Reinfeldt (born 1965) gained the majority of votes by just 1 per cent, ousting the Social Democrats, to bring the country its third youngest prime minister. Fears that jobs might be put in jeopardy or that the Swedish welfare system might be undermined by a change of government obviously had made little headway with marginal voters. Now it remains to be seen to what degree the government's policy to reduce the size of the social sector, employing some 30 per cent of the entire Swedish workforce, will be implemented. It also remains to be seen to what degree taxes, among the highest in Europe, will be reduced and the social welfare system streamlined, in particular, with respect to unemployment benefits, which threaten to undermine Swedish economic development. With unemployment running at 6 per cent, or 10 per cent, if people on sick leave and job training schemes are taken into account, the sums involved are considerable.

The new world order, almost a generation after the end of the Cold War, has brought new enemies. In consequence, Sweden's almost two-century-old political and military neutrality has receded into the background. Osama Bin Laden's statement that he had no bones to pick with Sweden did not prevent the country from supporting the war in Afghanistan against the Taliban and Al Qaeda, making it as vulnerable to Islamic extremism as any other. The admonitory example of Denmark, put in the firing line of Islamic fundamentalists because of a caricature of the Prophet Muhammad published in the Danish newspaper *Jyllandsposten* in 2005, brought home to Swedes new political realities and the dangers they entailed, were any further example needed.

Even at home, changes were taking place, albeit minor in scope: the final vestiges of privilege of the Swedish nobility, already largely symbolic, were finally eliminated in 2002. That said, Sweden remains a highly centralised country, politically and economically, one in which government regulations, whatever political party is in power, determine virtually all aspects of political and economic life. Indeed, governmental involvement seems to intrude to an ever greater degree in all aspects of life, from gender identity and rights to social initiatives for ethnic minorities. However laudable these may be – and some are in hot dispute – they have served to stifle private initiatives. In consequence, private charitable endeavours have remained at a low ebb. The popular expectation of most segments of society remains that the government will provide what is required for the resolution of most of society's ills, whatever they may be.

Ecological issues, along with economic ones, now dominate Swedish political debate. Global warming is a particularly hot issue, though media unity on the rightful solutions to invoke masks genuine scientific disagreement among meteorologists, academics and industrialists. Certainly, the hot summers of the late 1770s and early 1780s are comparable to those of today and it is by no means clear to many what, if any, significant degree human industry, as opposed to solar activity, has played a major role in the changes. That said, many Swedes prefer to take no chances in risking further destruction of the atmosphere and so, in Stockholm, buses now run on gas from anaerobic sewage.

Yet ecological concerns notwithstanding, Swedes in general love their aeroplane flights to the tropics and so a huge percentage of the population avail themselves of cheap transport, usually with charter flights, whatever the environmental cost. These, along with faster rail and road links, have certainly brought Sweden closer to the other countries of the world, especially its European neighbours. The opening of the Sound Bridge and Tunnel in 2000, linking

Sweden and Denmark, remains a potent symbol of the new age of co-operation, not only for the Nordic countries and Germany, but Europe as an organic whole.

The Swedish economy has also become more integrated with that of the rest of the world and many Swedish companies earn vastly more income abroad than in Sweden itself. As in the past, economic events outside Sweden and especially in America can exert enormous influences domestically too. The bursting of the world-wide 'dot com bubble' in 2000 which started in the United States affected Sweden in serious ways, causing its stock market to fall dramatically, in consequence of which many companies in that sector went into bankruptcy. Governmental intervention in the functioning of the economy also continues to play a major role: a planned merger of Volvo's lorry production with that of Scania to form a single company was prevented by the government, in order to avoid the creation of a monopoly, deemed harmful for the country's well-functioning market economy.

The still burgeoning telecommunications industry was and remains vulnerable to the wider global economy. Thus, when, at the turn of the millennium, the telecommunications industry world-wide was in a state of crisis, Ericsson, too, was no exception: it lost 30.3 billion crowns of its value in 2001 alone. However, in 2004 it merged with Sony and became once again a profit-making venture, international in scope. With its headquarters in Stockholm, it is just one of a number of such telecommunication industries based there, which has led some to nickname the city 'the Wireless Valley'.

If some problems, largely economic, have been resolved, others, particularly those of a social nature, have been less amenable to change. Alcoholism remains a serious problem, as in a number of other northern European countries. Indeed, the consumption of alcoholic beverages increased dramatically in Sweden in the new millennium, especially that of beer and wine, some 40 per cent greater that in 1996.

Unemployment, on the other hand, has remained relatively low. That said, job security has been on the decline, since few can rely on life-long tenure until their retirement, as had previously often been the case, at least in the first few decades of the post-war years. While this new job climate may have increased economic efficiency, it has also increased personal stress. Sweden's economic decline vis-à-vis the 1980s has sharpened this problem, since the country has not had the benefits of oil resources, like neighbouring Norway and Russia, to mitigate such ill effects. On the other hand, Sweden has been quick to invest in modern technology and development. In fact, more than 3 per cent of GDP is invested in such research and development, a proportion considerably higher than that invested in these areas even in the United States.

Academic research has also continued apace and, whilst the sciences remain clearly favoured, in investment terms, over the humanities, new ventures even there have been undertaken. Thus, a new translation of the Bible into Swedish was published in 2000, a highly challenging enterprise which involved some 250 scholars and for which funds of more than 67 million crowns were successfully provided.

While age-old ethnic divisions within the Nordic world have healed over, other racial and ethnic tensions have developed in their place. These include new sharper ones between native Swedes and immigrants from other parts of the world, especially the under-developed countries of the Third World, often in political and military turmoil. Stockholm's first mosque opened its doors near Medborgarplatsen on Södermalm in June 2000, a sign of religious toleration, but with growing threats of fundamentalist Islamic terror-ism world-wide and the public's increasingly anxious reaction, it is not yet clear how this new situation will come to affect traditionally liberal Sweden.

With respect to health and hygiene, Sweden's situation remains one of the best in the world. Although there is increased privatisation in medical care, public medical standards of treatment remain high, despite the fact that the greater demands made on public health care by an increasingly aged Swedish population have added strains to the system. Heart disease has declined relative to preceding decades and the country is one of the best fed anywhere. Furthermore, almost all the acute epidemical diseases of history have disappeared from Sweden: plague, leprosy, smallpox, malaria and cholera are known only as scourges of the distant past. It has been a different matter with AIDS, though this has now to a certain degree been contained through good sexual education and appropriate medical treatment for victims. That said, preparations have been made for the eventualities of new threats: the re-introduction of old epidemic diseases by bio-terrorism and the prospect of new influenza epidemics, such as that which might arise from so-called 'bird flu'. There is also the increasing problem of drug addiction, especially among the young, with its seemingly irresolvable social component. This has led to an increase in crime, not least within immigrant communities from the Third World, a minority of whom have been involved in the drug trade, along with a disproportionate presence in other forms of criminality. Yet the murder rate at the end of the last millennium in Stockholm remained low: only 3 per 100,000 people, or just slightly higher than in the UK in the same period. By comparison, in New York it was 16.8 and in Helsinki 12.5. On the other hand, in Rome it was only 1.7 and in Athens 1.4. So Sweden can hardly be boastful of an exceptionally good record. With respect to prostitution, the buying of sex was criminalised in 1999, but its sale was legalised.

Gender issues continue to be important. Gay and lesbian partnerships are now accepted in Sweden, even if outside major urban areas, traditional values and prejudices still prevail. In line with trends in the rest of Europe, marriage has continued to decline as an institution, with many Swedes, including a significant number of gay and lesbian parents, preferring to live and raise children together outside the institution.

Other aspects of traditional ways of life also remain under threat. While the Saami reindeer herders have survived the devastating effects of the Chernobyl disaster of 1986, other threats have served to circumscribe their traditional nomadic way of life further. For one thing, the pastureland available for their animals has been considerably reduced, for the so-called 'managed wildernesses' encouraged by modern ecologists mean that the wildernesses are now no wildernesses at all. The declaration by UNESCO which made areas of Swedish Lapland part of the Laponia World Heritage Site is a boon for tourists but not for the Saami in need of grazing land for their often over-populous herds. Moreover, the economic exigencies which have been obliging the herders to maximise the amount of meat that can be produced on a limited amount of grazing land have been at loggerheads with the 'needs' of nature in the wild. This situation has been further aggravated by the protection increasingly afforded to wolves by the Swedish government, in opposition to the wishes of herdsmen for whom wolves are a perennial threat, since the compensation awarded to those who lose reindeer to these predators is only a quarter of their true market value. Hydroelectric intrusions into grazing lands have also played a deleterious role.

Yet, as serious as these issues are for many Saamis, the overwhelming majority of their community are now preoccupied with different issues. This is natural since reindeer herding itself has become something of a private club for those who draw their livelihood from it: there was simply not enough land to make it possible for many of the rest to be engaged in such activities. In any case, many had already taken up other occupations, not least in factory work or tourism. With such diversity in the contemporary Saami community, it is not surprising that a dozen different local political parties have come into being, representing the spectrum of Saami political and other interests.

Sweden's role and identity in the European Union is, of course, now well established but it is still a matter of debate, sometimes a violent one. In 2001, Sweden took over the chairmanship of the European Union, but that same year angry protests erupted in Gothenburg when leaders of the European Union met in that city, injuring eighty people and causing damage in the region of 100 million crowns. More than a thousand people were arrested. Nonetheless, despite such grass-roots disgruntlement, Sweden's loyalty is demonstrated by its contributions to the European Union, unequalled by other countries, some 11 billion crowns, or 0.5 per cent of its GNP.

With respect to the United Nations, Sweden has maintained an unusually high profile dating from its inception at the end of the Second World War. It has kept two army battalions available for its service since 1964 and more than sixty Swedes have died under its flag, in a variety of peacekeeping assignments. In the Balkans Swedish forces played a particularly prominent role in Priština, in Kosovo, during the conflict there in 2002. More recently Sweden's diplomatic representative Hans Blix (born 1928), head of the International Atomic Energy Agency between 1981 and 1997, has taken a high, occasionally controversial role, with respect to the problems of Afghanistan, Iraq and most recently the conflict in Lebanon. Many may disagree with his conclusions, but few doubt the integrity with which he has represented Sweden, or the role of the country itself, as a peacemaker in the modern world and with social models of harmony that most of the nations of the world would do well to emulate.

APPENDIX 1

Chronology

829–30 and 851–2	missionary Ansgar arrives in Birka to proselytise
c.860	Rurik establishes himself at Novgorod, laying the groundwork for the establishment of Russia as a state
c.900	Olof conquers Hedeby, near Schleswig
c.1000	King Olof Skötkonung defeats King Olav Tryggvason of Norway in a sea battle at Svolder in the Sound, with the assistance of King Sven Tveskägg of Denmark
c.1022	Olof Skötkonung baptised at Husaby, in Västergötland
c.1027	King Anund Jakob defeated by the Norwegians at Helge, in Scania
1101	a meeting of the three Nordic monarchs at Kunghälla establishes the boundaries of Sweden, Norway and Denmark
1143	French Cistercians establish the Monastery of Alvastra in Östergötland
1160	martyrdom of King Erik Jedvardsson (St Erik)
1248	Birger Magnusson made Jarl (earl); establishment of a more efficient infrastructure for the Church in Sweden; priestly celibacy prescribed

1249	Birger Jarl leads crusade to Finland
1280	the Decree of Alsnö helps to consolidate a feudal order in Sweden along continental European lines, while introducing the estate system
1281	the Church's property is granted freedom from taxation
1306	Håtunaleken, in which King Birger Magnusson stood in a power struggle with his two brothers Erik and Valdemar for political domination
1317	Nyköping Banquet, a Christmas celebration, the occasion of which Birger Magnusson used to imprison Erik and Valdemar, who, by tradition, were then said to have been starved to death
1318	Birger Magnusson deposed by rebellion and forced to flee to Denmark
1319	election of King Magnus Eriksson at Mora, which provided the legal basis for Sweden's government and the relationship of king and country until 1719
1323	Peace of Nöteborg, the first territorial agreement between Sweden and Russia, defines the border between the two countries
c.1325	epic poem known as the Erik Chronicles is begun, focused upon the extended period commencing with the times of Birger Jarl up to the Nyköping *gästebud* (banquet).
1349	Birgitta (c.1303–73), daughter of magnate Birger Persson and widow of Ulf Gudmarsson, departs for Rome to secure the establishment of her monastic order
1349–50	the Black Death rages in Sweden
1391	Birgitta is canonised
1396	promulgation of the Nyköping Recess, according to which taxation was authorised only by virtue of a royal warrant and the confiscation of private property to satisfy the tax demands otherwise levied prohibited; goods previously so confiscated were to be returned

1397	declaration of the Kalmar Union, according to which Sweden, Denmark and Norway were united under one crown
1434	Engelbrekt Engelbrektsson leads an uprising against King Erik of Pomerania in Bergslagen and Dalecarlia, Erik Puke one in Norrland
1436	Engelbrektsson murdered
1437	Erik Puke executed
1436–8	Engelbrekt Chronicles are written, focusing upon discontent with Erik of Pomerania's rule
1450s	Karl Chronicles are composed, looking back on the period commencing in 1389, and continued to 1452
1451–5	war between Sweden and Denmark (truce 1453–5)
1477	Archbishop Jakob Ulfsson founds Uppsala University
c.1480–96	Sture Chronicles are written, in which the importance of Swedish independence from Denmark is stressed
1483	promulgation of Kalmar Recess, in which the supremacy of the Council is attested
1495	Russians attack Finland
1496	Svante Sture takes Ivangorod for Sweden
1506–9	war between Sweden and Denmark
1518	Danish navy under Christian II defeated at Brännkyrka by Swedes under Sten Sture the Younger
1520	Stockholm's 'Bloodbath' occurs on 8 and 9 November, in which many enemies of Christian II are put to death; Gustaf Vasa attempts to foment an uprising in Dalecarlia
1523	Gustaf Vasa enters Stockholm
1526	New Testament published in Swedish
1527	second uprising in Dalecarlia; Gustaf Vasa takes control over the Swedish Church
1531	Lutheran Reformer Laurentius Petri becomes Archbishop of Uppsala
1541	translation of the Bible completed

1542–3	Dackfejden revolt
1544	Convocation of Västerås confirms hereditary monarchy
1555	war with Russia
1561	the Council meeting in Arboga curtails the rights of the royal dukes; Estonia accepts Swedish sovereignty
1563–70	Seven Years War between Sweden and Denmark
1567	Erik has members of the powerful, noble Sture family, including Nils, Svante and Erik Sture, along with Abraham Stenbok, murdered, though blame was laid at the door of Jöran Persson
1570	Treaty of Stettin confirms the de facto order won by Gustaf Vasa; Älvsborg is returned to Sweden for cash; Frederick of Denmark relinquishes his claim on Sweden, Johan of Sweden on Norway; outbreak of war with Russia
1576	King Johan attempts to introduce a new Catholic-inspired liturgy, the so-called Red Book, to Sweden
1590	war with Russia in Estonia
1593	congregation of Uppsala establishes Lutheranism as the state Church of Sweden, rejecting the liturgy of the Red Book
1595	Treaty of Teusina delineates a northern border between Sweden and Russia in Lapland; re-establishment of Uppsala University
1596	peasant revolt against Klas Fleming, in Ostrabothnia, in Finland
1598	Sigismund defeated by Karl and his forces at Stångebro, by Kalmar
1599	Sigismund dethroned by the *Riksdag*
1600	Lindköping Bloodbath in which Karl's aristocratic opponents, Ture Bielke, Erik Sparre and Gustaf and Sten Banér are put to death, by order of the *Riksdag*
1604	Karl assumes the name Karl IX, having been confirmed as hereditary king at Norrköping, the previous year
1605	Swedish forces are defeated at Kirkholm, in Livland
1607	Gothenburg founded

1611	outbreak of the Kalmar War: the Danes occupy Kalmar, the Swedes Jämtland and Härjedalen; Axel Oxenstierna (1583–1654) appointed Chancellor
1612	Danes seize Älvsborg and the Fortress of Gullberg, cutting Sweden off from the North Sea
1613	peace between Sweden and Denmark effected by the Treaty of Knäred, the negotiations for which were facilitated by England, according to which Älvsborg was to be returned to Sweden on payment of a million *riksdalers*, that is, two-thirds of the value of the country's yearly crop
1614	Sweden and Holland sign military alliance in the Hague
1617	according to the Peace Treaty of Stolbova, Sweden receives Keksholm and Ingermanland; conversion to Catholicism criminalised
1618	beginning of the Thirty Years War in central Europe
1621	Gothenburg permitted to trade internationally; war with Poland in Livland leads to the capture of Riga; Uppsala University reopens
1626–9	war in Poland spreads to Prussia
1627	Dutchman Louis De Geer arrives in Sweden, establishing his own weapons factory and brass production; Sweden and Denmark come to the defence of Stralsund against the Habsburg General Wallenstein
1629	six-year truce between Sweden and Poland signed at Altmark
1630	Sweden enters the Thirty Years War
1632	5 April, General Tilly is mortally wounded at Lech; 6 November, King Gustaf Adolph falls at the Battle of Lützen; the Council assumes the reins of power in Sweden; University of Dorpat (Tartu) founded
1634	Wallenstein assassinated in Bohemia
1635	Saxony and Brandenburg make an independent peace with the Habsburgs; twenty-six-year truce agreed between Sweden and Poland

1636	France declares war on the Habsburgs
1638	colony of New Sweden founded in Delaware
1640	Åbo Academy founded
1642	Finnish translation of the Bible, commissioned by Queen Kristina, published
1643–5	war between Sweden and Denmark
1645	Swedes defeat Habsburg forces to the south-east of Prague
1646	Carl Gustaf Wrangel assumes control of Swedish military forces
1648	Prague captured and plundered by Swedish forces under Wrangel; Treaty of Westphalia ends the Thirty Years War, according to which Sweden receives parts of Pomerania, Rügen, Usedom, Bremen and Verden
1654	Queen Kristina abdicates; war erupts in Germany over Bremen
1655	reduction of the land of the nobility; renewed conflict with Poland; Fort Kristina, in New Sweden, captured by the Dutch
1656	Russia attacks Sweden's eastern Baltic territory
1657	Denmark declares war on Sweden; commencement of Karl X's military campaign from Poland and northern Germany through Denmark
1658	Peace of Roskilde confirms the cession by Denmark to Sweden of Scania, Halland, Blekinge and Bohuslan, along with the Baltic islands of Bornholm and the Norwegian province of Trondheim; siege of Copenhagen
1660	peace with Denmark: Bornholm and the province of Trondheim returned to Denmark; peace with Poland and Russia, the latter confirming the Peace of Stolbova
1666	Second Bremen War
1675	Battle of Fehrbellin, between Sweden and Brandenburg, in which Swedish forces were repelled
1680	absolute monarchy established in practice; introduction of Reduction

1681	Swedish law imposed on Scania; obligatory use of Swedish introduced for church services and in education
1682	State Council officially shorn of most of its powers and renamed the Royal Council; Karl XI is granted law-making powers and supervision over Reduction
1686	the Church Law promulgated, regulating many aspects of church organisation and practice
1689	king granted the right to levy taxes in times of war
1695	serious famine in Sweden caused by crop failure; publication of the official Swedish Hymn Book, attributed to Bishop Jesper Svedberg
1697	fire destroys much of the Royal Palace of Three Crowns, in Stockholm
1700	outbreak of the Great Northern War between Sweden, on the one hand, and Denmark, Poland-Saxony and Russia, on the other; victory for Sweden at Narva on 20 November
1701	Swedish victory over the Poles by the Düna River in Courland
1702	Warsaw, Klissow and Cracow in Poland taken by the Swedes
1703	Danzig (Gdansk) and Thorn (Torun) in Poland taken by the Swedes; St Petersburg founded in former Swedish Ingermanland by Peter the Great
1704	Russians recapture Narva; Swedes capture Lvov
1705	Sweden, under Lewenhaupt, victorious against Russia at the Battle of Gemäuterhof, in Courland
1710	Danes defeated at the Battle of Helsingborg; plague in Stockholm; Riga and Talinn fall to Russian forces
1712	Swedish forces successfully defend the country's north German possessions on Rügen and against the Danes in Mecklenburg
1713	*Kalabaliken* Revolt by the Ottomans against Karl XII's presence at Bender; Magnus Stenbock taken prisoner by the Danes at the Battle of Tönningen

1715	Karl XII finally returns to Sweden
1716	German diplomat Georg Heinrich von Görtz reorganises Sweden's finances
1718	death of King Karl XII at Fredrikshald, during the Battle of Fredkriksten's Fortress on 30 November 1718
1719	new regent, Ulrika Eleonora, accepts the end of absolutism; Sweden's eastern coast attacked by Russia; Bremen and Verden sold to Hanover
1720	various parts of Swedish Pomerania ceded to Prussia
1721	Treaty of Nystad ends the Great Northern War to Sweden's disadvantage, with large tracts of land, including Ingria, Estonia, Livonia and South Karelia, ceded to Russia
1731	founding of the Swedish East India Company
1738	introduction of a new steamlined legal code
1738–9	eruption of conflict within the *Riksdag* between the Hats, under Arvid Horn, and the Caps, under Carl Gyllenborg
1739	establishment of the Swedish Academy of Science
1741–3	renewal of war with Russia, after which South Karelia is lost to Russia
1747	beginning of the construction of the Fortress of Sveaborg outside Helsinki, under Augustin Ehrensvärd
1753	introduction of the Gregorian Calendar
1756	failed coup attempt fomented by Adolph Fredrik and Lovisa Ulrika
1757–62	Pomeranian War, in which Sweden fails to regain parts of northern Germany from Prussia
1766	political censorship abolished
1772	19 August, Gustaf III's coup reintroduces royal absolutism in Sweden
1782	Jews permitted to settle in four Swedish cities
1788–90	war with Russia
1788	Anjala Conspiracy opposing war with Russia crushed

1790	Battle of Svensksund
1792	16 March, Gustaf III shot by disaffected nobleman, Captain Jacob Johan Anckarström, at masked ball at the Royal Opera, with the support of other discontented figures
1804	Swedish alliance with Britain
1805–7	Pomeranian War between Sweden and France
1807	closure of the Swedish East India Company; free trade for Swedes granted for St Barthélemy
1808–9	war over Finland
1809	Treaty of Hamina: Sweden cedes sovereignty over Finland to Russia's Tsar Alexander I; royal absolutism abolished
1814	peace with Denmark, as a result of which Norway is ceded to Sweden
1815	Sweden obliged to relinquish its sovereignty over parts of Pomerania to Prussia
1827	new laws, the so-called *Laga skifte*, attempt to effect the consolidation of disjointed agricultural land into large units
1832	opening of the Göta Canal, begun in 1809
1834	cholera epidemic devastates many coastal cities
1846	guild system abolished
1853	telegraph lines between Stockholm and Uppsala opened for public use; gas lighting introduced in Stockholm
1855	November Accord between Britain, with its allies, and Sweden
1856	first railway line opens between Örebro and Ervalla
1857	toll on shipping passing through the Sound abolished
1858	single women over twenty-five years deemed of age to exercise property rights and the like
1862	railway line between Stockholm and Gothenburg comes into service
1863	Swede Alfred Nobel invents dynamite
1866	the estates system abolished

1867	introduction of a bi-cameral Parliament
1878	Swedish sovereignty over St Barthélemy and St Martin transferred to France
1880	Count Arvid Posse elected prime minister
1883	Themptander elected prime minister
1885	foundation of the Social Democratic Party
1891–1900	E. G. Boström, prime minister
1901	first award of the Nobel Prize; introduction of compulsory military service and the abolition of *indelning* (allotments)
1902–5	E. G. Boström returns as prime minister
1909	Great Strike
1911–14	Karl Staaff, prime minister
1913	Parliament introduces state pensions for the elderly
1914	Farmers' March in Stockholm; Sweden declares its neutrality in the First World War
1917	parliamentarism comes into practice
1920	Sweden joins the League of Nations
1921	death penalty abolished
1922	first woman (Kerstin Hesselgren) elected to Swedish Parliament; public radio broadcasting commences
1930	Archbishop Nathan Söderblom awarded the Nobel Prize for Peace
1939	Per Albin Hansson elected prime minister; Swedish neutrality declared after the outbreak of the Second World War
1940–3	German troops given permission to cross Sweden in sealed railway carriages
1946	Sweden joins the United Nations
1946–69	Social Democrat Tage Erlander, prime minister
1948	Count Folke Bernadotte, United Nations representative in Jerusalem, assassinated by Jewish terrorists
1954	establishment of Gothenburg University
1955	general public medical insurance introduced
1970	Swedish Parliament made uni-cameral
1974	Gunnar Myrdal wins the Nobel Prize for Economics; Eyvind Johnson and Harry Martinson share that for Literature

1986	Prime Minister Olof Palme assassinated; Chernobyl accident leaves radioactive fallout over much of Sweden
1995	Sweden joins the European Union
2000	Church of Sweden disestablished, thereby separating Church and state

APPENDIX 2

Monarchs and regents of Sweden

Yngling/Uppsala dynasty

+ *c.*994	Erik Segersäll
*c.*994–1022	Olof Eriksson Skötkonung
*c.*1022–50	Anund Jakob
*c.*1050–60	Emund the Old

Stenkil dynasty

*c.*1060–6	Stenkil
*c.*1070	Håkan Röde
*c.*1080–1110	Halsten and Inge the Younger
*c.*1110–20	Filip and Inge the Younger
1120–30	Interregnum

Sverker dynasty

*c.*1135–?56	Sverker the Elder
*c.*1156–60	Erik IX Jedvardsson the Holy
*c.*1161–7	Karl VII Sverkersson
*c.*1167–96	Knut Eriksson
1196–1208	Sverker the Younger Karlsson
1208–16	Erik X Knutsson
1216–22	Johan I Sverkersson
1222–9	Erik XI Eriksson
1229–34	Knut Holmgersson the Long
1234–49	Erik XI Eriksson Återkung ('King Again')

Folkung/Biälbo dynasty

1250–75	Valdemar Birgersson
(1250–66	Birger Jarl regent)
1275–90	Magnus Birgersson Ladulås
1290–1318	Birger Magnusson
(1290–8	Torgils Knutsson regent)
1319–63	Magnus Eriksson
(1319–32	regency for Magnus Eriksson)
1357–9	Erik XII
1362–64, 1371	Håkon

Mecklenburg dynasty

1364–89	Albrekt of Mecklenburg

Union and native regents

1389–1412	Margarete Valdemarsdotter
1396–1439	Erik of Pomerania
1441–8	Christopher of Bavaria
1448–57	Karl VIII Knutsson Bonde
1457–64	Christian I
1464–5, 1467–70	Karl VIII Knutsson Bonde
1471–97	Sten Sture the Elder (leader of the State Council)
1497–1501	Hans Johan II
1501–3	Sten Sture the Elder (leader of the State Council)
1504–12	Svante Nilsson Sture (leader of the State Council)
1512–20	Sten Sture the Younger (leader of the State Council)
1520–1	Christian II

Vasa dynasty

1523–60	Gustaf Vasa
1560–8	Erik XIV
1569–92	Johan III
1592–9	Sigismund
1604–11	Karl IX

1611–32	Gustaf II Adolph
1644–54	Kristina
(1632–44	Axel Oxenstierna regent)

Pfalsk dynasty

1654–60	Karl X Gustaf
1672–97	Karl XI
(1660–72	regency under Dowager Queen Hedvig Eleonora and five royal counsellors)
1697–1718	Karl XII
(1697	regency of royal counsellors)
1719–20	Ulrika Eleonora

Hesse dynasty

| 1720–51 | Fredrik I |

Holstein-Gottorp dynasty

1751–71	Adolph Fredrik
1771–92	Gustaf III
1796–1809	Gustaf IV Adolph
(1792–6	Duke Karl regent)
1809–18	Karl XIII

Bernadotte dynasty

1818–44	Karl XIV Johan
1844–59	Oskar I
1859–72	Karl XV
1872–1907	Oskar II
1907–50	Gustaf V
1950–73	Gustaf VI Adolph
1973–	Carl XVI Gustaf

APPENDIX 3

Prime ministers

1876–80	Louis De Geer, Independent Liberal
1880–3	Arvid Posse, Farmers' Party
1883–4	Carl Johan Thyselius, Independent Conservative
1884–8	Robert Themptander, Independent Liberal
1888–9	D. A. Gillis Bildt, Independent Conservative
1889–91	Gustaf Åkerhielm, Protectionist Majority Party
1891–1900	Erik Gustaf Boström, 1st term, Farmers' Party
1900–2	Fredrik von Otter, Independent
1902–5	Erik Gustaf Boström, 2nd term, Farmers' Party
1905	Johan Ramstedt, Independent
1905	Christian Lundeberg, Protectionist Majority Party
1905–6	Karl Staaff, 1st term, Liberal Coalition Party
1906–11	Arvid Lindman, 1st term, General Electoral Union
1911–14	Karl Staaff, 2nd term, Liberal Coalition Party
1914–17	Hjalmar Hammarskjöld, Independent Conservative
1917	Carl Swartz, National Party
1917–20	Nils Edén, Liberal Coalition Party
1920	Hjalmar Branting, 1st term, Social Democratic
1920–1	Louis De Geer, the Younger, Independent Liberal
1921	Oscar von Sydow, Independent
1921–3	Hjalmar Branting, 2nd term, Social Democratic
1923–4	Ernst Trygger, National Party
1924–5	Hjalmar Branting, 3rd term, Social Democratic
1925–6	Rickard Sandler, Social Democratic

1926–8	Carl Gustaf Ekman, 1st term, Freeminded People's Party
1928–30	Arvid Lindman, 2nd term, General Electoral Union
1930–2	Carl Gustaf Ekman, 2nd term, Freeminded People's Party
1932	Felix Hamrin, Freeminded People's Party
1932–6	Pehr Albin Hansson, 1st term, Social Democratic
1936	Axel Pehrsson-Bramstorp, Farmers' League
1936–9	Per Albin Hansson, 2nd term, Social Democratic
1939–45	Per Albin Hansson, 3rd term, Social Democratic
1945–6	Per Albin Hansson, 4th term, Social Democratic
1946–51	Tage Erlander, 1st term, Social Democratic
1951–7	Tage Erlander, 2nd term, Social Democratic
1957–69	Tage Erlander, 3rd term, Social Democratic
1969–76	Olaf Palme, 1st term, Social Democratic
1976–8	Thorbjörn Fälldin, 1st term, Centre Party
1978–9	Ola Ullsten, People's Party
1979–81	Thorbjörn Fälldin, 2nd term, Centre Party
1981–2	Thorbjörn Fälldin, 3rd term, Centre Party
1982–6	Olaf Palme, 2nd term, Social Democratic
1986–91	Ingvar Carlsson, 1st term, Social Democratic
1991–4	Carl Bildt, Moderate Party
1994–6	Ingvar Carlsson, 2nd term, Social Democratic
1996–2006	Göran Persson, Social Democratic
2006–	Fredrik Reinfeldt, Moderate Party

SELECTED FURTHER READING

Baldwin, Peter. *Contagion and the State in Europe, 1830–1930*, Cambridge, Cambridge University Press, 1999.

Carlsson, Harry G. *Out of Inferno. Strindberg's Reawakening as an Artist*, Seattle, Washington University Press, 1996.

Grell, Ole Peter, ed. *The Scandinavian Reformation. From Evangelical Movement to Institutionalisation of Reform*, Cambridge, Cambridge University Press, 1995.

Grell, Ole Peter and Andrew Cunningham, eds. *Health Care and Poor Relief in Protestant Europe*, London and New York, Routledge, 1977.

Griffiths, Tony. *Scandinavia*, Kent Town, South Australia, Wakefield Press, 1991 and 1993.

Helle, Knut, ed. *The Cambridge History of Scandinavia, volume I: Prehistory to 1520*, Cambridge, Cambridge University Press, 2003.

Hope, Nicholas. *German and Scandinavian Protestantism, 1700–1918*, Oxford, Oxford University Press, 1995.

Johnson, Amandus. *The Swedish Settlements on the Delaware, 1638–1664*, volumes I and II, New York, D. Appleton, 1911 (reprinted 2005).

Kent, Neil. 'Gustaf III and Italian Culture', in Shearer West, ed., *Italian Culture in Northern Europe in the Eighteenth Century*, Cambridge, Cambridge University Press, 1999, pp. 187–206.

Light and Nature in Late 19th Century Nordic Art and Literature, Acta Universitatis Upsaliensis, Ars Suetica 13, Uppsala, 1990.

The Soul of the North: a Social, Architectural and Cultural History of the Nordic Countries, 1700–1940, London, Reaktion Books, 2000 and (in paperback) 2001.

The Triumph of Light and Nature: Nordic Art 1740–1940, London, Thames and Hudson, 1987; published in Swedish by Bonniers in 1987 (English version reprinted in paperback in 1992).

Klinge, Matti. *The Baltic World*, Helsinki, Otava, 1994.

Koerner, Joseph Leo. *Caspar David Friedrich and the Subject of Landscape*, London, Thames and Hudson, 1990.

Levack, Brian P. *The Witch-hunt in Early Modern Europe*, 2nd edn, London and New York, Longman, 1995.

Lundh, Christer. 'Households and Families in Pre-industrial Sweden', *Community and Change. A Journal of Social Structure, Law and Demography in Past Societies*, 10/1 1995, pp. 33–68.

Michalski, Sergiusz. *The Reformation and the Visual Arts. The Protestant Image Question in Western and Eastern Europe*, London, Routledge, 1993.

Ranger, Terence and Paul Slack, eds. *Epidemics and Ideas. Essays on the Historical Perception of Pestilence*, Cambridge, Cambridge University Press, 1992.

Roberts, Michael. *The Early Vasas: a History of Sweden, 1523–1611*, Cambridge, Cambridge University Press, 1986.

From Oxenstierna to Charles XII: Four Studies, Cambridge, Cambridge University Press, 1991.

Ruong, Israel. *The Lapps in Sweden*, Stockholm, Swedish Institute for Cultural Relations with Foreign Countries, 1967.

Rydén, Göran. 'Iron Production and the Household as a Production Unit in a Nineteenth-century Sweden', *Continuity and Change. A Journal of Social Structure, Law and Demography in Past Societies*, 10/1 1995, pp. 69–104.

Salmon, Patrick. *Scandinavia and the Great Powers, 1890–1940*, Cambridge, Cambridge University Press, 2002.

Wadström, C. B. *An Essay on Colonization particularly applied to the Western Coast of Africa with some free thoughts on Cultivation and Commerce, also Brief Descriptions of the Colonies Already Formed, or Attempted in Africa, Including those of Sierra Leona and Bulama*, London, 1794.

Whitaker, Ian. *Settler and Nomad in Northern Torne Lappmark, Polar Record*, 21/133, London, 1983.

INDEX

CAMBRIDGE CONCISE HISTORIES